Women in India: Motherhood and Multiple Identities

Women in India: Motherhood and Multiple Identities

Swapan Kumar Pramanick
Samita Manna

SERIALS PUBLICATIONS
NEW DELHI (INDIA)

First Published - 2010

ISBN: 978-81-8387-358-1

Published by

SERIALS PUBLICATIONS
4830/24, Prahlad Street, Ansari Road
Darya Ganj, New Delhi-110002 (India)
Phone : 23245225 Fax : 91-11-23272135
E-mail: serials@sify.com

Contents

Section Three

Women: Dual Identity

Section Four

Women in Politics

Preface

Motherhood often creates a crisis in the feminist's world of thought as they think that women's subordinate status is partially created by men due to her motherhood. So an attempt is made by the radical feminists to delete the very significant identity 'mother' associated with 'motherhood' and 'mothering'. Gender equality and gender justice can be established through providing equal education, equal employment, ensuring equal social and legal rights and also ensuring greater privileges for them by which the subjugated status of women over a period of time could be eliminated. For Indian women, in particular motherhood deserves a high esteem though working women often face dilemma in the social life if they are mothers. Yet, they wish to become 'mothers'. The biological and emotional urge for motherhood comes in conflict with the social and work- place responsibilities. Women development does not mean that they have to be at par with men eliminating their feminine qualities of which motherhood is a major attribute.

The present work is a collection of eleven articles which have been thematically arranged into four sections. Each section has its own theme related to the topic of this book. Each of the authors in each article has tried to highlight gender problems according to their own thoughts and ideas. Among these articles, a few are based on field studies. So along with the established wisdom and the theoretical debates of the authors, the empirical works also lead to new insights and ideas to create new useful materials and facts for the present generation. We hope that this treatise will provide new ideas among the academicians, researchers and readers. It will come in handy for researchers and members of the general public.

As editors our first generally acknowledged debt is to all the authors of this book whose contributions have helped us to publish this book.

We would like to acknowledge further the active encouragement and cooperation extended to us by Prof. Pralay Kumar Deb and Dr. Amal Kumar Mallick who enthused us to publish this book.

We are also deeply obliged to Ms. Nandini Saha, Reader, Department of English, Jadavpur University, for her enthusiastic help and cooperation during the time of preparation of the manuscript.

We, the editors, would also want to thank Mr. Jha, the publication manager of the Serial Publishing house.

S.K. Pramanick
S. Manna

About the Contributors

PRALAY KUMAR DEB had his Master's and Ph.D degrees from the University of Calcutta. He was formerly Professor of English and Dean, Faculty of Arts and Commerce, University of Kalyani. He is currently Part-time teacher in English at Presidency College and Bethune College. He is the author of Jonson and Congreve: A Study of Their Comedies and Gateway to Culture: Eases on Literature, Society and the Arts. His essays in criticism published in various journals (both English and Bengali), have won the acclaim of distinguished scholars here and abroad.

BARUN KUMAR CHAKRABORTY, M.A, Ph.D, D. Litt, was formerly Professor and Head, Department of Folklore, University of Kalyani, West Bengal. He has written 50 books and is a regular contributor to various journals and periodicals. He is an established Folklorist, Critic and Academician.

DR. BISWAJIT GHOSH is Professor and Head of the Department of Sociology, the University of Burdwan. He has published more than forty research articles in reputed journals and edited books. His areas of interest include Sociology of Development, Gender Studies, Industrial Sociology and Society and Culture in India. He has edited/compiled a book on 'Trafficking in women and children, Child Marriage and Dowry: A study For Action Plan in west Bengal' published by Unicef and Govt. of West Bengal in 2007.

DR. NANDINI SAHA (M.A., Ph.D) is a Reader at the Department of English, Jadavpur University. Her areas of specializations are Nineteenth and Twentieth Century British fiction, Literary Theory and Criticism, and British Postmodernist fiction. Her doctoral dissertation was on the British Postmodern novelist John Fowles. Her current research includes papers on Mahasweta Devi, on the correlation between historiography and narrativity.

DR. SYED ABDUL HAFIZ MOINUDDIN is a Reader in the Department of Political Science with Rural Administration, Vidyasagar University, West Bengal. He is also the Teacher-in-charge of the Department of Sociology of the same university. Dr. Moinuddin has done his research on 'Divorce and Muslim Women in West Bengal' and obtained his Ph. D. from the University of Calcutta in 1997. He has since been publishing articles in reputed sociological Journals in the country and has published a number of books in this area.

DR. SANDIP KUMAR GHATAK is presently working in Asansol Girls' College, Burdwan University as Reader and Head of the Department of Political Science. He has already published more than 25 articles in different national and international journals. He is also associated with some nationally reputed academic bodies. His areas of interest are Women Studies and Sociology.

SOUMYAJIT PATRA is a Lecturer in the Department of Sociology at Vidyasagar University. He has obtained Ph. D from the University of Kalyani. Soumyajit Parta was awarded Research Fellowship from the Ministry of Welfare (Government of India). His research area includes tribal culture, gender issues and sociology of religion. Recently Soumyajit Patra was invited to present a paper in an international seminar on 'Alternative Expressions of the Numinous' held at the University of Queensland (Australia).

PANCHALI CHAKRABORTY was a student in the Department of Sociology, University of Kalyani and she secured first position both in her Graduation and Post graduation Examinations. Panchali obtained her Ph.D from the University of Kalyani. Her papers in different reputed journals have made her well known in the academic world.

BHASWATI ROY (SARKAR) was a Fellow in a UGC sponsored project. She was awarded Ph.D. by the University of Kalyani for her dissertation on the problems of working women. Bhaswati has also published papers in many reputed journals.

Introduction

I

WOMEN IN INDIA: MOTHERHOOD AND MULTIPLE IDENTITIES

During the last two decades many issues relating to gender have proliferated throughout the world. Gender discourses are not only confined to social scientists but the interested persons from different areas have come into fore and through different dialogues they have been trying to formulate different paradigms for changing the status of women. Under the domain of patriarchy women are the subordinate group though constitutional safeguards are equally rendered to men and women both.

The following statement will bear out the position of Women.

> Women constitute half the world's population, perform nearly two-thirds of its work hours, receive one-tenth of the world income but own less than one-hundredth of the world's property (Evans 1994: 2).

Again as Simone de Beauvoir points out,

> The woman worker in France, according to a study made in the years 1889–93, received only half the pay of a man for a day's work equal to that of a man. ... In America in 1918 a woman got only half a man's wage.... Between 1911 and 1943 women's wages in France were raised a little more rapidly than the men's but they remained definitely lower (Beauvoir 1997:147).

This is absolutely true. Feminism as a concept has developed from the sense of inequality. Women's oppression and subordination help to develop "feminism". Women's international year 1975 and the international decade 1975-1985 played crucial role in creating awareness throughout the world in a new dimension. The status of women is changing and women are playing multiple roles effectively. Often different issues related to role conflict may be the subject of an important academic and intellectual discourse for the modern elite.

"Most women unquestioningly accept that mothering is an exclusive female activity and if they can not attain that state or do justice to it, though they have attained it, feel they have failed their essential vocation" (Geetha 2002:123). Like other institutions, motherhood is also a social institution. From the very childhood, the girl child develops within herself the desire to be a mother. This starts when the little girl begins to play with her dolls and like her mother she pretends to be a mother too. Society for its own interest creates different customs, traditions, norms, duties, expectations separately for boys and girls. The process of socialization starting from the birth of a child constructs one's perception, thought, desire and willingness, and as a result, 'femininity' and 'masculinity' are also constructed.

Motherhood brings profound changes in a woman's life. Woman holds subordinate status as a wife, but her status changes when she becomes a mother. Motherhood denotes security for the woman. Till today not only in rural India but also in urban areas where extended families exist, a woman just after marriage as wife maintains a subordinate status not only to her husband but also to the other female members like mother-in-law and sister-in-law. Within the norms of patriarchy, the women themselves are sometimes responsible for causing harm to other women. As wives, women have no voice, no freedom, and little education; they simply imitate the roles performed by their elders. It will be wrong if it is said that there are no exceptions, but there is no alternative for women. Kakar (1990) points out that mother-in-law and sister-in-law often create hindrance for the development of intimacy between wives and husbands. But, motherhood/parenthood helps to moderately free the husband and wife from such constraints. A new romantic as well as lovable relationship is potentially established between the husband and wife as the interference of the other members are lessened due to their attainment of the stage of motherhood/fatherhood.

Motherhood, when established by the birth of the first child, is the most secure status for a woman, as also confirmed by Caplan (1985, cited in Puri 1991: 157). Caplan (1985) and Puri (1991) also suggest that women's statuses are most secure as mothers of a male child. Within the conjugal family, motherhood promotes integrity between husband and wife, by becoming a father, he develops a soft, loyal and lovable relationship with his children.

> Across cultures, the mother's role is a dynamic and powerful one. Women have and continue to utilize the power they wield over their children to their advantage. One may argue that this is a pyrrhic sort of power, exercised well within the long shadow of patriarchy. Yet in actual life, this power earns reward and authority. This is especially evident in the Indian context, at least in the influence mothers command with grown up sons, the authority that older women, especially mothers-in law, enjoy over young women, and most important in the pride with which mothers persuade and entreat her daughters to accept and live out the destinies and vocations which had propelled their own lives (Geetha 2002: 125).

From the very childhood, male and female children are classified by their distinctive roles and status. Women are respected as they bear the burden of childbirth. Not only in human society, even in plant and animal kingdoms, females are conferred a high esteem. Pregnant mothers in all societies are assigned a high status as they are the creators of society. The attraction between male and female is universal, spontaneous and natural. Even in a garden, where the female flowers have honey, flies, birds and other insects come and carry the pollen grains to help in bearing the fruits, which is the process of the cosmic world. We, the humans, are not separate entities distinct from the kingdom of plants and animals. Human beings are also a part of this cosmic world. Hence this symbiotic relationship between male and female helps to maintain a stable and harmonious condition of the cosmos.

Motherhood is a blessing for womankind. Wifehood is glorified and made meaningful by motherhood. Popular local sayings like *Putrabati Bhaba* (may you be the mother of a son) are often used by elders to bless married women. Several such adages and local texts are also prevalent in Indian folk society where younger women are always identified by the elder women in terms of their status as either their motherhood, wifehood or at least by their womanhood. In patriarchal society the male child is the bearer of the family line. All important social functions of Indian families are only performed by the male child. "The son rescues the souls of the deceased ancestors from the hell into which they might fall without his birth" (Prabhu 1940: 242). In this connection I would like to refer to Magaret Mead (1939). She observes that cultural norms of the society are very important to develop 'maleness' and 'femaleness' within an individual varying from society to society and culture to culture. In Indian society a woman always stands in relation to others. In this context, a few lines from *Manusmriti* is worth mentioning.

> Her father protects (her) in childhood her husband protects (her) in youth.... And her sons protect (her) in old age; a woman is never fit for independence. (*Manusmriti*, Buhler's translation: 1964)

It is really astonishing that this statement was written in 300 B.C. but till today, women are largely unchanged in their respective status and role. The Indian society is structured in such a way that the women have no way to come out from it. Motherhood will be incomplete or the bliss of motherhood would be denied if she fails to give birth to a male child. Even in earlier Vedic periods when women were free in society, male child[1] was still welcome. Even in the Rigveda there is no such rejoicing over the birth of a daughter (Macdonell, quoted in Das, 1962). The educated and affluent families are no exceptions to this rule. Another popular saying used in Indian society is *Putrarthe Kriate Varja* (wifehood is meaningful only if you beget a male child). Entering the new era of twenty first century, the attitude of the parents regarding their preference for a son remains unchanged. At the birth of a son, frequent conch-shells are blown or drums are beaten and sweets are distributed among themselves. In this context I would like to quote a few lines from a Maharastrian girl's experience, where she compares herself "to a white sweet-scented Jasmine (Jai) and the boy to a big,. strong smelling thorny leaf (Kevada)". She then asks, "Did anyone notice the sweet fragrance of a Jai? The hefty kevada however has filled the whole street with its strong scent" (Karve 1968, cited in Ghadially 1996: 47).

Nevertheless the mother is the most venerable person in this world–even more than the father[2]. More than one Dharmasastra writers have declared that the father is a hundred times more venerable than the teacher, but the mother is a thousand times more venerable than even the father (Prabhu 1940: 273). Motherhood is envisioned as the natural outcome of womanhood. Interestingly the educated, financially independent, professional women also celebrate their motherhood.

> If a woman can not be a mother, she feels guilty, as if her body has betrayed itself and her. Women also imagine that whatever else they are or may do their ultimate destiny is linked with motherhood. Thus successful professional women who have decided to stay single, women who long to get married and have a child, but who cannot for whatever reason, at some point in their lives, all of them feel inadequate, unfulfilled and some less of a woman"(Geetha 2002:123).

Women throughout the world are not at par with their male counterparts. They are identified as the 'second sex' (Beauvoir

1997). Sex is a form of stratification that identifies women as a separate class. In this context, Firestone (1972) argues, "Unlike economic class, sex class sprang directly from a biological reality." Now the question is why do women tolerate male dominance?

> For feminists, the fact of biological difference (particularly post-Freud) was deeply problematic, since as long as difference existed, so would the congruence of female biology and female inferiority. The very body in which feminists themselves lived was one labeled by men as 'feeble' and 'unstable'. A considerable tradition read the binary of difference as inferiority/superiority. Men, for example, were the sex capable of advanced moral reasoning whilst women had innate qualities of nurturance and care for others. Within this context, it was inevitable that women would wish to demonstrate that they were in every way the equal of men and that impact of biological difference was much exaggerated (Evans 1994 :4).

By nature male are aggressive, female are not like that. Whereas men have more physical strength and little emotional attachment, females are mentally soft and passive. The biological difference between male and female is universal. The social construction of 'male' and 'female' is developed through culture. Actually the debate starts between the 'naturalist' and 'nurturalist' out of the statement defined by Sigmund Freud[3], 'Biology is destiny'. Mostly the Feminists and particularly the Radical Feminists often deny Freud's statement. The main cause of women's subordination is her 'mothering'. Motherhood is often described as a stage of complete segregation in which the women have only authority to be the queen of her restricted domain.

Long battles have been waged by feminists to delete the subordinate status of women. So according to feminists, to minimize the gap between male and female, the first step to be taken is where normal motherhood should be discarded. The children would not be allowed to take birth in their mothers uterus. Another argument regarding equality between male and female is to practice lesbianism whereby the women will attain sexual freedom. Male as a dominant class tend to show his dominance over female as inferior class. This domination can be eradicated only when 'sex' as a class disappears and also through ignoring heterosexuality and by practicing lesbianism. But this can only be followed as theoretical debate and discourse. These radical thoughts have only few takers as these are full of debatable arguments. Besides, western society, if we are to study Indian society, a completely different picture will be revealed.

Preference for sons is a longing for the mother, and with the exception of a few urban educated mothers, this is a common feature existing till today all over India. Paradoxically the mother-daughter relationship, particularly after marriage of the daughter, intensifies with deeper sense of warmth, love and intimacy, better understanding of each other emotionally as both mother and daughter now belong to the same class – both being wives of their husbands and the home managers of their individual house. The status of subjugation brings mother and daughter closer in a common psycho-social relation. Ross (1961) also mentions that a very special relationship tends to develop between an Indian girl and her mother.

It has already been observed that motherhood and mothering are the natural outcome of females' biological make-up. Women are the subjugated section of our society as they do not get equal rights in education, health, parent's property, decision making process and even she has no control over her own earnings and own body. In this situation women have to depend on others.

According to Adrienne Rich, there is a distinction between motherhood as 'experience' and motherhood as 'institution'.

> Rich argues that the experience of motherhood–'the *potential relationship* of any woman to her powers of reproduction and to her children'–has been taken from women's control and has become subject to the institution of motherhood, 'which aims at ensuring that potential–and all women–shall remain under male control' (Rich 1977: 13, cited in Lawler 1996).

Motherhood has been explained by many feminists and others as the mere resultant effects of patriarchal society. But nonetheless motherhood also has its own significance which is totally ignored in such discussion. Collins (1991), in her analysis of Black women's mothering, demonstrates some of the ways in which motherhood can be valued without falling into stereotypical depictions of male and female nature. Sometimes it has been observed that mothers have to bear hardship but it has its own autonomy and satisfaction which can not be ignored. Even in our rural society where women hardly get their equal rights like the male, motherhood has its own place. In poor families the girl child often falls a victim to trafficking (Ghosh 2007:35-36) but not the male child, this type of mentality is developed due to the poor socio-economic status. Apart from all such gender discrimination in rural Bengal, the rural women enjoy their motherhood. The pregnant woman is highly welcomed as it is thought that she would be the mother of a son. Through the birth of a son, the parents can gain Moksha (Salvation) as he maintains the link between the two worlds–past and future. In all rural societies, the pregnant mothers receive special attention; feasts and ceremonies are arranged in different months for her safety and satisfaction. In Indian society, after child birth, different purificatory functions are arranged of which *Norta* and *Ekusha* are important intended to give rest to the lactating mothers. (Bhowmick 1966, 1974; Manna 2000, 2003). Recently many changes have taken place in Indian society and the women have become more vocal and visible today that they were in the past.

Hinduism provides a conception of the world in which women are necessary but harmful. Traditionally, this potential for harm has been controlled through religious laws prescribing women's proper behaviour and bringing them under the control of men. Yet women (and the mother especially) do control others; the mother in Hindu thought becomes the Hindu woman in control of herself. As such, she provides an alternative role to that of a dutiful wife (Jacobson and Wadley 1999: 129).

Sex difference has played an immense role in the formation of authority and its legitimacy. Male domination is a universal feature irrespective of a country's civilization. The biological instinct is supreme, and can not be denied. The ultimate motto is to gain love and peace. So by nature one will be aggressive and the opposite will be submissive. This is the law of nature, where opposites will attract, live together and procreate. Though Radical Feminists[4] often say that if we put aside the biological differences these women will be at par with the male. But is it possible to diminish the gap between the two?

Societies are an integral part of the dynamic world. The recent wave of globalization has changed the basic structural part of society as well as its functional manifestations. Men and women are the actors where society is a theater hall–they play according to their assigned status and obligations, under the domain of patriarchy. Now the question is whether globalization could be the sole responsible factor for deleting the subordination of women? On the other hand this subordination is attained not through the process of socialization but due to the stratification on the basis of sex. Male domination is a universal feature irrespective of a country's civilization. Biological instinct is supreme and hence by natural law the male and female have distinctive roles. Otherwise motherhood would lose its charm.

> Discriminations against women may be viewed as arising from the generally ascribed status "female" and from the specially ascribed status of "wife". "mother" and sister (Finlay 2007 :298).

> By a young girl, by a young woman or even by an aged one nothing must be done independently even in her own house.... She who controlling her thoughts, words and deeds, never slights her lord, resides (after death) with her husband (in heaven), and is called a virtuous wife" (*Manusmriti* trans. By Buhler 1964; cited in Ghadially 1998: 30).

In these two quotations stated above by two different authors, namely Finlay and Manu, we see how both the West and the East considered woman as an appendage to her husband though in one case an existing fact is being stated while in another women's subordination is normatively prescribed. Ever since the later Vedic period, women were totally confined within the four walls. The oppression, exploitation and humiliation persisted in an extreme form and its ultimate result was the practice of the customs of *sati* which continued for hundreds of years. It was the nineteenth century that started a process of change in the lives of the women. Active participation of women in the Indian National movement started the first wave of women awareness in India. Through many historical upheavals, the dominance of patriarchy continued and changed its forms and figures differently. By the second half of the nineteenth century there were reform groups in all parts of British India. They focused attention on the inhumane practices of *Sati*, female infanticide, polygyny, child marriage, purdah, prohibitions on female education, *devadasis* (temple dancers wedded to the gods), and the patrilocal joint family. Their activity acted as a stimulus and as an encouragement for reform-minded individuals in other areas, and gradually reformist organizations with an all-India identity began to emerge (Forbes 1996: 19).

Till today in India, where a majority of the population live in rural areas dominated by caste type of stratification, the lack of literacy is overpowered by traditional beliefs and practices. Rules of patriarchy prevail to control these women. In ancient Indian literatures we find innumerable examples of illustrious women in their roles as wife and mother. These are Sita, Savitri, Gandhari, Draupadi, Kunti and Sakuntala, etc. All were remarkable and glorious for having maintained their wifehood and motherhood inspite of several hardships. Wifehood and motherhood were not always bliss to them. Sometimes these appeared before them as crises but with devotion and toleration they created their ideal model character of Indian women.

Women in Indian society are currently changing their position in remarkable ways. They are playing myriad roles in various spectra of social, political, economic, and professional life. Eventually in the last two decades, the Indian female population has received much attention from our government. Global contacts and many positive effects of information technology have enabled Indian women to come much closer to the mainstream of population. To say about 'women in India' is a really very complex task. Indian society, unlike western society, has its own distinctiveness. It is not so easy to generalize the women under the multifarious complex parlour of Indian society. The hierarchies and inequalities exist through caste, class, power, religion, race and many other divisions amidst diversities. Subordinate status of women is unparalleled and is widely accepted. But the nature of subordination is to be examined contextually. The main task as a feminist is to study 'the structures of oppression'.

Throughout the world the position of women is now complex and paradoxical. The situation is quite the same when we discuss the position of Indian women because Indian culture and its heritage are unique in nature. In India, women play the most vital role in maintaining the family and the larger society. The life of woman is significantly characterized as that of wifehood and motherhood. These two enlightened statuses make her a superwoman, having the ingredients of 'Tyaga' and 'Seva'- self-abnegation and service. These are the significant qualities of Indian woman and through these qualities she creates a real bondage of love, happiness and peace. Being an ideal wife she can establish harmony at home which will ultimately lead to a greater peace in society i.e, microcosm vis-à-vis macrocosm. Being a mother she creates a new world. Children are nourished, loved and cared by her.

> It is through the mother that a new life is shaped and released into the world. It is the warmth of a mother's love that first put its imprint on the offspring...when mothers become shy of their motherhood and lose their motherliness 'Matrudevo Bhavo' lost its meaning too. Mothers lost their hold on children, families lost their sanctity, societies lost their cohesiveness and the nation its integrity (Lakshmi Kumari, 1997).

Indian society had its glorious past, where women were free and equal like the male folk. Women and men were happy. They shared their thoughts commonly, distributed their labour equally and maintained real harmony in their homes and society. But gradually those golden days were over with the advancement of civilization. The male folk, through their physical strength and intention occupied the dominant status, began to exploit the women's inherent qualities of love, affection and submissiveness and kept the women within the four walls. Various customs, laws and religious dicta also made the women feel insecure, dependent and a burden for the family and society at large.

> For an Indian woman, imminent motherhood is not only the personal fulfillment of an old wish and the biological consumation of a lifelong promise, but an event in which the culture confirms her status as a renewer of the race and extends to her a respect and consideration which were not accorded to her as a mere wife (Kakar 1988: 68).

In Indian society, even today, from family to office, a girl is identified by her relationships with other male members, as she is referred to by her father's name (in the case of unmarried girls) or by her husband's (in the case of married girls) and in her old age by her son's. So if we observe critically, women will always be known throughout her life in relation to another male member. She is fully dependant on him. So it is spontaneous and natural for her to desire a son.

In her family she has observed her father's dominance, after marriage she accepts her husband as the ruling authority. So in the same way unconsciously she wants to be a mother of a son who one day would be a husband and a father. Being a mother she will control him and will feel joy that she is the mother of a son. This is the social conditioning that develops her psychological and cultural behaviour. So the personality system is directly linked with the social system.[5]

> For the Indian mother ... the son is the major medium of self expression. It is her motherhood that the

> traditional family values and respects; her wifehood and daughterhood are devalued and debased. The women's self-respect in the traditional system is protected not through her father or husband, but through her son. It is also through the son–and for that matter on the son–that she traditionally exercises her authority (Nandy 1988:74).

Ashis Nandy in his article 'Woman Versus Womanliness in India' rightly points out that "all forms of conservatism and protests against modern western encroachments on the Indian society have taken shelter in and exploited the symbol of motherhood" (ibid : 74).

Throughout India, the concept of motherhood is venerated. The words 'mata' and 'Ma' (mother) connote warmth, protection and life-giving power. Ideally a child is expected to honour his mother. The cow is worshipped in North India as 'Gao Mata' (mother cow). 'Sitala' deity is the powerful local goddess who is responsible for the cure and protection of the villagers (Manna: 2003).

We would like to conclude with a quote from the case study by Jyoti Puri (1999), where she reaffirms the finding that the concept of motherhood is not and should never be considered as a monolith. Besides her subordination, Indian woman, not only in her own country, but in the other countries too, is identified by her intrinsic qualities of motherhood. Nine months and nine days she bears the troubles of bearing her child, her breast milk is the first feed for her baby; she also endures the pain of delivery. But she forgets everything when she touches her child, perceives the sensation of her child's soft skin against hers. She forgets her pain and sorrows when she watches the child's divine smile and feels the pleasure of the suckling of her breast. She never feels tired of changing diapers or other untiring work for her children that keeps her busy the whole day. This mother-child relationship is filled with divineness. In Puri's study on 54 anonymous women who depicted their narratives of which 23 of the married women are mothers. She observes:

> Motherhood is the other role through which middle-class women attempt to secure their positions as wives and daughters-in-law. In the narratives of these women on the meaning of motherhood, or its aspects such as pregnancy, child birth, and breastfeeding, no monolithic account emerges. Instead, they express themselves in ways that draw upon, qualify, and question hegemonic notions of motherhood and womanhood. In contrast to these prevailing hegemonic expectations, these women's narratives on aspects of motherhood are more nuanced, complex, and nor easily categorized... these narratives also suggest ways in which motherhood may be a means to subvert the limits of their positions as wives and daughters-in-law. It is in this respect that these narratives more clearly deviate from prevailing notions or scholarly literature on marriage and womanhood (Puri 1999: 154).

II

Women are no longer only confined to their role as 'perfect wife' but multiple identities can be observed while they come forward to take up the challenges of the larger society. The articles incorporated in this work attempt to show the diversities of women's experience both at home and outside. Thematically these writings have been arranged in four sections but all these sections share the common point of showing how women are facing subordination through patriarchal norms and how they are trying to come out of it. Attempts have been made by the authors to assess the multiple roles of women besides motherhood in their various domains of socio- political and economic life. We hope that these writings will unearth the 'actual' normal practices about their social roles in the perspective of contemporary society.

The first section of this treatise deals with the literary representation of women as 'mother'. This section is headed by the name **Women as 'Mother' in literature.** There are three articles written by three eminent academicians who have tried to understand women as they have been treated in various literary works for identifying their multiple identities. Many changes have taken place over a period of time in women's life but there is a common point of agreement viz. the challenge of motherhood of women and how women have faced it. It is a biological experience and has a psycho-emotional feeling attached with it when a woman becomes a mother. Her motherhood distinguishes her from the male folk. In the three articles the contributors have selected those literary works for analysis where motherhood has been manifested in the feelings and the activities of women. Each of the writers has tried to trace out the woman as a separate entity for their particular inherent qualities. According to the narration of each author, motherhood is understood differently considering the socio-economic circumstances in which the woman lives since the practice of mothering is defined by the society.

The first article entitled *Dialectics and Resolution: A Paradigm of the Mother Cult in Tagore's Sacrifice* by Prof. Pralay Kumar Deb is based on the analysis of Tagore's famous writing 'Sacrifice'. The poet wrote this play, the English version of which was published in 1914, with the intention of putting an end to the sacrifice of living animals in order to propitiate God with their blood. It was a part of the living tradition of Bengal – the cult of 'Shakti Puja' that the mother Goddess has to be worshipped in this manner. In an extremely dramatized form, the poet draws our attention to the meaninglessness of violence and propagates his life- long philosophy of peace, non- violence and kindness organized on the basis of his knowledge of the spiritual heritage of India. The author here points out that Tagore's real intention is to depict the real image of the mother goddess-being the creator and benefactor of the earth. God cannot propagate violence. The mother, in the last analysis, play the role of a protective mother. They nurture and nourish and provide care. It is through universal love and humanism that one can really worship the Mother-God as worship of God implies love and concern for the universe. 'Sacrifice' does not mean sacrifice of blood through killing. It implies sacrifice of one's ego, his selfishness, sacrifice of cruelty and, in the last analysis, sacrificing one's pride and selfishness for the cause of community. The 'protective mother' demands love from us, 'love that makes the human divine and the divine human', and it is this love which makes him move on from darkness to light, from hostility to peace, from destruction to creation. The mother cult assumes the creation of the 'Religion of Man, which is above all religious dogmas'.

The second article, *In the name of the Mother: The Role of Woman as Mother* by Dr Nandini Saha, portrays a series of illuminative characters of mothers in four different stories of Mahasweta Devi as translated by Radha Chakravarty. The stories in this article are selected to show how mothers are overwhelmed with the feelings of motherhood. In these four stories, mothers exhibit their affectionate characters having the traits of love, sacrifice, devotion and self-denial. In the story *Ma from Dusk to Dawn*, the author narrates the role of a tribal mother, who sacrifices her whole life for her son after the death of her husband. Throughout the day she labors hard to earn for her son and after dusk she becomes the mother who cooks the rice to feed her "idiot son" even by depriving herself. But, alas, due to her chronic starvation, she invites her death and has to leave her son forever for whom she sacrifices her whole life. The author's second story is '*Sindhubala*' which was published in 1971. In this story, Sindhubala is identified as a *devangshi* woman. Her life is full of pathos without being a wife or a mother, but in spite of all, she performs the role of a mother curing all ailing children, as she supposedly possesses a mystical power. At last, she is blamed as an evil woman as she fails to cure the child whom she sees as her own. Here Sindhubala's primary identification rests on her failure to be a 'biological' mother. The next story *Jamunabatis Mother* is purely a story of a beloved mother who saves every penny to buy small gifts for her two-year-old daughter. But all in vain, Jamunabati is no more to receive the gifts from her mother. She dies of dengue fever and the money which her mother saves for buying her a gift, she uses for the funeral pyre of Jamunabati. This then is "A narration of deprivation, disillusionment and death, the story charts the gradual awakening of Jamunabati's mother from escapist self-delusion to a harsh confrontation with the reality of her predicament" (as quoted by the author from Chakravarty 2004). The last story of the collection is titled *Giribala* who is a helpless mother. She is an ideal mother who likes to protect her children with all her care and love but unfortunately due to poverty, Aullchand, the husband of Giribala, sells his two daughters. Being a mother Giribala is dumbstruck with grief. Finally Giribala leaves home and her husband decides to work as a maidservant in a town with her two children. So, in this story Giribala is not only a mother with all qualities of motherliness but finds out an independent source of livelihood also.

Prof. Barun Chakraborty has attempted to find out the changing role of women starting from *Charyapada* in the medieval age to Bani Basu's *Ekushe Pa*, which was published in the year 1994. Prof Chakraborty in his article initially undertakes a systematic understanding of the role of women in Bengali literature and finally he analyses one story in depth. His study reflects the changing role of women over a period of time. From several Bengali works of literature he has tried to analyse the role of women. From the oldest specimen of Bengali *Charypada* to the most recent novel written by Bani Basu's *Ekushe Pa*, he has systematically analysed the changes that have taken place in women's life. In *Charyapada* times, women were not mere appendages to men. Women were not their captive only for doing their home-management and child caring and rearing. They enjoyed considerable freedom, but gradually, women became subordinated under the rule of patriarchy. Husbands were treated as the replica of God. Qualities like devotion, sacrifice, *Patibrata, Sahamaran,* and chastity came to be recognized as the attributes of an ideal woman. 'Be like Sita, Sabitri' were the ideals for women and the names like Damayanti, Behula are often mentioned as examples to be emulated. The image of a 'Sati sadhhi' woman became the role model of a perfect wife. Women were abused to sacrifice their freedom. In the 19th century this role model of women began to be questioned. Tagore's *Mukti* (Salvation) is a poem taken from *Palataka,* the collection of poems. Here the author has depicted the real captive condition of a woman; how she was alienated from her family and ultimately she committed suicide to achieve freedom- freedom from the daily chores of bondage and drudgery. Characters like Sohini is taken from the story *Laboratory* by Tagore, Jasoda from *Sahartali* by Manik Bandopadhyay where they showed themselves differently from the archetypal characters of females of a traditional society. They are brave, independent and outspoken in speech and show attributes like that of a man. Manojini, a female character has been shown in a manner where a woman has freedom over her body as she thinks that sexual urge is like most primitive urges like that of food. So she does not hesitate to fulfill the sexual demands of her close male friends. Tilottama Majumder's *Chander Gaye Chand* is also a relevant example where the two girls Shreyoshi and Debrupa maintain lesbian relations. Finally the author states the outlook of contemporary society where the girl likes to go for a 'live together'. In this way, through different episodes he presents the changing role of women over a period of time.

In another section of this article, Chakraborty analyses a story *Sagar Sangam* where the protagonist Dakshyayani expressses her endured toleration, generous motherhood by finally accepting Batashi, as her own daughter who was basically a young child of a prostitute. She is in conflict with her self between her long cherished superstition and her eternal motherhood. At last, motherhood succeeds over superstition. In this way ultimately the reflection of motherhood supersedes the whole social character of Dakshyayani.

The second section of the book is entitled **Status of Women: An Overview**. The paper on *Context and Issues of Gender Discourse Today: The Case of West Bengal* by Prof. Biswajit Ghosh has been included as it gives a broad overview of the position of women in modern society, particularly in the context of West Bengal. In this paper, the author primarily focuses on the ever increasing problems of gender equity and gender violence with special reference to West Bengal. Though the Constitution has guaranteed right to equality between men and women, it is found that the female members of a family are subjected to all round deprivation even today. Women's oppression as well as their devalued position in the society is the central part of the debatable issues among academicians and policy planners. It is shown that even today a girl child is deprived of better health, nutrition and educational facilities and above all the right to equal treatment vis-à-vis a male child. All these reinforce the notion that girls are a burden and can easily be disposed of through early marriage. Dowry system, sexual harassment by elderly male relatives, as well as domestic violence as a post marital torture by husbands and in laws is the most common form of violence against women. This paper is informative and well documented for a proper understanding of sex ratio, child sex ratio, literacy and other indicators for assessing the status of women with special emphasis to West Bengal. The author has drawn our special attention to violence against women in West Bengal also inspite of the fact that this is a state where the condition of women is better than many other states. He argues in favour of dealing with the phenomenon in a holistic manner. As he says that "The real inhibiting factor of 'powerlessness' of women can be tackled by such 'holistic empowerment".

The third section of the book is highlighted by the issue on **Women: Dual Identity,** consisting of four different articles. *Problems of Working Mother: a Dilemma in Motherhood* is the first article written by one of the editors with her scholar Bhaswati Sarkar dealing with the issues related to gender equality and gender justice in the contemporary society. This study is purely an empirical work done in the Kalyani township wherein 385 working women were taken as sample of the work. The working women perform the dual roles-at office and at home-and often feel guilty for not having given adequate time to either place. Even the childless mother is marginalized among the mothers. Majority of the respondents (58.72%) perceive that they can manage their dual roles successfully. 35.58% respondents have opined that they manage their dual responsibilities moderately. These respondents try utmost to adjust themselves with the duality of their lives and try to manage both the activities. On the contrary, 5.72% of the respondents think that their dual roles hamper both their role in family and their role in the office. Majority of the respondents are of the opinion that in future if their dual roles at all affect their families, they will sacrifice their career for the sake of their children, husbands and families.

Widowhood: Crisis in Social Identity is written by Ms. Panchali Chakrabarty. The study was conducted among the Bengali Hindu widows residing in Naihati, North 24 Parganas in West Bengal. To know the socio-economic status of the widows, 300 widows were selected through random sampling. Having lost their husbands, these women feel depressed, deprived of love and all kinds of support of husbands on the one hand and social banishment on the other. This creates a feeling of loneliness and a sense of social ostracism among them. The study also reveals that the majority of the widows-both unemployed and employed- follow the rites, rituals and life-style pattern of the Hindu widows. Illiterate widows (62.61%) are more conservative in most cases. A liberal attitude is seen among 55.33% widows who have no faith in *Pap, Punya, Dharma, Adharma* as mentioned by them. But most of the respondents believe that widowhood is a consequence of sin committed or evil done by them in their previous life. The widows are marginalized group among the already marginalized women. They maintain a sub-cultural status. Except a few, majority of the women face tremendous socio-economic problems, economic hardship, along with social distance arising out of the traditional beliefs, practices, that relegate them to the status of sub-womanhood in our society.

In the third article of this section entitled *Awareness of Tribal Mothers toward Child Health: An Enlightening Motherhood,* the author has tried to assess the changing role of tribal mothers after the implementation of special and intensive welfare programs of ICDS and IPP for poor and illiterate people in rural and urban societies respectively. After the initiation of ICDS program, there has been a significant transformation in rural areas. Tribal mothers are now well aware about the necessity of the vaccination program for their child's health.

To look into the matter, an indepth survey was conducted among three tribal communities of Nadia District of West Bengal living in different rural and urban areas. In some of these villages ICDS, have been implemented by the Government of India to improve the health situation of the people. This study shows how the major tribal people of Nadia District-namely the Santal, the Munda and the Oraon have accepted this program and moved a step forward towards integration with the mainstream. In all the villages where ICDS centers have been opened, the tribal mothers have accepted it readily. All pregnant mothers and all children have been immunized though in a few cases they have stopped immunization. The rate of admission in the ICDS schools is also very satisfactory. The Santals are more advanced in this regard.

The paper on *Islamic law of Marriage and Divorce: Subjugated Womanhood by SAH Moinuddin,* is the fourth article of the third section of this collection. In this article the author has examined the nature and application of Islamic law of marriage and divorce as far as Muslim women are concerned. In Islam, marriage is not a sacrament but a civil contract between two adult members-male and female. Islamic law, though talks about the consent of women in marriage, really ensures dominance of men over women through marriage as it is practiced in Islamic societies. Muslim women face various forms of inequality and injustice. As a result, they virtually constitute subjugated section of the society. Muslims are very traditional and conservative in nature as religion pervades every aspect of their life. A Muslim man can have up to four wives at a time without any legal protection to the women against the exercise of this privilege. Polygamy is not a cause for seeking divorce by a Muslim woman. Divorce is very easy in their society. Men have absolute freedom to get divorce and the restrictions which are there, are only procedural in nature. There is little consolation in the fact that there is a provision of returning *mahr,* a sum of money to his wife which the husband accepted during the time of marriage when divorce is declared.

But, here also, in reality there are rare cases of individuals who return *mahr*. But actually there is no necessity of such divorce as Muslims can keep four wives at a time. So, he simply discards her or ill-treats her. By and large, it can be stated that Muslim law is fettered with inequalities and the women in every case are considered less equal. The author also has shown in his study that only 2 out of 128 women got *mahr*. So, the Islamic law of marriage and divorce reflects a subjugated womanhood and there is little change in the situation even today.

Women in Politics is the final section of this book consisting of three articles written by three sociologists. The status of women in Indian society has been changing a lot. Women are no longer confined within the four walls. They are on the move. The participation of women in politics in India is the resultant effect of the Constitution (73rd amendment) Bill which was accepted in 1993, stipulating one third right of representation to women in Panchayat Raj institution (local self government). Women's political empowerment is becoming a central issue at present. Democracy means the equal participation of men and women in all spheres of life and at different levels of decision making. Gender equality-political and social is enshrined in the Fundamental Rights of the constitution, together with equality of opportunity to employment and appointment in office. Political equality includes not only the equal right to franchise but also the more important right to gain access to the formal institutionalized centers of powers. Independence brought with it the opportunity for equality in the social and political spheres, through the instrumentality of the Constitution.

In the paper entitled *Women and Politics in India–Quotas as Antidote to Marginalization*, Prof Swapan Kr. Pramanick has tried to examine three important but related issues connected with the participation of women in politics with reference to empirical studies done in rural areas in a few states in India.

1. The increasing marginalization and the peripheralization of women in politics in India accompanied by a

situation where politics itself is greatly marginalized due to non-participation of decent people including women.

2. The paradoxical attitude of male dominated politics and political parties towards the question of reservation for women in the political arena on the one hand, and their lip service to the cause of women, on the other.
3. The nature and effect of 33 per cent reservation of seats and offices for women in Panchayats.

The analysis has been made with particular reference to the situation prevalent in the state of West Bengal. Under the leadership of Mahatma Gandhi, the first political movement of women started in pre-independence days when women joined the freedom struggle in hundreds and thousands. But in the post independence era, the adverse attitude of the major political parties towards granting position to women in politics and the norms of patriarchy, have alienated women from politics. That can be shown if one analyses the percentage of women representatives in Parliament and the State Assemblies.

Ultimately the reservation for women in politics has created a new horizon for women. The opportunities have opened up. A large number of women, along with SCs and STs, get a chance to enter the political arena to take part in political processes. The social base of 'representative democracy' is thereby spread out throughout the country. This has also led women to legitimize and reinforce their role in the public sphere, particularly in formal governmental structure. This process has intensified and opened up a new arena for women. With this process, women have been experiencing an increase in their self esteem, confidence and motivation which help them for better understanding and greater coordination with the larger society. The author has shown how the whole process of participation of women in politics through reservation has falsified the traditional conservative stand that women are only ideal homemakers and that they are incapable of participating in the political process.

In his paper *Women and Contemporary Justice: Populism through Reservation* Soumyajit Patra argues that without changing the attitude of society towards women, mere reservation of seats in election will hardly bring any positive impact. The author talks about a sincere attempt that should be made for changing the value system, belief pattern and cultural practices and internalization of these through proper socialization. One major step towards this radical transformation may be the introduction of gender equality awareness right from the primary level of formal education. Over and above, 'conscientisation' can be developed in this way. Finally, the author raises a question about effectiveness of this reservation policy in a highly stratified society. As the backward classes are also internally differentiated, this has given birth to the claim of quotas within the quota. Therefore, reservation is not the only solution. In a democratic set up, it is desirable that the entire electoral system is open, secular and rational. And through this process only one can ensure a fair political participation both for men and women.

Sandip Kumar Ghatak, in his paper on *Political Participation among the Women in West Bengal – its Nature and Extent* has mentioned the importance of party membership, attending public meetings, casting votes, political discussion with peer groups, regularity of reading newspaper and magazine etc. in analyzing the nature of participation. Till today, the position of women among all the recognized political parties both in national and state levels is not at all encouraging. Political parties are not prepared to share power equally with women while they nominate their candidates in any election. Even the topmost position of the party is often monopolized by men. In the top decision making committees in all parties, women take part in negligible number. In local level politics their participation is also not satisfactory at all. The author argues that, with a view to improving the position of women in law making body, a major role should be played by political parties. Women constitute half of the population and it is only through their participation that a real democracy can be operationalized.

NOTES

1. One of the authors of this book frequently visits different parts of the states for conducting her field work since 1980s till date. Her native place is a remote village named Amdabad, Nandigram Thana, Purba Midnapur. And her in-laws' house is also in the district of Hooghly, village Balarampur, Thana Pursura. As a participant observer she has personally observed that in each and every house of these two districts, the parents eagerly wait to welcome their sons but not their daughters. The sounds of the conch shells still remind the author about her feminine exclusion. For further examples see: Manna, Samita. 2000. *Fair Sex in Tribal Cultures*. New Delhi: Gyan Publisher. Though the tribals were once free regarding their preference for male child, but now due to the contact of caste people gradually they are also in some cases eager to get male child.
2. Domination of the patriarchal family exists in majority of the states of our country. Even in Assam state which is dominated by patriarchal family but there the daughters are welcomed graciously by their parents. Even there is no dowry and each family is supposed to accept their daughter as Lakshmi, the goddess of wealth. One University Professor once told me during the time of interrogation about the status of women in Assam, that in their area there is a common proverb "Sata Putra Sama kanya" (one daughter is equivalent to hundred sons).
3. Freud outlined his theory of sexual and emotional development by assuming a fixed, 'normal', mode of social masculinity and femininity in which 'normal' masculinity and 'normal' femininity had predictable social paths. For example, in an age where contraception was unreliable it was entirely reasonable to suppose that 'normal' heterosexual intercourse led to 'normal' motherhood and fatherhood. Whether individuals wished for this or not, such was the direct impact of biology on destiny (Evans 1994 : 31).
4. "Radical feminism rejects the male- dominated society as a whole and claims that women when freed from the dominance of patriarchal relations- should aim to transform the existing social order radically even to develop their own social institution. This radicalism is based on the assumption that women have different experiences and interests than men and that women have radically different orientations than those characterizing

traditional and contemporary patriarchal society (Alvasson and Billing 1997: 22-23).

5. "A social system is a system of processes of interaction between actors, it is the structure of the relation between the actors as involved in the interactive process which is essentially the structure of the social system" (Parsons 1964: 25).

REFERENCES

Alvasson. M and Billing, Y. D. (1997), *Understanding Gender and Organizations.* New Delhi: Sage Publications.

Beauvoir, S.D. (1997), *The Second Sex.* London: Vintage.

Bhomick, P.K. (1966), *The Lodhas of West Bengal.* Calcutta: Puthi Pustak.

Bhomick, P.K. (1974), *The Socio-cultural Profile of Frontier Bengal.* Calcutta: Puthi Pustak.

Buhler, G. (1964), The Laws of Manu (Trans.), in Muller, M.ed, *Sacred Books of the East,* Vol. XXV, Delhi: Motilal Banarasidas.

Caplan, P. (1985), *Class and Gender in India; Women and their Organizations in a South Indian City.* London: Tavistock Publications.

Collins, P.H. (1991), *Black Feminist Thought: Knowledge, Consciousness and the Politics of Empowerment.* New York: Routledge.

Das, R.M. (1962), *Women in Manu and Hissevem Commentators.* Varanasi: *Kanchana Publication.*

Evans, M. (1994), The Women Question. New Delhi: Sage Publication.

Finlay, B. (2007), *Before the Second Wave : Gender in the Sociological Tradition.* New Delhi: Dorling Kinders (India).

Firestone, S. (1972), *The Dialectic of Sex.* London: Paladin.

Forbes, G. (1996), *The New Cambridge History of India.* Cambridge: Cambridge University Press.

Geetha, V. (2002), *Gender.* Calcutta: Stree.

Ghadially, R. (1988), *Women in Indian Society.* New Delhi: Sage Publications.

Ghosh, B. (2007), *Trafficking in Women and Children, Child Marriage and Dowry: A Study for Action Plan in West Bengal,* Government of West Bengal and UNICEF.

Jacobson, D. and Wadley, S. S. (1999), *Women in India:* Two Perspectives. Delhi: Manohor.

Kakar, S. (1988), 'Feminine Identity in India', in R. Ghadially (ed): *Women in Indian Society*. New Delhi: Sage Publications.

Kakar, S. (1990), *Intimate Relations: Exploring Indian Sexuality*. Chikago: University of Chikago Press.

Karve, I. (1968), Kimship Organization in India. Bombay, Asia Publishing House.

Mead, M. (1939), *From the South Seas*. New York: William Morrow.

Lakshmi Kumari, M. (1997), *The Role of Women in Society: Sita Must Live*. New Delhi: Sterling Publishers Pvt. Ltd.

Lawler, S. (1996), 'Motherhood and Identity', in T. Cosset, A. Easton and P. Summerfield (eds.) *Women Power and Resistance*. Philadelphia: Open University Press.

Manna, S. (2000), *The Fair Sex in Tribal Cultures-Problems and Developlment*. New Delhi: Gyan Publishing House.

Manna, S. (2003), *Crystallisation of Caste in Frontier Bengal*. New Delhi: Classical Publishing Company.

Nandy, A. (1988), 'Woman versus Womanliness in India. An essay in Social and Political Psychology in Rehana Ghadially (ed.): *Women in Indian Society*. New Delhi: Sage Publications.

Prabhu, P.N. (1940), *Hindu Social Organization*. Bombay: Popular Prakashan.

Puri, J. (1999), *Woman, Body, Desire in post-colonial India: Narratives of Gender and Sexuality*. New York: Routledge.

Ross, A.D. (1961), *The Hindu Family in its Urban Setting*. Toronto: University of Toronto Press.

Section One

Role of Women as Mothers in Literature

1

Dialectics and Resolution: A Paradigm of the Mother-cult in Tagore's *Sacrifice*

Pralay Kumar Deb

While dozing off the weary hours in a railway carriage, Tagore, at the age of twenty-four, dreamt of a little girl deeply shocked at the sight of a blood-streak running down the steps of a temple. Vainly she tried to wipe out the blood-streak, but the memory of her agonizing effort haunted Tagore throughout his life. His immediate response to the merciless slaughter of animals in the name of religion found expression in his second novel *The Saint-King*. The continuing train of thought achieved a new dimension of significance in *Sacrifice*, originally a Bengali poetic drama, later translated into English prose to the exclusion of all the melodramatic excesses which somewhat obscured the main focus of interest in the original.

The English version of *Sacrifice*, published in 1917, attests to Tagore's maturity of vision; it may be regarded as the distillation of his life-long philosophy of peace, non-violence and kindness, organized on the basis of his knowledge of the spiritual heritage of India. The great fulfilling chant of his life-of his invocation to the divine sanctities of human love-enriched with the associations of Upanishadic messages and Buddhist precepts-has been crystallized in the thematic structure of the play. He depicts the tragedy of Jaisingh, torn in a conflict between his loyalty to King Govinda and his love for Raghupati, the Brahmin priest who has brought him up as his son. King Govinda forbids sacrifice in the temple of Goddess Kali and Raghupati becomes infuriated at the violation of 'laws laid down in scriptures'[1] so much so that he goes on to plan the deposition and even murder of King Govinda. Unable to satisfy Raghupati's frenzied desire for royal blood, Jaisingh sacrifices his own life at the altar of the Goddess, thus extinguishing the flames of retributive passion which engulf the whole being of Raghupati. Love emerges triumphant, the graceful blessing of the Mother, as is evident in the happy reconciliation between King Govinda and Queen Gunavati and in Raghupati's contrition that makes him discover in Aparna 'the last gift of Jaisingh (p. 187).

Tagore's primary intention in the play is to expose the meaningless atrocity of animal sacrifice, committed in wild transports of primitive lust for blood, with the deliberately false or superstition-dominated assurance of placating the anger of 'the dread Mother' (P.134) wearing a necklace of human skulls. And he succeeds in spotlighting the supreme importance of love which, sweetened by compassion, triumphs over the violent excesses of ritualism and initiates a new phase of human religion in the history of dehumanized Shakti-worship. In the thematic structure of his play, however, alongside his disapprobation of the hysterics of murderous ferocity, there is an attempt to explore the dialectics implicit in the paradigm of the Mother-cult by dramatizing it in the conflicting personalities of King Govinda and Raghupati. The dialectics is resolved with the self-sacrifice of Jaising; the tragic universe is re-integrated, the moral and cosmic harmony re-established with a true recognition of the loving identify of the Mother.

The English version of *Sacrifice* does not contain any Act-division, and in spite of its organic symmetry in the collation of plot-mechanics, it is reminiscent of the technique of a Jatra performance, unfolding a continuous sweep of action oriented towards the inevitable. The centre of action is the conflict between King Govinda and Raghupati, the one altruistic, forgiving and scarcely conscious of his regal glory and the other vindictive, uncompromising and always prompted by the blatant arrogance of his Brahmin lineage. The specifically dramatic element of conflict, the classical *agon*, between an apostle of *sophrosyne* and an embodiment of *hubris* forms the nucleus of good theatre, at once exciting and elevating, but what is generally missed in the evaluation of Tagore's play is that his conflict is not merely between two opposed personalities having opposed points of view (as is the conflict between Dionysus and Pentheus in Euripides' *Bacchae* or between Henry and Becket in Anouilh's *Becket on L'Honneur de Dieu*) but, in a deeper sense, between two opposed principles of the age-old Mother-cult, namely violence and love. Principles have, however, been fused into personalities in the play, and the uniqueness of Tagore's contribution to the development of religious drama in Bengal consists in his deep-searching analysis of the Mother-cult through the presentation of ideological characters reacting to and clashing with one another on a non-allegorical plane.

Raghupati, supported by Queen Gunavati who wants to extricate herself from the 'barren waste of childlessness' by her offerings of 'the red bunches of hibiscus and beasts of sacrifice', (p. 106) expresses his unshaken faith in the Mother's lust for destruction. To Jaising he says:

The world is ceaselessly killing; and the great Goddess Kali, the spirit of ever-changing time, is standing with her thirsty tongue hanging down from her mouth, with her cup in hand, into which is running the red life-blood of the world, like juice from the crushed cluster of grapes. (p.147)

King Govinda, who is in sympathetic communion with Aparna, the unfortunate beggar-girl, contemplates, on the other hand, the vision of an all-loving, all merciful Mother who can be offered only flowers and who can be approached for saving the weak and helpless from the grip of the strong and cruel. Towards the end of the play, when Gunavati says. 'The Goddess is no more', he affirms his faith in the humane nature of the Mother : 'She has burst her cruel prison of stone and come back to the woman's heart.' (p. 187).

And what he says is echoed in the address that Raghupati makes to Aparna : 'Come, child, come, Mother. I have found thee'. (p. 187) Raghupati and King Govinda suggest the antagonistic forms of the Mother-cult, which are, however, resolved in the end, as they have been in the Bengali imagination, yielding a homely harvest of inalienable faith.

The image of Goddess Kali that Raghupati worships is the image of 'the Terrible',(p.179) the raging and shrieking Mother, thirsty for blood, glorying in the carnage wrought by Herself. The citizens of Tripura, uncritical heirs to centuries of ritualism, also worship this image, singing the hymn of the Goddess in ecstatic excitement:

The dread Mother dances naked in the battle field,
Her lolling tongue burns like a red flame of fire. (p.134)

They sing of her dishevelled dark tresses sweeping away the sun and stars and of the red streams of blood running from her cloud-black limbs, recalling the description of Goddess Chamunda in Bhabahuti's *Malati-Madhava*. Raghupati, along with his followers, pays homage to the Mother who devours time, destroys evil, drenches herself in the blood of 'countless killings'. (P.147) His idea of the terrible aspects of the Goddess looks back to the tradition-consecrated ambit of Tantric meditations on the Shakti-cult. It should, however, be remembered that in the scriptural incantation it is mentioned that the Goddess, who is four-handed, carries in her upper left hand a sword and in her lower left hand a severed human head, while her upper right-hand offers courage and her lower right hand bestows blessings. Raghupati, who is obviously concerned with the implications of the sword and the severed human head, prays for courage and divine blessings, not for the salvation of his soul, but for wreaking vengeance on King Govinda. His prayer to the Goddess as he awaits the return of Jaising with eager yet tremendous expectancy is characteristic of his mental attitude:

"Do not allow thy repute to be lost, and thine enemies to laugh at thee. If thy children must lose their pride and faith in their Mother, and bow down their heads in shame before the rebels, who then will remain in his orphaned world to carry thy banner?" (p. 180).

It is Aparna, whose pet goat 'has been brought by force to the temple to be killed', (p.107) who first raises her voice of protest against the customarily-accepted destructiveness of Mother Kali. She addresses the Mother directly: "Mother, art thou there to rob a poor girl of her love? Then where is the throne, before which to condemn thee?"(p. 108).

King Govinda cannot redress her grievance forthwith, but he takes steps, forbidding sacrifice to the Goddess, and this he does because, as he says to Raghupati, 'Mother came to me, in a girl's disguise, and told me that blood she cannot suffer'. (p. 111) Mother came to him, as he informs Gunavati later, 'Not with her petition, but with her sorrow'. (p. 155) King Govinda envisions the loving kindness of the Mother, conceives of her as the mother of all earthly creatures suffering the buffets of pitiless greed, blind ignorance and overweening pride, and prays to her to be a pattern of affection: 'Mother, do nor raise your sword and lick your lips for blood; do not set brother against brother, and woman against man.' (p. 155) He does not question the Mother's will, but he tells her that 'when King's blood is shed by a brother's hand, then lust for blood will disclose its demon face, leaving its disguise as a goddess' (p. 156). Profoundly disturbed by Chandpal's information that his brother Nakshatra has promised Raghupati to bring blood to the Goddess, King Govinda thinks of the hideous enormity of the sin planned to be committed, but his spirit of submission to the Mother remains as humble as ever: 'If such be your wish I bow my head to it'. (p. 156) He loves the Mother, discovering her filial affinities to the exclusion of her furies of destruction, and prays to her for the well-being of all: '... let your creatures live in peace.' (p. 155) His contemplation of the essentially human aspect of the Mother reminds us of the soulful lyrics of Shakta composers like Ramprosad and Kamalakanta.

An interpretation of the basic theme of *Sacrifice* could have been made in the manner in which Hegel interprets that of Sophocles' *Antigone*, in the *Phenomenology*[2] and *Aesthetics*[3], as illustrative of a collision between two equally justified principles of 'the ethical substance', if only Raghupati were disinterested in his application of the divine concept. In Sophocles' play both Antigone and Creon are destroyed, one commits suicide and the other is hurled into the measureless caverns of despair, providing the restoration of the 'harmony of the spirit' (*Geist*) in the end. In Tagore's play, however, Raghupati suffers while the King wins and the antithetical scheme of confrontation between them is resolved only with the self-sacrifice of Jaising. Ragupati's devotion to Mother Kali is deep-seated and unquestionable, but he takes advantage of it to reinforce his Brahmin image on several occasions. In fact, his religious fervour has been smothered by his bigoted conviction in caste superiority. Consider the following extracts from his speeches to Jaising, Queen Gunavati and King Govinda respectively:

(a) But there remain the Brahmins, though the gods be absent; and the King's throne will supply fuel to the sacrificial fire of their anger. (p.117)

(b) Oh, the evil age, when the Brahmin's futile curse recoils upon himself, to sting him into madness. (p.120)

(c) Sceptic, are you so certain in your mind that Brahmins have lost the ancient fire of their sacred wrath? (p.137)

Raghupati believes in the power of the Brahmin's curse, prides himself on his being a Brahmin, suffers abjectly as he has to shame his Brahminhood by kneeling before the King. He is indeed a fanatic, like Chanakya in D.L Roy's *Chandragupta*, bent on asserting the supremacy of the Brahmins in the degenerate ethos when 'The King's throne is raising its insolent head above the temple altar'. (p.117) He has the greatest lesson of his life when Jaising, his cruel, ungrateful 'darling', kills himself in his presence–the lesson of love which obliterates the distinction between a Brahmin and a Kshatriya and shows the victory of whatever is positive in life. Raghupati unlearns hatred and learns humility.

The absolute of truth is achieved through a rejection of the destructive cult of violence, the sordid folly of revenge. Raghupati discovers his way to the positive, transcending a series of negatives. After the self-immolation of Jaising, realizing the futility of his Brahmin fundamentalism and the emptiness of his religious hegemony, he throws away the image of Goddess Kali and denies her existence outright. To Queen Gunavati he says, 'Goddess there is none...She is nowhere,- neither above, nor below... No, there is none... Nothing, nothing'. (pp. 183-5) When King Govinda asks about the image, he answers in a similar vein, 'The Goddess is nowhere' (p. 186) Like King Lear in Act V. scene iii of Shakespeare's play, who utters the word 'never' no fewer than five times, Raghupati, the wreck of a man by now, forlorn and helpless in his unassuageable anguish, harps on the nothingness of the stony image of delusion which he seems to have filled with all his 'impotent dreams'. (p. 183) King Lear suffers and then dies in a world where evil has been pushed to its most malignant extremes, but Raghupati is redeemed in a world of human sensitivity as Aparna calls him 'Father' and he responds to her call–the call that Jaising has left behind him in her sweet voice. Raghupati gets to understand that love is the centre and circumference of life–that it enshrines truth and conquers death. Jaising wanted to drink at the fountain of love in 'this unanswering void, truthless, merciless, and motherless'. (p. 166) He wanted to hear from Aparna something which would 'overflow this life with sweetness, flooding death itself'. (p.167) Without any hesitation, misgiving or ambiguity he confided to her that she was his Goddess, for she was all sacrifice: 'You bring to me your sacrifice every moment, as a mother does to her child.' (p. 160)

In hours of spiritual conflict Jaising had the love of his sweetheart. Raghupati has the love of his daughter (who plays the role of a protective mother) when his son has left him–love that makes the human divine and the divine human. And it is this love which makes him move on from darkness to light, from hostility to peace, from destruction to creation. The Mother-cult assumes the character of the Religion of Man which is above all religious dogmas, Hindu and other. Fittingly enough, Tagore, who knew the need of the war-obsessed world around him better than any other Indian except Mahatma Gandhi, dedicated his play to 'those heroes who bravely stood for peace when human sacrifice was claimed for the goddess of war'.

NOTES AND REFERENCES

1. Rabindranath Tagore, *Sacrifice and Other Plays* (London, Macmillan, 1917, Reprinted 1970), p. 111. All subsequent page references to the play are to this edition.
2. Tr. J.B. Baillie (London, George Allen & Unwin, rev. ed. 1931), pp. 484-92, 739.
3. Cited in the translation by F.B. Osmaston, as *The Philosophy of Fine Art* (4 vols, London, G. Bell and Sons Ltd., 1920), pp. 215. IV. 323-4.

2

In the Name of the Mother: The Role of Woman as Mother

Nandini Saha

In the Name of the Mother (2004) is a collection of short stories by Mahasweta Devi, translated into English by Radha Chakravarty. The four stories in this collection deal with the exposition of the ideas of motherhood. Mahasweta Devi, popularly known for her novels on the tribal and marginalized communities, has here dealt with the mythicized idea of 'motherhood' related to all its ramifications in terms of class and caste. These stories were first published earlier and have been brought together in this volume, as the translator Radha Chakravarty feels, "The stories in this volume are linked by a common thread: the idea of the mother" (blurb). 'Ma, from Dusk to Dawn' ('*Shanjh-shokaaler Ma*') was first published in 1970, 'Sindhubala' ('*Sindhubala*') in 1971, 'Jamunabati's Mother' ('*Jamunabati'r Ma*') first published in 1972 and 'Giribala' ('*Giribala*') in 1982.

> In the definition of ideal womanhood that has evolved in the decades following Independence, the elision of femininity and maternity has become a determining feature. Motherhood is deified, but paradoxically, the myth of mother's quasi-divine status is premised upon her capacity for voluntary self-sacrifice.[1]

In the Introduction to this volume the translator explains how the idea of the 'mother' has at different periods of history served various political and social purposes. The stories in this volume represent the 'mother' figure, at times even as quasi-divine, in order to reiterate her status "premised upon her capacity for voluntary self-sacrifice". The stories fictionalize the concept of motherhood and its social relevance with particular reference to the marginalized and lower strata of society. These tales narrate the interrelatedness of the existence of the woman/mother as an individual with her specific socio-cultural background, her role as mother superseding her roles as daughter and wife, and the process of realization of her 'self' through her struggle for her children. I will attempt in my paper to show how, in spite of attempting to subvert the conventional notions of motherhood by presenting an "ambivalent concept with both restrictive and emancipatory potential" (x), Mahasweta Devi appears to be reiterating and valorizing the self-sacrificing image of the 'mother' which is conducive to the traditional concept. Much in the same vein the translator Radha Chakravarty comments on Mahasweta Devi's 'chronicling of truth':

> Her representations of the maternal thus reveal a deep ambivalence. While seeking to expose the hypocrisy latent in discourses of maternity, she does not reject the values of love, care, and responsibility that are traditionally associated with the maternal role. (viii)

In 'Ma, from Dusk to Dawn' the story revolves around the transformation of a woman with strong ancestral ties to the mother donning the 'robe' of a mystical healer to feed her son. The narrative begins with the death of Sadhan Kandori's mother Jati Thakurni. Jateshwari or Jati Thakurni as she is later renamed, a descendant of the ancient tribe of Jara the hunter, also known as the Pakhmaras or bird hunters, marries herself in to the Kandori caste of her husband Utsav Kandori. The Kandoris by profession "wove reeds into delicate mats" (14). In spite of the fact that her husband belongs to a higher caste, Jateshwari, contrary to the usual mindset of Hindu women, fails to identify herself with her husband's caste. Conversely she feels herself being haunted by the curse of her tribe and when her husband dies due to consumption of illicit liquor at her son's rice-eating ceremony, she believes it is the curse that kills him. Since Jara's arrow had killed Lord Krishna in pre-historic times, his tribe had been banished from their land in Dwarka and cursed to roam around from place to place without a permanent home, living on crematorium grounds and their members had to marry within their caste or the ancient curse would kill those who married them. Jati believes that it is this curse that kills her husband because she had dared to run away and marry outside her tribe. After the death of her husband Jati finds herself not only alone but also strangely enough, the author comments "Jati was now free" (22). The man, for whom she had dared to leave her people and probably taken a curse on herself and her family by doing so, she somehow feels relieved by his death! Jateswari did not want to climb up the social ladder as Utsav had planned to by changing his name (and thus their caste) through affidavit to Utsav Das from Utsav Kandori. Jati is much too attached to her historic tribe, even its curse, to want to give it up only to move up the social ladder and belong to the 'gentleman' class. There is a strong assertion of her tribal identity as against the rise in social hierarchy that would lead to a loss of that indigenous tribal identity.

The presence of her young son, Sadhan, who appears like a "frightened bird... clasped to her breast" (22), ties her to her identity of Jati Thakurni till her last. The red cloth and the small trident given to her by the old sanyasi of the Hanuman temple in the heart of the Kharagpur station coolie slums, where Jati takes shelter after her husband's death, helps her to transform from the descendant of the accursed Jara the hunter to Jati Thakurni, the woman with mystical healing powers. She rises in social staus: first by marrying Utsav who was by birth a "weaver of fine mats, of a higher caste than the Pakhmaras, the bird hunters" (20-21), Jateshwari's tribe, and then by Utsav's working as a coolie at the Kharagpur railway station, Jati rises in caste as well as class. But her constant awareness of the curse of her Jara tribe, keeps her connected to her ancestors in spite of her marriage and movement away and her climb higher up the social ladder. But it is as a mother that she finally reaches the highest rung, where she is worshipped as a goddess from sunrise to sunset. She becomes Sadhan's 'mother' only after sunset and till the sun rises again, thus 'Ma from dusk to dawn'. In her last moments she wants to call her son and make him sit near her but she cannot because it is daytime and her devotees all flock around her. "They're the ones who supply the rice all year round, keep Sadhan alive. One day, Jati had turned Thakurni at her own will. And it is as Thakurni that she must die today." (10) The concept of the supremely powerful mother-Goddess is subverted here by depicting the helplessness of the mother who is forced to become a 'goddess' to feed her son and in the bargain loses the freedom to even express her motherly affections.

"After much thought she became Thakurni. Or else she could not have saved her idiot son.... Jati realized that without donning the armour of the supernatural, she would have nothing to protect her." (27) She has no work, no home to call her own when she leaves Kharagpur and reaches Howrah. To ward off the advances of men Jati uses the red cloth of the sanyasi. Sadhan, an "idiot boy, his brain remained undeveloped even at thirty. Built like a bull, his body contains nothing other than the stomach.... There's only the stomach." (3) To provide for the hunger of this bull-sized son of hers, Jati transforms herself to Thakurni, the woman with mystical powers who has cures for ailments and ways of redemption from one's sins. Jati Thakurni recalls the "antidotes and remedies learnt from her grandmother and prescribes medicines from time to time" (26), and in return her devotees give her offerings of rice that helps her to feed her son and satisfy his unending hunger. Through the day she earns the rice to feed her son and after dusk she becomes the mother who cooks that rice and lovingly feeds her son. The red cloth that the old sanyasi drapes on her misleads people to treat her as a "sadh'i", but helps her find a way to survive. Utsav's ambitions of belonging to the gentleman class and his efforts thus do not help Jati, nor is she able to rejoin her tribe after her husband's death. Symbolically her failure to find her tribesmen after Utsav's death is how she is discarded by her tribe for having failed them by marrying outside their clan. It is through what she has learnt from her grandmother of the ancient tricks of natural remedies, the teachings of her ancient historic tribe, and nothing of the upcoming caste and class, that saves her and her child.

Ironically Jati's transition during the day to the woman with mystical powers is for rice and she herself dies due to starvation. She not only ignores her personal desires as a woman when she whispers to herself "Curse this beautiful face" (26) and rejects all advances of men, but she also disregards even her basic need for food to survive. Whatever she earns as offering she feeds her bull-sized son. On the third day of her illness the doctor diagnoses Jati's disease as being highly contagious. The author comments: "Even today, in the land of India, no cure has been found for it. The name of this disease is starvation. Eating nothing, starving, feeding all the scraps to Sadhan, Jati Thakurni's nerves had dried up." (9) The story ends on an extremely poignant note when Sadhan runs away with the rice that has been arranged for Thakurni's *shraddha* ceremony. He needs to cook rice to keep his *shanj-shokaaler Ma*, dusk-to-dawn mother, close to him. On his way home Sadhan cries and urges his mother, "'Ma, you make your own way to heaven. Sadhan will cook rice now, eat it. Please forgive him.'" (32) We know Thakurni would also rather have him cook rice and eat it than perform a grand *shraddha* ceremony in her honour. She was foremost the self-sacrificing mother and that is what she lived and even gave her life for.

"Sindhubala, plain of face, dark of skin" (33) is how the second story of the collection, with the title 'Sindhubala' begins. Her father loved his dark daughter and planned to buy a son-in-law for her. He had ambitions of becoming a builder from a mason and planned to "bait a son-in-law with hard cash" (34) and build a room or two for them on the roof. It is her mother Panchumi who thought of her daughter as the one with the "bulging forehead, snub nose, black skin" (34), a daughter who she brings up alone on "*muri* and *khoi*", and even gets her married with a fanfare and a feast. The well meaning and loving father dies untimely and the mother who did not think too highly of Sindhubala is the one who eventually brings her up, gets her married and after Sindhu is deserted by her in-laws, finds a means of survival for both herself and her daughter. The highly imaginative and ambitious father is contrasted with the practical and down-to-earth mother of Sindhubalā. Even Panchumi's fears about her daughter's looks are proved true when Sindhu's mother-in-law brings her back complaining that her son is going astray for the want of a "beautiful bride" (34). The high wall that Sindhu's father had built around the house as if to protect his wife and child from the world is broken by Sindhu's mother to open a shop in the corner where she sits frying "*khoi-muri-chola*" and makes popcorn and sells it. Metaphorically the wall had anyway broken to expose the mother-daughter duo to the trials and tribulations of life with the death of Sindhu's father. Sindhu's mother keeps saying "Work hard never rest/Your fortunes will prosper/Your home'll be blest" (36). It is Sindhu's mother who takes on the gendered role of the 'active male' rather than Sindhu's father. Again it is she who decides how much she will charge for Sindhu's mystical services. She even asks for the money in advance.

Sindhubala, married at fourteen, but left by her husband barely three years after marriage, is forced to touch ailing children with her 'auspicious' feet, even though she shudders to do so, because she is paid for the cure. This becomes the only source of income for the mother and daughter. Though she has failed to bear a child of her own, she is seen to possess supernatural powers that cure ailing children. In spite of being labeled the one who is "born divine, a *devangshi* girl" (37), she nevertheless finds herself trapped in a "sterile, barren body" (39) as well as in a "sterile, barren household" (38). To Sindhu her home seems "much too ordered, much too clean and sparkling" (ibid) without the presence of children. She would rather go away to her husband as she longs for her non-existent conjugal life with Sanneshi. She does not like "sitting around as a *devangshi* woman" (39). She would rather be a regular wife and mother than this woman with supernatural healing powers. In fact she even has misgivings about her powers of healing. She asks her mother if it is not a sin to touch children with her feet, since Hindus are taught not to touch sacred objects with their feet. And children are regarded as god-like creatures. She is scared as to the consequences if something went wrong with any of the children she tries to cure. This 'business' of curing children with her feet seems to be lucrative and Panchumi has no qualms in cooking up stories to help continue with the act. Panchumi refuses Sanneshi when he comes to take Sindhu back saying, "My daughter now sits at home and raises a hundred rupees' worth of clothes and money. Why would we say goodbye to all of that?" (42) The act of being possessed by the goddess on Tuesdays and Saturdays has become a routine for Sindhubala, an intoxicating habit. "This addiction is an invisible enchanted wall. A wall that stands between Sindhu and all of life's realities" (40)–the realities of being a wife and a mother.

Sindhubala gives up "pretending to be a goddess" (44) the day Sanneshi curses her for being a sorceress and killing his son by casting an evil spell. All her years of being barren seemed to be quenched when they brought Sanneshi's son from his second marriage to her to be healed. She touches him with both hands over and over again, that she usually does not do, and prays so that he is cured. The child seems to be her own, the one she never has. But with the death of the child, Sanneshi firmly believes that Sindhu is evil. It is because of her evil spell that his children fail to survive. Henceforth Sindhu gives up on healing children, no matter what everybody says. She decides that if both the ordinary and the holy have to eventually meet with death, she would rather die an ordinary being. She is hurt that the man she loves thinks her evil and blames her for the death of his child. The irony of this story lies in the fact that the man who is responsible for Sindhubala becoming a *"devangshi"* girl, blames her at the end for being the evil sorceress not knowing that this 'mystical woman' act is all a pretense needed to earn bread for Sindhu and her mother. Like in the earlier story, here too the pangs of hunger lead the mothers, Jati and Panchumi, to tread the path of the supernatural. While in the earlier story it is the mother herself who dons the robe of the woman with mystical powers, here the mother makes her daughter don the robe. And as for Sindhubala her failure to be a mother leaves her at the end even without the 'robe' of the mystical healer. The author here then valorizes the 'mother' over all other identities of a woman.

The next story 'Jamunabati's Mother' does not deal with women and their quasi-divine powers. It is the story of how a mother works day and night to save every penny to buy small gifts for her two-year old daughter. It is the story of the lives of people who live in slums and how they make ends meet but are helpless in the hands of the illness that Mahasweta Devi terms in 'Ma, from Dusk to Dawn' as the "disease" that affect countries like India. It is the story of the population that live and survive in dire poverty "in the fields and farms, on the streets and pavements, beside the railway tracks" (52) and for whom the author bitterly comments: "Several lakhs of people like them must be immediately discarded, so that this country, this city, might become beautiful" (46). According to the translator Radha Chakravarty, the story "presents the ruthless consumerism of the modern city, where a two-year-old girl is regarded as "completely superfluous" because her father, a bottle washer and her mother, a seller of incense, "don't seem to be of any use to the world."[2]

Mahasweta Devi's caustic wit is seen working at its best here. In this story the author speaks of a family who live in the slums and survives by earning on a day-to-day basis. Jamunabati and her parents belong to the class of people who are "expendable... [because they] don't seem to be of any apparent use to either society or the world at large" (45). In fact they are "no more than the brackets in a mathematical equation. If you don't get rid of them, you can't begin to solve the problem" (ibid). Jamunabati is the thin, dark-skinned, 'with wisps of curly hair' and with a "coin tied around her waist" to keep her safe from the evil eyes of all, two-year old girl for whom her mother strives. Jamunabati's father cleans bottles at a chemist's and the mother goes from shop to shop selling incense sticks. They manage to employ a babysitter to look after Jamunabati when her parents are away, who has to be given four *rotis* everyday and "an extra two bucks" (47) as her payment. Rakhali, the babysitter, loves the little girl and takes good care of the child in her parents' absence. It is on one of Jamunabati and her mother's regular visits to the market, which is essentially the back lanes of the market, where they get to buy "cracked eggs, half-rotten potatoes, stale brinjals, very cheap"(ibid), when Jamunabati points to a doll that she wants. The doll cost nine rupees and sixty paise. But even after staying up at nights and making paper bags from the old newspapers Rakhali helps to buy from a few households, Jamunabati's mother manages to save only six rupees. But with this money she saves for the doll she has to instead buy Jamunabati's health drink that the doctor prescribes for her when she gets fever: "That stuff. Haven't you seen it in the movies? Twenty-three vitamins stuffed into a single container?" comments Jamunabati's father, which cost 'fourteen rupees'. Jamunabati's mother then gives up the eight rupees she has saved and asks her husband to get the other six and buy what the doctor has prescribed. But the doll never gets bought. It is then a red dress she spots in a shop. Though "her body can't cope" (49) with the strain, Jamunabati's mother's goal is to now save twelve rupees for that dress, so she stays up at nights to make paper bags as well as chop betel nuts, the new job that she has taken on to earn the extra amount.

In the guise of telling a story about Jamunabati's mother's struggle to work and overwork herself to fulfill her dreams for her daughter, the author questions the system of society. No amount of extra work can save her daughter's life. Although the money she saves allows her to pay for her daughter's funeral who dies of dengue fever. All her dreams to buy a doll or a dress for her daughter are eclipsed by the need for healthy and nutritious food, through the course of the story. The "timid, thin and weak" (50) father of Jamunabati is incapable of either doing extra work to earn extra money or do something to ensure the well being of his family. He is not only "timid, thin and weak" (50) in Jamunabati's mother's dreams but is also "timid, thin and weak in reality" (ibid).

The constant refrain that runs through the story is how such "expendable" people like these three of the emaciated and malnourished family are a hindrance for the 'growth' and 'progress' of the state. Within the framework of the author's attempt to question the governmental laws and system regarding attitudes towards the poor, the author also narrates the individual efforts of the mother. Neither the mother nor the father has a name but they nevertheless perform their duties that the not-so-nameless authorities fail to perform. Jamunabati's mother's unending efforts to earn and save for her daughter are all in vain. Her daughter first keeps falling ill due to lack of proper nutritious food and then finally dies due to dengue, the new menace in the city caused by unclean and unhygienic living conditions that help to breed mosquitoes. While it is a story yet again about a weak father and a struggling but stronger mother, it is also a caustic satire on the so-called progresses of the cities in the name of "*garibi hatao*". The author ironically drafts how it is just a slogan and nothing much is done at the level of concrete reality to eradicate poverty or help poor people to live better. Thus the story ends with an extremely loaded query by the author on behalf of people like the characters of this story: "With so many scientists, so much planning, such a lot of gas and so many chambers–was it not possible to arrange something?" (55) To quote Radha Chakravarty again, "A narrative of deprivation, disillusionment and death, the story charts the gradual awakening of Jamunaboti's mother from escapist self-delusion to a harsh confrontation with the reality of her predicament." (JSL 66) And also that "it is the sight of her daughter's dead body that strips Jamunaboti's mother of her last remnants of illusion. The body of the child functions here both as a token of defeat and as a site for the emergence of a new insight that establishes the link between private sorrow and collective social trauma." (JSL 67) Thus the translator charts the development of the 'self' of the mother alongside the delineation of the social issues.

The last story of the collection is titled 'Giribala'. This is the story of the helplessness of a mother. The issue of poverty and the way in which it determines the lives of the mothers in marginalized groups has been dealt with in the earlier stories of this collection. "A girl's by fate discarded, lost if she's dead, lost if she's wed"–is the scathing refrain that haunts this entire story. When Giribala's father, a prosperous bamboo trader, gets her married to the "ganja fiend" Aullchand, he does not realize the predicament that is to meet his daughter's fate. Even the truth about Aullchand's character from Bangshi fails to convince Giri's parents enough to refuse to send their daughter with Aullchand when he returns to take back his fourteen-year old bride. Living in the keeper's ramshackle hut in the corner of the orchard of the babu's land and working as a maidservant, Giri struggles to make ends meet. But she manages to give birth to three daughters and a son and gets the operation done to prevent further childbirth that of course enrages the vagabond Aullchand.

The story sadly but bitterly revolves around the rampant and flourishing flesh-trade that steals mothers of their teenage daughters like Giri's Belarani and Paribala. When her father for four hundred rupees sells off the twelve-year old Bela, everybody consoles Giri by saying that Bela is after all her father's property, as all adolescent girls are. And to Giri,

> Amidst this numbing grief, the truth suddenly flashes across her mind. Nobody is willing to give much thought to a girl-child. She, too, should not worry. She, too, is female. Her father too had surrendered her to a monster without making any enquiries first. (67)

The babu who Giri's father approaches for help, to find Bela, explains: "This is a new racket that's begun. All this talk of marriage is just a front for girl-trafficking. The racket's in full swing all over Murshidabad." (67) In depicting the sordid reality of girl trafficking and the apathetic authorities, the author delineates the strength of the mother. When she loses Bela, Giri runs from pillar to post trying to find her daughter while Aullchand sits around crying. And she also tries to get her younger daughter married off to a decent man before any untoward incident can take place. But when she loses Paribala again to the menace of the traffickers, she does not look for her because she knows it will be futile. As the babu's pishi comments: "She's the mother of a girl-child, after all! ... Don't I know why you shed no tears? Small sorrows make you weep but grief turns you to stone." (77) And with Pari, Giri's younger daughter, meeting with the same fate as her sister, Giri decides to leave her husband and work as a maidservant and bring up her two other children in the town. As she realizes at the end that if she had the courage to leave her husband and home earlier she could have saved her daughters from being sold off.

This story, unlike the others in the collection, is more about the helplessness than the strength of the 'mother'. Nevertheless the character of Giri, whose tale begins with the comment that "It had never struck anyone that Giribala might have a heart and mind of her own" (56), does show some effort to defy the norms and leave her husband's home to save her children. The home that Giri has always dreamt of possessing is built by Aullchand from the money he gets by selling his two daughters but Giri refuses to live in that house. She rather takes to the road, vows to work as a maidservant in the town and bring up her son Rajiv and youngest daughter Maruni, while Aullchand "glances at Maruni furtively" (77), probably hoping to earn some more money through her. Giri finally manages to muster up enough courage to leave the 'monster' of a man to the disapproval of all: "Everyone is convinced that it's not Aullchand but Giribala who's at fault." (78) "What happened to Bela and Pari was common practice these days. But why leave your husband and go away? What kind of woman was that?" (ibid) Probably the answer would be that such a woman is a mother, a mother for whom the well-being of her children is of prime importance.

> The stories in this volume present a range of responses to the discourse of motherhood, exposing in particular the intersecting forms of exploitation to which women in certain underprivileged sections of Indian society

are subjected. The stories also describe the strategies often evolved by women to survive and circumvent the forms of containment inflicted upon them by society. In more than one story, the central figure is a woman who awakens, through a painful experience related to motherhood, to a deeper awareness of the social injustices she ought to resist.

Much like the other stories of Mahasweta Devi on and about women where she criticizes the gendered concepts of woman and exposes the exploitation of women, the stories in the volume *In the Name of the Mother,* while delineating the ambiguous status of the all-powerful mother also represents the mother adhering to conventional notions of the role of a mother. Two of the stories in the collection show how the role of the 'mother' overshadow their existence in the world as women who possess mystical healing powers, the other two stories are about the specific roles of the mothers in their struggle against hunger. On the one hand the quasi-divine mothers are allotted power in being able to heal others, on the other hand that same power is eclipsed by their alternate role as mother. While the woman is shown to juggle her various roles, her role as 'mother' seem to minimize and dominate over the other roles. All these women seem to arrive at a self-realization through their estrangement from their husbands either through death or otherwise, and through their acceptance of their roles as mother. Thus motherhood is valorized over marriage here. With the mothers of these stories donning the robe of the supernatural mystical healers, the myth of the 'mother-figure' as goddess is shattered. Again as Radha Chakravarty points out, "Each narrative indicts the collective stereotyping that perpetuates the myth of divine motherhood, even as it recognizes the value of genuine mother-love." (xi) Apart from this the usual elements of a Mahasweta Devi narrative with its emphasis on the exposition of the exploitation of the marginalized, whether it be the tribal and minority groups in society or their women who then are 'twice exploited' -once as a member of their social group and as a member of the 'second sex'. Finally in this volume of stories it is the explication of the identity of the woman as 'mother' that gets precedence over and above all her other identities as an individual by her own right, as a daughter, or as a wife.

NOTES

1. Mahasweta Devi, *In the Name of the Mother*. Calcutta: Seagull Books, 2004, viii. All further references in the text with page nos.
2. Radha Chakravarty, "Reading Mahasweta: Shifting Frames" in Journal of the School of Language, Literature and Culture Studies, Jawaharlal Nehru University, New Delhi, ed GJV Prasad. Delhi: Pencraft, Spring 2004, 65-66. All further references to the text as JSL.

3

The Changing Role of Women in Bengali Literature

BARUN KUMAR CHAKRABORTY

Literature is the manifestation of contemporary social life. So if one is interested to be acquainted with the social life of Bengal, he is required to go thoroughly through the contemporary Bengali literature. The oldest specimen of Bengali literature is *Charyapada*. The people, portrayed in *Charyapadas* used to perform certain duties based on manual labour. As for example, women would drive the boats, they were experts in it. They would collect money from the passengers of the boat. They would prepare country liquor. Savar women (women of the hunting class) used to go to forests after getting properly dressed for a walk. They enjoyed that kind of freedom. In *Charyapadas* the joint family life of the Bengalees has been depicted.

Women always want that their husbands should be lovers of home. But women themselves were not always very loyal to their husbands. To many, the out side of courtyard was considered to be their own courtyard. During the day they were afraid even of their own shadow, but at night they could easily go out of their home when all were asleep (Chakrabarty 1390).

In *Sri Krishna Kirtan* we notice that Radha was married to Ihon during her childhood. She was residing at Ihon's home even before the completion of her eleven years. Early marriage was then customary in Bengal. Women of milkman class used to sale milk and curd in the market. So they used to go out of their residence. Of course mother-in-laws would not always allow housewives to go out side every now and then. Radha would cook various items for her husband Ihon (Bhattacharya 1999).

A few decades ago, when elderly women blessed others, they used to say 'be like Sita, Sabitri'. We may add a few names to this list like Damayanti, Behula etc. This proves that they were idols to the fair sexes. Since childhood, an Indian girl is taught to be an ideal house wife. Husbands are treated as the replica of God. A wife should follow her husband in every walk of life. Her first and foremost duty is to obey her husband, satisfy him even at the cost of her own self or life. If the husband is not loyal to his wife, if he has attachment to other women, still, wife should not desert him, dishearten him. If the husband tortures her physically it is her noble duty to bear with this torture whether it is physical or mental. In other words, a wife is one who sacrifices everything including self comfort, prestige, honour, in spite of facing tremendous humiliation from her husband, she must not protest it. Such a wife is considered to be an ideal one. Such one is considered *Sati Saddhi*.

Tagore's *Mukti* (Salvation) is one of the important compositions of *Palataka*, the poetry collection. The speaker of the poem speaks herself. The poem is a frank confession of the speaker's long monotonous life of twenty two years. When she was only nine, she came to her husband's residence as his life partner. She earned appreciation from all quarters for her ideal qualities befitting a house wife. Every one praised her attributing *Sati, Lakshmi* etc. But according to the speaker, she had to materialize the desires of others. She had no freedom, no choice. Her routine life was full of monotony.

Randhar pare Khawa abar khawar pare randha
Baish bachchar ek chakatei badha.

After cooking, she had to take her meals and after taking daily meals she had to be busy with cooking again. Thus she had to maintain the cyclic order of the life.

Even the unfortunate lady could not have the sweet company of her husband up to her satisfaction....

Tumi aste apish theke, jete sandhyabelai
Parai kothai Satarancha Khelai

Her husband after coming from his office, used to go to play the game of chess somewhere in the neighborhood every evening. No, she did never object to it. She did never protest for long twenty two years. Now when she is listening to the knocking of her death, she feels inspired as if the spring has at last come to her. To her, death seems to be as sweet as anything. At least she will not have to shoulder the drudgery of a housewife. She wants freedom. She is in need of salvation. The poem is a distinct protest on the part of all the house wives against the prevailing system, Tagore 1321 B. Tagore's 'Letter from a wife' *(Strir Patra)* depicts practically the same feeling shared by the lady of *Mukti*. Of course Mrinal seems to be more dignified, more logical, more sensitive, more protesting. *Mukti*'s heroine was married at the age of only nine, while Mrinal was married at the age of twelve. Mrinal admits that she is quite intelligent. She conceived but she was so unfortunate that she could not become a mother. At least she could have received a shelter in her monotonous life if her daughter had survived. She compares her position in the family with the cows confined to a particular place devoid of any freedom.

Bindu was the sister of Mrinal's elder brother in law's wife. She was compelled to leave her home due to the torture received from her cousins. She took shelter in Mrinal's father in law's house. Mrinal came forward for her help against the will of the members of her family. To get rid of Bindu, she was married to a mad man. Bindu escaped with great difficulty. But unfortunately, she was again sent to her mad husband's residence. She committed suicide. Her suicide was protest against the prevailing social system. In this society women are compelled to believe that husband is all, he is the salvation to his wife. She should not be allowed any freedom. She should only discharge her responsibilities allotted to her, faithfully and sincerely.

Mrinal after discharging her duty for long twenty years at her father-in-law's house, left for *Sri-Kshetra*. She in her letter addressed to her husband assures, 'you may think that I die... don't worry, I don't like to cut such old jokes with you.....I too will survive, I am saved'.

No, before Mrinal no fair sex could have dared to make her husband stand in *Kathagara* (a small wooden enclosure where a convict stands) like this. The language used by Mrinal is so prosaic, so logical that it is completely free from emotion. Like an experienced lawyer Mrinal not only on her own behalf but also on behalf of all women has protested against the inhuman orthodox rites imposed on the women by the patriarchal society (Tagore 1321 B).

Sohini is the principal character of the story *Laboratory*. By birth she was a Punjabi, but she was married to a Bengali scientist. Sohini is a unique type by herself. She is very bold, courageous. She is determined to protect the laboratory established by her husband, thus she wants to keep her husband's memory alive. She admits that she is not loyal to her husband so far as the tradition of the society is concerned. She could never be molded by merely the name of her late husband. Sohini admits 'I am from Punjab. I can use the knife very smoothly. I can even kill my daughter and the proposed son-in-law'. She never sheds tears for the sake of love, but on the other hand she can sacrifice her life for love or take away any body's life. What is not to be obeyed, I must not obey that, I must fight to the last, and I must win ultimately (Tagore 1347 B).

Jasoda is striking character. She is the principal character of the novel *Sahartali* (1941) by Manik Bandyopadhyay. Her personality, commanding attitude, unique leadership, love for the labourers, easily arrest the attention of the readers. Jasoda is strong and stout. Her physique is masculine in 2character. She attends the meeting of labour organizations. She addresses them The workers admire her, respect her, even they depend on her decision. But she is not a political character. She is devoid of petty sentiment. She has control over emotions. She runs a very big kitchen which is similar to community kitchen of the socialist outlook. Even the mill owner can not ignore her. Satyapriya, the owner, tries to manage her to run his industry smoothly. She can stop production in the mill, on the other hand she knows by dint of her practical experience when the workers should go on strike as a protest against the authority (Bandyopadhyay 1941).

Manik Bandyopadhyay's *Pratibimba* is a political novel, better to say novelette. Banbihari Das is a party comrade. He is in the jail for the last six months. He is a lecturer by profession. His wife is Manojini. She is also a party comrade. After the imprisonment of her husband, she is requested by her parents, brothers and sisters to go with them, but she discards their request. She rents a house along with some other party members and starts residing there. She is not deeply shocked for her husband's imprisonment. Manojini does not believe in so called chastity. Sitanath loves monojini. Monojini is senior to him by three or four years. One night when all are asleep Sitanath expresses his love to Monojini. He embraces her, Monojini does not protest loudly. She tries to pacify his urge. She admits that she does not love Sitanath. She is not excited at his behavior. Monojini confesses that in respect of social life she maintains equality; she does not maintain any artificial barrier at the time of mixing with male members of the society. When Tarok asks Monojini if he demands her sex, Manojini without least hesitation answers, 'I have no objection, if you want, enjoy it'. Monojini considers Sitanath to be an asset of the party. If under circumstances he leaves the party, the party would face a great loss. To monojini sexual urge is equal to the urge for food. It is very insignificant to her. Anybody may appeal to her to satisfy his sexual urge. To her purity of body or sexual purity is meaningless. For instance once she was surrounded by a group of people with a definite purpose at the evening, she was not frightened. She knows even the women have only one life. She admits she is not afraid of anything (ibid 1941).

Tilottama Majumder's *Chander gaye Chand* was published in Saradiya Anandabazar, 1409 (B). This novel deals with adolescents. Sreyoshi and Debarupa are two friends residing in the same hostel; Sreyoshi loves Shubhrasil, a medical student who happens to be a resident of Lovepur, Birbhum. He is not handsome but he paints wonderfully. But Debarupa is hostile to these affairs of Sreyoshi. She insists Sreyoshi not to indulge Subhrasil, but in vain. Debarupa asks Sreyoshi not to put on bra at night, but Sreyoshi rejects this. Debarupa urges that she herself will put off it. She also says that Sreyoshi must not be shy before her as because she is herself a woman. It is clear that both of them enjoy each other, some sort of physical relation develops between them. Of course Debarupa's attachment with Sreyoshi is greater than that of Sreyoshi. Not so called morality has been followed; no chastity of women's body has been honoured. Impulses have been given proper importance. In this novel we must not forget that the novelist belongs to the fair sex, she admires love; this love should not be confined to heterosexual relation only. Even a girl can love another girl, not necessarily that she must love a boy.

The novelist has presented an unusual crisis in the novel. Once Sereyoshi comes to Sruti and requests her to help her. Her lover kissed her neck and has left a mark there. Sreyoshi knows that Debarupa will not tolerate it. So she uses leucoplast to conceal the mark. Debarupa ultimately detects the mark and created mental pressure on Sreyoshi. She announces no body will be allowed to do anything for Sreyoshi herself (Majumder 1409 B.).

Tilottama Majumdar's *Ektara* is another interesting novel, published in the Anandabazaar Saradiya in 1413 (B). Debarati is the central character of the novel. The novelist has shown her gradual changes due to varied circumstantial impact. We come across crude behaviour of Debarati's so called dear ones. At the very beginning of the novel we find that the eldest maternal uncle of Debarati who happens to be big officer of the Railways requests Debarati to purchase a Benarasi according to her own choice, which will be a gift of her maternal uncle in her marriage and assures that he will make payment. But he refused to pay two thousand rupees considering it expensive and out of his limits. Debarati's parents took exception to this behavior and reminded him that it was out of his own volition that he had wanted to gift a saree. Naturally this shakes Debarati a lot. Her mother protests against her eldest brother and told him that she had not wanted it from him. She told him "You yourself assured that you would present her a Benarasi. Even you yourself asked her to purchase it....you need not give a single farthing. Still she will be married". Debarati's eldest maternal uncle shows his manners only for five hundred rupees. There are people in our society who very often make commitment but fail to materialize them.

Ritaban falls in love with Debarati. He proposes her and she readily accepted his proposal. This was the first love affair in Debarati's life. She, of course, was then at the adolescent period. Ultimately we find Ritaban rejected her and started thinking of his bright future. Debarati was naturally very much disappointed. She wanted to know the reason why Ritaban had changed his mind, but he could not answer. He had no proper answer. This shows how rapidly a young man can change his decision, he cannot stick to an inference, on the other hand a lady is loyal to her beloved.

Our society demands much from the women. They should be loyal to their husband, father-in-law, mother-in-law and others. They are expected to take up all the burden of running the household like cooking, cleaning, washing etc. but in return they get only criticisms, insults and misbehavior. Our society teaches our women to be like Sita, Sabitri, Damayan etc. They would never think for themselves.

Debarati marries Nil. It was a love marriage, still after marriage Debarati faces various problems. She comes to know that she has been deceived by Nil. He is not a qualified man as he claimed to be before, besides he draws now three thousand five hundred rupees and not eight thousand accordingly to his own declaration. He gives up his job and starts business but he can not become successful. Debarati does everything at Nil's house, but in return she receives only adverse criticism, insults and does never receive respect which she deserves. Even she is not allowed to use the toilets used by other members of the family. When she conceives, Nil takes her to a Nursing home and abortion is done there; she cannot enjoy conjugal life like other couples. During her seven years of married life the last two years she had no physical relation with her husband. Her mother-in-law insults her every now and then but Nil never protests. When her ornaments are stolen yet again she is condemned for it and suspected for this crime. The insult reached the highest point when Nil took her to a business magnet for his personal enjoyment. When the business magnet came to understand that Debarati was the wife of Nil he condemned Nil and gave her lift to her residence. All these helped Debarati to be the symbol of protest. Ultimately she left Nil's house and took shelter in a ladies' hostel. She tried to earn her living by working in snatches at various publishing houses.

Debarati never use symbols of a married woman like bangles of conch shell and vermilion. When Sanjiban Bandyopadhyay, a writer, tells her that family becomes happy owing to woman's virtues, Debarati questions how can a woman be happy?

Debarati is astonished as Sanjiban Bandyopadhyay does never ask her about her curiosity, intellect, whether she has interest in art and culture or in music. He only wants to know whether Debarati performs her responsibility as expected from an ideal house wife. But he does never inquire whether Nil looks upon his father-in-law and mother-in-law as his parents. What measures have been taken by him to make his wife happy? Debarati rightly concludes the fact that women and men differ from each other by their respective roles and responsibilities assigned by the society

> Debarati: I want to disregard the society. I want to hate it. I want to believe that there must be a better world. I must achieve it.

Last but not the least; let us cite the case of Saumitri Mukherjee. She had been to Samsingsol, a beautiful village She decided to stay there. She was not followed by her husband when she was asked to rethink her decision she replied.

> Soumitri: I am after all Saumitri Mukherjee. I know to shoulder my own responsibility. I am also the wife of Anandya like other social identities, but still I have got

every right to take my own decision and I do not bother whether my husband is with me or not.

How logical Saumitri is? Her reasoning is quite justified. Our male oriented society only wants that womenfolk should be rational, logical but they do not need to be so. Here males have been argued to be responsible husbands. They cannot and they should not guide the wives all the time on all occasions. Women should have their own free will and freedom.

Earlier children have been seen revolting against parents in Bengali novel. But the present one is not a simple expression of mere impulses. This emerges from a grounded rationality in an adolescent mind that judges the interpersonal relationship from a strongly humanitarian point of view (Majumder 1413 B.).

Bani Basu's *Ekushe Pa* is another interesting novel, published in the year 1994. It depicts the storm and stress period of the adolescence. The social structure is changing, the so called morality, values of life is not being observed rigidly. That is why the teenagers express their impulses without fear or hesitation. Ritu a teenager falls in love with Parthapratim, a celebrity in the field of drama. But Parthapratim is pretty senior to Ritu. Ritu reached Delhi alone to meet Partha at Kamalanagar. After facing much trouble somehow she reaches her destination, but she disovers another Partha who is completely a different man. He is lunatic. Here she also discovers Partha's life partner. She believes in live-together. She did not marry Parthpratim. Let us quote a few lines from the conversation between Ritu and partha live-in partner.

"Are not you afraid of him. How do you live with him"?

"Fear"? She laughed, "why should I be afraid? This is for the time being.He will then be all right. Again he will work like storm, he will go abroad, and he will write plays, he will paint, so long...so long". Ritu listened silently.

Ritu asked "How long does he remain in this state? How long has he been suffering from this before marriage"?

"Marriage? Oh, are you speaking of me? Ritu tells suppose this has been going on before marriage. Then you can easily apply for divorce". The lady laughed at her, told, "yes you are hundred per cent correct. You are very bold and calculative... listen Rituparna, we are not married. I can leave him any day at any moment"

Then?

"Then? You are asking me". She gave stress on the word 'you', then told slowly. "This is exclusively my own choice" (Basu 1400 B.).

Ritu a teenager eagerly went to Parthapratim who happened to be like her father. She wanted to live with him, but situation compelled her to come back. Bishnupriya a character of the novel criticizes her father for his misbehaviour with her mother. She speaks with herself. "Are parents above all criticisms? Are they god and goddess of the heaven? I notice, everyday I notice, my father is a cruel man, my mother cannot sleep at night, almost every night she even does not take her meal only due to misbehavior of my father and shall I not be able to speak against it..."

Parents are also objects of criticism, they should be judged rationally, this kind of argument did never exist in our society before. But nowadays the temperament of the children has changed in the global society, parents are like others, subjects of criticism, they are also answerable for their misdeeds.

SAGAR SANGAM-THE PORTRAIT OF ETERNAL MOTHERHOOD

Premendra Mitra's versatility in the domain of Bengali literature is known to all. He was a successful novelist, a short story writer of rare repute and over and above he was a poet. Mitra also occupies a very high position in the field of Juvenile Literature. *Sagar Sangam* is a representative species of Mitra's innumerable short stories.

The principal character of the story 'Sagar Sangam' is Dakshyayani. She lost her husband in her tender age. Afterwards she follows religious rites and rituals very rigidly. She is spirited and formidable. She is respected by all not so much for her attachment to religious activities, but for the sharpness of her language. Presently we find her in a pilgrimage to sagar. She is traveling by boat. Dakshyayani is very annoyed because she has been compelled to be the co-passenger of a group of prostitutes. She thinks that she has been thus deceived by Lakshman the arranger of the pilgrimage. She abuses him and curses him angrily.

In the boat Dakshyayani comes across a girl of tender age 'Batashi'. She does not like her because of her caustic tongue, besides she happens to be the child of a prostitute. Dakshyayani is saved from drowning caused due to an accident. Somehow she is escaped from danger and she is rescued along with Batashi. Everybody recognizes them mother and her daughter. Somebody praise Dakshyayani for saving Batashi's life. In fact very tightly Dakshyayani catches hold of Batashi's tunic. This proves how much affection she possesses towards the child. Dakshyayani in the first phase tries to make them understand that they are mistaken. The girl is not her own child but all are in vain. Realizing her danger Batashi starts weeping. She feels that her rescuer does not like her. She has none to look after. The old boatman enjoys the matter humorously and tells Dakshyayani that Batashi is not her daughter and in the same way the boatman instigates the child by saying that Dakshyayani is not her mother.

The old boatman advices Dakshyayani to catch hold of Batashi's hand, otherwise she may fall. Daksyani follows it. Thus she reaches the bank of the river safely. She is shocked; she comes to understand that only one or two of the boatmen have survived. Others including the passengers of the boat have drowned. She is also informed that she jumped into the river from the broken rudder in order to save the life of Batashi.

Mitra very interestingly treats the episode. He has explained the attitude of Dakshyayani from psychological point of view. She faces a conflict, conflict between her long cherished superstitions and eternal motherhood. Consciously she ignores Batashi and considers her unholy, defiled but she feels attachment for her from her sub-conscious state of mind.

The prostitutes are looked down upon by the society even now a days. They are considered to be unholy though they serve the society in their own ways. Besides in many cases women become the victims of men's covetousness and finding no other alternative, they accept prostitution as their livelihood. It is a matter of great regret that society hardly tries to trace out the reason behind one's acceptance of unholy livelihood. Even the children of prostitutes are looked down upon by the society. Not only mothers, but also their children are untouchable to the member of the society. We hate them and do not have sympathies for them. Dakshyayani has been guided by this long cherished superstition. To her, Batashi inspite of being unfortunate, is undesirable and almost untouchable, for being the daughter of a prostitute. Sometime her motherly affection surfaces, but her conscious mind overrules it. Mitra very artistically has drawn those pictures in which the conflict of Dakshyayani has been depicted. While Batashi is following Dakshyayani from behind, she falls down. Dakshyayani is provoked to scold her but she remains silent. She realizes Batashi is a little girl, she is weak. She catches hold of her hand and notices that both her legs are trembling. Dakshyayani asks her if she can walk. Batashi ensures that she can walk herself but after walking for sometime, she becomes senseless. Dakshyayani takes her in her lap.

That is the month of Paus, the winter season. Dakshyayani asks Batashi to lie down. She assures her that she will not even touch the blanket as a portion of it Batashi has already used. Dakshyayani sleeps keeping safe distance from Batashi. At dawn she discovers Batashi has placed one of her hands on her neck. At first Dakshyayani thinks to be aloof from her but she can not. Her motherly affection prevents her. Rather she places the blanket on Batashi covering her body so that she may sleep well.

In the morning Dakshyayani collects some parched rice and moa. She asks Batashi, whether she is hungry and to go and wash her face quickly. When Batashi makes an attempt to go to the nearby pond, Dakshyayani asks her, 'can you go alone or shall I accompany you?' She warns her to proceed very cautiously. She cooks food and shares it with Batashi, but very interestingly she does not take Batashi's assistance in cooking.

Dekshyayani resolves to get rid of Batashi the moment she will step down at Ganga Sagar. When the boat starts to rock, she becomes nervous, she closely embraces her and requests the boatman to leave them on ground.

Ultimately they reach Ganga Sagar. Here Batashi addresses her as mother. Dakshyayani is not irritated any more for such intimate approach. Suddenly Batashi fell ill. Most reluctantly she permits the volunteers to take Batashi to the hospital. She thinks if Batashi dies, that will be better for her. But when she thinks that Batashi is sinking, she becomes restless. She prays to Almighty so that the life of Batashi is saved. She decides her Batashi will survive; she will be able to face all sorts of criticisms, adverse comments most boldly. Even, she makes up her mind, if she is not permitted to stay at her father in law's residence for Batashi, she will live close to that place.

Batashi fails to recover. She ultimately dies a premature death. Doctor assures Dakshyayani that Batashi's cremation will be done by them. But they need Batashi's identity, her age, father's name etc. Dakshyayani keeps silent for a moment then she assures the doctor that she herself will provide everything in black and white, as she being a married Hindu lady cannot express everything verbally.

The story ends here but the clear indication we get that Dakshyayani enters her name as the mother of Batashi. Thus she sheds off the shackles of superstitions and inhibition of mind. The motherhood is crowned here. Social distances crumble down before the motherly affection. Here we can clearly hear the voice of eternal motherhood. Now Dakshyayani has no hatred for Batashi, daughter of a prostitute. In fact she finds herself in the place of Batashi's mother, the cherished place of all the mothers of all the ages.

REFERENCES

Bandyopadhyay, Manik (1941), Pratibimba, a Novel in Manik Rachanabali. Kolkata: Bangla Academy.

Bandyopadhyay, Manik (1941), Sahartali, a Novel in Manik Rachanabali. Kolkata: Bangla Academy.

Basu, Bani (1400B), Ekashe Pa, a Novel. In Sradiya Kolkata: Ananda Publishers Private Limited.

Bhattacharyya, Amitra Sudan (1999), Baru Chandidasher Sri Krishna Kirtan Samagra. Kolkata: Dey's Publishing.

Chakraborty, Jahnavi Kumar (1390B), Charyagitir Bhumika, Calcutta.

Majumder,Tilottama (1409B), Chander Gaye Chand, a Novel. In Anandabazar Patrika Saradiya, Kolkata: Ananda Publishers Pvt. Limited.

Majumder,Tilottama (1413B), Ektara, a Novel In Anandabazer Patrika, Saradiya, Kolkata: Ananda Publishers Private Limited.

Tagore, Rabindranath (1347B), Laboratory, a Short Story in Galpaguchcha. Kolkata: Viswa Bharati.

Tagore, Rabindranath (1324B), Mukti; a Poem from Palataka. Kolkata: Viswa Bharati.

Tagore, Rabindranath (1321B), Strir Patra. In Galpaguchcha. Kolkata: Viswa Bharati.

Section Two

Status of Women: An Overview

her younger daughter married off to a decent man before any untoward incident can take place. But when she loses Parubala again to the menace of the traffickers, she does not look for her because she knows it will be futile. Aghorbala thus rightly comments: "She's the mother of a girl-child, after all.... Don't I know why you shed no tears? Small sorrows make you weep but grief turns you to stone." (77) And with Pari, Giri's younger daughter, meeting with the same fate as her sister, Giri decides to leave her husband and work as a maidservant and bring up her two other children in the town. As she realizes at the end that if she had the courage to leave her husband and home earlier she could have saved her daughters from being sold off.

This story, unlike the others in the collection, is more about the [illegible] the [illegible] of the mother. Nevertheless the character of Giri, whose tale begins with the comment that "it had never struck anyone that Giribala might have a heart [illegible] [illegible] home [illegible] leave her husband [illegible] [illegible] The home that Giri has always dreamt of possessing is built by Aulchand from the money he gets by selling his two daughters but Giri refuses to live in that house. She rather takes to the road, vows to work as a maidservant in the town and bring up her son Rajiv and youngest daughter Maruni, while Aulchand "glances at Maruni furtively" (77), probably hoping to earn some more money through her. Giri finally manages to muster up enough courage to leave the 'mehal' of a man to the disapproval of all: "Everyone is convinced that it's not Aulchand but Giribala who's at fault." (ibid) "What happened to Bela and Pari was common practice these days. But why leave your husband and go away? What kind of woman was that?" (ibid) Probably the answer would be that such a woman is a mother, a mother for whom the well-being of her children is of prime importance.

> The stories in this volume present a range of responses to the discourse of motherhood, exposing in particular the intersecting forms of exploitation to which women in [illegible]

4

Context and Issues of Gender Discourse Today: The Case of West Bengal

BISWAJIT GHOSH

The issues of gender equality and gender justice are today matters of intense scrutiny and debate all over the world. This is equally true in an essentially patriarchal society like India where the Constitution has guaranteed right to equality between men and women. Largely speaking the primary source of violence in a patriarchal society is the family. A female member in a family is subjected to all round deprivation. There is a tacit complicity of the family and community in women's oppression as well as their devalued position in the society. As a girl child, she is deprived of better health, nutritional and educational facilities & above all bequests *vis-à-vis* a male child. All these reinforce the notion that girls are a 'burden' and can easily be disposed off through early marriage or if necessary through payment called 'dowry'. Frequent evidences also show adolescent females being subjected to sexual harassment by elderly male relatives. In such cases traditional family norms & values under the dictates of the patriarch subdue voices of protest. Post marriage torture by husband and in-laws, commonly known as 'domestic violence', is the most common form of violence against women. This paper primarily focuses on the ever-increasing problems of gender equity and gender violence in Indian society with special reference to West Bengal.

It should be noted at the outset that domestic and other types of violence against women is not limited to mental and physical tortures but has deep-rooted impact on the children in the family, who witness such incidents. According to WHO the impact of such 'family violence' on public health is intense and alarming. Physical assault, mental depression and abatement to commit suicides, as a result of family violence, cause a dearth of efficient female labour. Often a victim of such violence falls prey to traffickers and is forced to become a sex worker. Along with the problem of neglect of girl child under the patriarchal social structure, such gender violence cause substantial loss of human resource as well as income of a nation and calls for immediate social remedy. The loss of human and social value emanating from the violence against women has also been given much importance by both national and international agencies.

Given this context we are dismayed by the fact that women in India still constitute a large chunk of our population who continue to be exploited in many spheres. Despite the fact that women's role in the productive economy has been increasing over time, a girl is yet perceived to be a burden of the family in many parts of India. As per the Hindu law, daughters require extreme financial investments with no material returns. Hence they are 'liquidated' even before birth. Thus, rates of female foeticides and infanticides are high in some parts of the country. Declining Child Sex Ratio (CSR), which largely explains prevalence of female foeticides and infanticides, is alarmingly a general trend in India today and in the states like Punjab (793), Haryana (820), Delhi (868), Gujarat (878), Himachal Pradesh (897), and Rajasthan (909), the fall is very sharp as per the 2001 Census. It is praiseworthy that in spite of certain demographic compulsions, West Bengal is almost bereft of the problems of female foeticides and infanticides. The state also did not have any history of pernicious Sati in memorable past. In terms of CSR, West Bengal is second in the country after

Kerala. But, we should not be content with this, as CSR in West Bengal has declined from 1,008 in 1961 to 963 in 2001.

The primary evidence of gender inequality is reflected through the general sex ratio across states over time. The average number of women per thousand men in India has increased from 927 to 933 in between 1991 and 2001. But this ratio has remained much below the national average for many Indian states like Delhi (821), Haryana (821), Punjab (874), Uttar Pradesh (898), Madhya Pradesh (920), Gujarat (921), Bihar (921) Maharashtra (922) and Rajasthan (922). For Mizoram and West Bengal this ratio was below the national level in 1991, but rose above that in 2001. Historically, however, West Bengal's sex ratio had always remained below the national figure mainly due to influx of male migrants from neighbouring states. But in 2001 the state could increase its tally for the first time to 934.

While making a comparative assessment of West Bengal's position vis-à-vis other states on gender issues, it should be kept in mind that the state has been in the forefront of social reform and political movements in pre-independent India. Men and women fought equally for freedom and independence. Again, the state has for the last 30 years witnessed several state sponsored development programmes like land reforms, decentralized planning at the district and Panchayat level, introduction of 33 per cent reservation for rural women in the local bodies. The state government has also spent a substantial proportion of its budget provisions towards social upliftment of weaker section and particularly for educational expansion. Consequently, it is argued that the demographic profile of the state shows certain upward trend to some extent and the uphill task to achieve gender justice is more appropriate to a state like West Bengal (Bagchi 2005:15). In a study on Gender Empowerment Measures (GEM) for different states in the country, West Bengal is ranked 7th in a list of 16 states (Mehta 1996).

Another health related index to measure gender development is Infant Mortality Rate (IMR) for girls. Levels of IMR are acknowledged as basic indicator of the quality of life in a society. It is noteworthy that West Bengal has consistently had lower levels of IMR for both boys and girls than the national average. In 2001, West Bengal's IMR for the girls was 49 which was fourth in the country after Kerala (9), Himachal Pradesh (36) and Maharashtra (48). The comparative figure for the country as a whole was 66. The state has also been successful to bring down both the birth and death rates significantly. The decline in the birth rate has been nearly double than that of the national average over the period 1990-2001. West Bengal's ranks among 15 major states in the country in birth (22.7) and death (8.3) rates were 7th and 2nd respectively in 2001. Table 1 gives a brief idea about the comparative standing of West Bengal, the 4th populous state in the country, in certain selected aspects of gendér development. The table identifies the major areas where policy decisions and action plans are to be strengthened to extend gender justice further. It appears that while West Bengal could perform better so far as sex ratio, child sex ratio, literacy and other health related indexes are concerned, there remain areas of serious concern like declining work participation rate for women[2], poverty and crimes against women.

Table 1

Major Indicators of Gender Development in West Bengal

Indicator/Year	*Rate in India*	*Rate in West Bengal*	*Rank among 15 Major States*
Sex Ratio, 2001	933	934	6
Child Sex Ratio, 2001	927	963	2
Female Literacy, 2001	54.16	59.61	5
Gender Disparity in Literacy Rates, 2001	0.216	0.167	11
Enrolment Ratio for Girls, (VI- VIII), 1997	40.1	40.5	9
Female Life Expectancy at Birth, 1996-2001	64.20	64.19	9
IMR for Girls, 2001	66	49	4
Under Five Mortality, 1997	95	68	4
Neonatal Mortality, 1998-99	43	32	3
Work Force Participation Rate for Women, 2001	25.68	18.32	15
Crime Against Women, 2006	1,64,765	12,785	6
Population Below Poverty Line, 1999-2000	26.10	27.02	6

Source: Census, 2001; India: Social Development Report, 2006; and NCRB, 2006.

SOCIAL AND DEMOGRAPHIC PROFILE OF WEST BENGAL

Let us first look into the social and demographic profile of contemporary West Bengal in brief to delve deep into the problem of gender justice and gender inequality in a Bengali dominated society. With a population of about 82 million in 2001, West Bengal is the 4th populous state in India. It is a matter of great concern that the state accounts for 7.8% of country's population having a share of only 2.7% (88,752 Sq. Km) of the total geographical area. West Bengal has six out of ten most populous districts in the country. Consequently, the density of population (903) in the state is the highest among the Indian states[3] although around 72% of the people live in rural areas.

This means that even in the rural areas of the state, competition for scarce natural and societal resources is intense. One cannot discuss the problem of gender development in West Bengal with out reference to this aspect. Again, the Scheduled Castes (SCs) and Scheduled Tribes (STs) population in the state constitute 23.20 and 5.50% of the total population respectively. However they respectively constitute 28.6 and 5.8% of population in rural areas, and 19.9 and 1.5% of population in urban areas. Among the minorities, the Muslims are the dominant section and they account for about 25.25% of total population in the state. But in rural Bengal, Muslims constitute 29.17% of population. The recently published Rajinder Sachar Committee Report has revealed that the Muslims are still a deprived lot in the country and 'very small' proportion of government and public sector employees are Muslims, concentrated in lower level positions. Thus, the socially and economically backward sections like SCs, STs and minorities together account for more than half (53.95%) of the population in the state and an overwhelming majority (63.17%) in rural Bengal in 2001. Hence, the problem of societal development in general and gender development in particular is more severe in West Bengal than many other states of India.

It appears from Table 2 that West Bengal had 17.77% decadal growth rate of population during 1991-2001 and consequently the density of population also increased by adding 136 more people per square kilometre during the same period. District wise, Kolkata had the lowest growth rate of 4.11 and Uttar Dinajpur had the highest rate of 28.72. But population control has conversely affected the Child Sex Ratio at Kolkata (see Table 7). It is important to note that five of the six North Bengal Districts (Uttar and Dakshin Dinajpur, Malda, Darjeeling and Jalpaiguri) had higher population growth rate than that of the state average. This shows that in-migration into the region due to geo-political and economic reasons is continuing despite having slacked and undergone a spatial diffusion to other parts of the state in recent years. Also districts like Murshidabad, North and South 24 Parganas, and Nadia had much higher rates. The density of population is highest in Kolkata (24760), followed by six other most populous districts like Howrah (2913), North 24 Parganas (2181), Hooghli (1601), Nadia (1172), Murshidabad (1101), and Burdwan (985) in 2001.

Table 2
Population, Area and Density of Population by Districts in West Bengal

State/Districts	*Area (Sq. Km)*	*Population*		*Density of Population*	
		1991	*2001*	*1991*	*2001*
West Bengal	88752	68077965	80176197	767	903
Burdwan	7024	6050605	6895514	861	982
Birbhum	4545	2555664	3015422	562	663
Bankura	6882	2805065	3192695	408	464
Midnapur (E+W)	14081	8331912	9610788	592	683
Howrah	1467	3729644	4273099	2542	2913
Hooghli	3149	4355230	5041976	1383	1601
Purulia	6259	2224577	2536516	355	405
24-Parganas (N)	4094	7281881	8934286	1779	2182
24-Parganas (S)	9960	5715030	6906689	574	693
Kolkata	185	4399819	4572876	23783	24718
Nadia	3927	3852097	4604827	981	1173
Murshidabad	5324	4740149	5866569	890	1102
Uttar Dinajpur	3140	1897045	2441794	604	778
Dakshin Dinajpur	2219	1230608	1503178	555	677
Malda	3733	2637032	3290468	706	881
Jalpaiguri	6227	2800543	3401173	450	546
Darjeeling	3149	1299919	1609172	413	511
Cooch Behar	3387	2171145	2479155	641	732

Note: The figures for 2001 have been revised on the basis of final census data.
Source: Director of Census Operation, West Bengal.

In another vital index of population below the poverty line, West Bengal has secured 6th position among 15 major states during 1999-2000 (see Table 3). Estimates based on the NSS Consumption Survey (30 days recall method) show that West Bengal had 27.02% of population below the poverty line during 1999-2000 as compared to the 26.10% of population at the all India level. Table 2 demonstrates the differences in rural and urban poverty levels of 15 major Indian states in between 1993-94 and 1999-2000. It exhibits that West Bengal is 6th and 5th in total and rural poverty. The proportion of population below the poverty line in rural West Bengal was 31.85% in the state in 1999-2000. Such concentration of poor people in rural areas is a matter of great concern[4]. Going by the Planning Commission's assessment, West Bengal is 9th and 8th among

Table 3
Percentage of Population Below Poverty Line by Residence in Major Indian States, 1993-94 –1999-2000

	Rural		*Urban*		*Combined*	
States	*1993-1994*	*1999-2000*	*1993-1994*	*1999-2000*	*1993-1994*	*1999-2000*
A. Pradesh	15.92	11.05	38.33	26.63	22.19	15.77
Assam	45.01	40.04	7.73	7.47	40.86	36.09
Bihar	58.21	44.3	34.5	32.91	54.96	42.6
Gujarat	22.18	13.17	27.89	15.59	24.21	14.07
Haryana	28.02	8.27	16.38	9.99	25.05	8.74
Karnataka	29.88	17.38	40.14	25.25	33.16	20.04
Kerala	25.76	9.38	24.55	20.27	25.43	12.72
M. Pradesh	40.64	37.06	48.38	38.44	42.52	37.43
Maharashtra	37.93	23.72	35.15	26.81	36.86	25.02
Orissa	49.72	48.01	41.64	42.83	48.56	47.15
Punjab	11.95	6.35	11.35	5.75	11.77	6.16
Rajasthan	26.46	13.74	30.49	19.85	27.41	15.28
T. Nadu	32.48	20.55	39.77	22.11	35.03	21.12
U. Pradesh	42.28	31.22	35.39	30.89	40.85	31.15
W. Bengal	40.8	31.85	22.41	14.86	35.66	27.02
India	37.27	27.09	32.36	23.62	35.97	26.1

Figures are estimated by Planning Commission on the basis of NSS Consumption Survey (30 days recall method)

Source: 1. Compendium of Environment Statistics, 1997 (Central Statistical Organization)
2. Planning Commission: News and Events.

the major Indian states in rural and urban Human Poverty Index respectively in 1991. More importantly, state wise data on unemployment (current daily`status) in the 1990's indicate that in rural areas unemployment levels were very high in West Bengal along with Kerala and Tamil Nadu. The levels were even higher for females in Kerala, West Bengal and Assam (Council For Social Development, 2006: 10). A significant part of the state is relatively more backward economically and also tends to be less advanced in terms of human development. These include (a) large part of six northern districts namely, Darjeeling, Jalpaiguri, Cooch Behar, Malda, Uttar and Dakshin Dinajpur; (b) the three south-western districts namely, Purulia, Bankura and Birbhum; and (c) the Sundarban areas of the two 24 Parganas districts in the south of the state. Majority of such districts also figure prominently in any discussion on crimes against women (see Table 12). Irrespective of such spatial backwardness, the aggregate State Domestic Product (SDP) of West Bengal in 2000-2001 was Rs. 17,860 Crores in current prices and per capita SDP was about Rs. 16072 (Govt. of West Bengal 2004 : 5). This is higher than the national average. West Bengal is a fastest growing state in India with a compound annual growth rate of 7% and per capita growth of 5% during 1993-94 and 2000-01 (West Bengal Human Development Report 2004: 5). But the state is faced with the problem of low rate of employment generation along with decline in crop prices for farmers since 1990. In an economy that is heavily dependent upon agriculture, writes West Bengal Human Development Report 2004, such problems along with worsening coverage and quality of public services, 'have had particular impact upon the conditions of women' (2004: 7). In other words, West Bengal represents a 'mixed picture' (WBHDR 2004: 13) in development as also revealed through Human Development Index and Gender Development Index due to variations across districts stated in Table 4.

Greater population pressure has put inevitable stress on basic infrastructure as well as on the provision of health and education services in the state. Yet, as Table 5 indicates, there has been rapid decline in birth rates, death rates and infant

Table 4
Selective Development Index in West Bengal by Districts, 2001

Districts	*Per capita DDP (Rs.) at current prices*	*HDI Value*	*HDI Rank*	*School Enrolment Rate*		*GDI*	*GDI Rank*
				Male	*Female*		
Burdwan	17537.98	0.64	5	64.9	56.8	0.560	7
Birbhum	12791.72	0.47	14	62.5	52.5	0.435	14
Bankura	15741.64	0.52	11	69.4	51.9	0.494	10
Purulia	13044.67.	0.45	16	66.2	42.0	0.424	15
Midnapur (E&W)	15526.01	0.62	7	74.4	67.0	0.578	4
Hooghli	16279.65	0.63	6	71.2	61.7	0.581	3
Howrah	15591.44	0.68	2	73.8	63.3	0.570	5
24 Parganas (N)	14768.32	0.66	3	72.6	66.5	0.564	6
24 Parganas (S)	13630.22	0.60	8	69.6	56.4	0.521	8
Nadia	16211.46	0.57	9	68.0	60.3	0.506	9
Murshidabad	13392.39	0.46	15	53.9	45.8	0.423	16
Kolkata	33299.50	0.78	1	77.92	77.8	0.642	1
Uttar Dinajpur	11182.86	0.51	13	57.2	42.0	0.478	12
D. Dinajpur	14579.19	(Com)	(Com)	(Com)	(Com)	(Com)	(Com)
Malda	14777.20	0.44	17	45.9	37.2	0.416	17
Jalpaiguri	16749.07	0.53	10	60.6	43.2	0.492	11
Cooch Behar	13855.35	0.52	11	65.7	51.9	0.471	13
Darjeeling	18529.18	0.65	4	71.5	68.8	0.600	2

Source: West Bengal Human Development Report 2004: 13-14 & 219-220

mortality in the state over the last two decades. The all India figure for these vital rates are much higher[5]. Again, the Life Expectancy at Birth (LEB) for women in the state has outstripped that of men, thereby making amends for the general sex ratio. Expectation of life at birth for women has gone up from 54.70 in 1981 to 64.19 in 1996-2001. The state is one of the better performing states in the country in this respect even though certain districts like Malda, Cooch Behar, Birbhum and Murshidabad show a LEB below 60 (WBHDR 2004: 11-12).

Table 5
Birth (live), Death and Infant Mortality Rates for West Bengal, 1981-2002

Particulars		*1981*	*1991*	*1999*	*2000*	*2001*	*2002*
Sample Registration System							
Birth rates per	Rural	37.0	30.3	22.9	23.0	22.8	22.6
1000	Urban	20.0	18.5	14.3	14.0	13.8	14.1
population	Combined	33.2	27.0	20.7	20.6	20.5	20.5
Death rates per	Rural	12.2	8.9	7.2	7.1	7.0	6.9
1000	Urban	6.9	6.7	6.8	6.7	6.4	6.4
population	Combined	11.0	8.3	7.1	7.0	6.8	6.7
IMR per	Rural	98.0	76.0	55.0	54.0	53.0	52.0
1000	Urban	44.0	47.0	40.0	37.0	38.0	36.0
population	Combined	91.0	71.0	52.0	51.0	51.0	49.0

Source: Registrar General of India.

Similarly, sex ratio has improved from 917 in 1991 to 934 in 2001. Table 6 informs that it is highest in Birbhum and lowest at Kolkata. Perhaps in case of a big metropolis like Kolkata this imbalance is well explained by the presence of a large number of single males who are mostly migrants living in the city without their families. Like Kolkata, sex ratio is also comparatively low at other urban-industrial districts like Howrah and Burdwan. In between 1991 and 2001 however, all these districts have significantly improved theii number of females per 1000 males. With regard to the Child Sex Ratio, as has been mentioned earlier, West Bengal however could not restrict the general declining trend seen in respect of the country. As Table 7 shows, the decline is more prominent in two districts, namely Kolkata and Dakshin Dinajpur. The Table also demonstrates that Muslims of the state as a whole and particularly of districts like Kolkata, Murshidabad, Cooch Behar, Dakshin Dinajpur, Birbhum, South 24 Parganas, Hooghli and Nadia had better sex and child sex ratio. This forces us to deduce that there is an inverse relationship between levels of socio-economic development and sex ratio/ child sex ratio. The experience of some developed states in the country, as has been discussed earlier, also repeats the same story.

Table 6
Population by Sex and Sex Ratio in the Districts of West Bengal, 1991-2001

State/Districts	1991 Male	1991 Female	1991 Sex Ratio	2001 Male	2001 Female	2001 Sex Ratio
West Bengal	35510633	32567332	917	41465985	38710212	934
Burdwan	3186833	2863772	899	3588376	3307138	922
Birbhum	1313285	1242379	946	1546633	1468789	950
Bankura	1437515	1367550	951	1636002	1556693	952
Midnapur (E+W)	4284954	4046958	945	4916370	4694418	955
Howrah	1982457	1747187	881	2241898	2031201	906
Hooghli	2271792	2083438	917	2589625	2452351	947
Purulia	1142771	1081806	947	1298078	1238438	954
24-Parganas (N)	3818197	3463684	907	4638756	4295530	926
24-Parganas (S)	2962214	2752816	929	3564993	3341696	937
Kolkata	2445328	1954491	799	2500040	2072836	829
Nadia	1989841	1862256	936	2366853	2237974	946
Murshidabad	2439342	2300807	943	3005000	2861569	952
Uttar Dinajpur	987771	909274	921	1259737	1182057	938
Dakshin Dinajpur	632969	597639	944	770335	732843	951
Malda	1360541	1276491	938	1689406	1601062	948
Jalpaiguri	1453194	1347349	927	1751145	1650028	942
Darjeeling	679323	620596	914	830644	778528	937
Cooch Behar	1122306	1048839	935	1272094	1207061	949

Source: Census 2001.

Table 7
Sex Ratio and Child Sex Ratio (0-6) by Religion in the Districts of West Bengal, 2001

	All Religion		Hindu		Muslim	
State/Districts	*Sex Ratio*	*C S R*	*Sex Ratio*	*C S R*	*Sex Ratio*	*C S R*
West Bengal	934	960	932	956	933	968
Burdwan	922	956	921	955	920	961
Birbhum	950	964	948	960	952	968
Bankura	952	953	951	953	924	952
Midnapur (E+W)	955	951	954	948	953	965
Howrah	906	956	905	955	910	958
Hooghli	947	951	944	950	958	955
Purulia	954	964	953	963	935	966
24-Parganas (N)	936	964	932	959	929	968
24-Parganas (S)	947	951	944	950	958	955
Kolkata	852	931	739	918	1043	995
Nadia	946	972	947	968	948	971
Murshidabad	952	972	943	961	958	976
Uttar Dinajpur	938	965	927	958	950	972
Dakshin Dinajpur	951	966	949	966	956	967
Malda	948	964	944	961	950	965
Jalpaiguri	942	969	939	968	941	973
Darjeeling	937	962	930	956	868	987
Cooch Behar	949	964	947	962	954	969

Census of India, 2001.

The growth of literacy by sex and community in different districts during 1991-2001 is unfolded in Tables 8, 9 and 10. The state had the highest-ever decadal percentage increase in female literacy (13.66%) in the last census decade. But district wise growth rate discloses that the achievement is not evenly distributed across the state. Thus, Cooch Behar, Jalpaiguri, Dakshin Dinajpur, Murshidabad and Malda have achieved an outstanding decadal growth rate in literacy between 15 and 21%. This could not be done in districts that had literacy rate above 60% in 1991. So far as the crucial index of women literacy is concerned, West Bengal's level had always remained above the all India equivalent. In 2001 the state could achieve the highest decadal percentage increase of female literacy by 13.05% and reach the rate of 59.61 as against the all India equivalent of 54.16%. This enabled the state to skip the ladder

Table 8
Literacy Rate by Sex in West Bengal Districts, 1991- 2001

	Persons		*Males*		*Females*	
State/Districts	*1991*	*2001*	*1991*	*2001*	*1991*	*2001*
India	52.10	65.38	64.13	75.85	39.29	54.16
West Bengal	57.70	68.64	67.81	77.02	46.56	59.61
Burdwan	61.88	70.18	71.12	78.63	51.46	60.95
Birbhum	48.56	61.48	59.26	70.89	37.17	51.55
Bankura	52.04	63.44	66.75	76.76	36.55	49.43
Midnapur (E+W)	69.32	74.90	81.27	84.91	56.63	64.42
Howrah	67.62	77.61	76.11	83.22	57.83	70.11
Hooghli	66.78	75.11	75.77	82.59	56.90	67.21
Purulia	43.29	55.57	62.17	73.72	23.24	36.50
24-Parganas N)	66.81	78.07	74.72	83.92	57.99	71.72
24-Parganas (S)	55.10	69.45	68.45	79.19	40.57	59.01
Kolkata	77.61	80.86	81.94	83.79	72.09	77.30
Nadia	52.53	66.14	60.05	72.31	44.42	59.58
Murshidabad	38.28	54.35	46.42	60.91	29.57	47.63
Uttar Dinajpur	34.58	47.89	45.24	58.48	22.85	36.51
Dakshin Dinajpur	46.40	63.59	56.75	72.43	35.33	54.28
Malda	35.62	50.28	45.61	58.80	24.92	41.25
Jalpaiguri	45.09	62.85	56.00	72.83	33.20	52.21
Darjeeling	57.95	71.79	67.07	80.05	47.84	62.94
Cooch Behar	45.78	66.30	57.35	75.93	33.31	56.12

Source: Director of Census operations, Census of India, 2001, West Bengal.

by one position leaving Gujarat behind as compared to 1991 and become 5th among 15 major states. Notwithstanding such performance, female literacy remains feeble in Purulia (36.50), Uttar Dinajpur (36.51%), Malda (41.25%), Murshidabad (47.63%) and Bankura (49.43). It is important here to note that the enrolment rate for girls (shown in Table 2) in all these districts along with Jalpaiguri, Cooch Behar and Birbhum varied between 37 and 52 only. This was highest in Darjeeling (69), followed by Midnapur (67) and Kolkata (66.8). Gender differences in enrolment becomes evident by the fact that among the boys this rate is as high as 77.9 (at Kolkata). Again, there is a sharp decline in the male to female ratio in respect of enrolment to class VIII from 78.3% in 1973 to 55.8% in 1993 notwithstanding gradual increase in Gross Enrolment Ratio in the state (Bagchi and Guha 2005: 53). In the 2001-2 academic session, the percentage of girl students in a class of 100 was 48.08 in the primary, 42.66 in the middle, 40.42 in the secondary, and 37.08 in the higher secondary sections (Census, 2001). According to a study the mean years of schooling for girls and boys in West Bengal during 1998-99 was 3.5 and 5.2 respectively and these figures come close to the national average of 3.4 and 5.3 for girls and boys respectively (Tilak 2006:37). This gender differential in education explains our failure particularly in checking high dropout rate for girls in spite of some efforts through special schemes.

Table 9
SC and ST Literacy in West Bengal by Districts, 2001

	SC			ST		
		Literacy			Literacy	
Districts	*Percentage*	*Total*	*Female*	*Percentage*	*Total*	*Female*
West Bengal	23.02	59.61	46.9	5.5	43.4	29.15
Burdwan	26.98	51.99	39.59	6.41	41.83	28.19
Birbhum	29.51	45.74	33.05	6.74	61.2	18.17
Bankura	31.24	42.92	27.11	10.36	49.6	31.13
Midnapur (E+W)	16.4	63.57	49.84	8.31	47.05	30.83
Howrah	15.42	61.13	51.4	0.45	52.06	42.19
Hooghli	23.58	56.1	44.73	4.21	45.45	31.94
Purulia	18.29	45.15	26.35	18.27	42.64	23.4
24-Parganas (N)	20.6	70.79	61.41	2.23	46.09	33.27
24-Parganas (S)	32.12	67.36	54.21	1.23	43.29	29.88
Kolkata	6.01	70.54	62.26	0.21	76.39	67.07
Nadia	29.66	63.09	53.94	2.47	40.63	29.2
Murshidabad	12	48.91	39.27	1.29	35.79	25.01
Uttar Dinajpur	27.71	50.06	35.71	5.11	28.68	17.63
Dakshin Dinajpur	28.78	54.55	42.09	16.12	55.14	30.12
Malda	16.84	51.17	38.87	6.9	32.16	19.63
Jalpaiguri	36.71	61.87	49.62	18.87	42.59	30.67
Darjeeling	16.09	62.43	50.31	12.69	55.48	45.85
Cooch Behar	50.11	64.35	52.29	0.57	55.31	43.3

Source: Census of India, 2001.

Table 10
Percentage of Female Literacy by Religion and Residence in the Districts of West Bengal, 2001

	All Religion			*Hindu*			*Muslim*		
State/Districts	*Total*	*Rural*	*Urban*	*Total*	*Rural*	*Urban*	*Total*	*Rural*	*Urban*
West Bengal	59.61	53.16	75.74	63.09	55.68	78.31	49.75	47.87	59.23
Burdwan	60.95	56.1	69.29	60.97	55.1	69.92	61.39	60.41	64.38
Birbhum	51.55	49.7	70.2	51.88	49.23	72.5	50.97	50.62	58.25
Bankura	49.43	47.56	71.91	50.88	48.82	72.59	46.96	46.64	53.63
Midnapur (E+W)	64.42	63.03	75.95	66.41	65.05	78.03	54.36	53.62	60.05
Howrah	70.11	64.55	75.78	72.82	66.31	79.31	60.78	59.05	62.74
Hooghli	67.21	62.09	77.46	67.51	61.02	79.31	67.31	69.41	59.81
Purulia	36.5	33.24	64.91	37.56	34.22	65.14	34.14	29.56	59.46
24-Parganas (N)	71.72	60.99	80.37	75.11	62.94	82.39	58.13	58.11	58.2
24-Parganas (S)	59.01	56.15	73.7	62.94	59.45	79.26	50.27	49.06	57.97
Kolkata	77.3	–	–	80.15	–	–	63.61	–	–
Nadia	59.58	54.96	75.7	64.46	59.65	76.72	44.03	43.66	52.91
Murshidabad	47.63	45.67	60.75	55.72	51.14	73.22	32.76	32.85	31.87
Uttar Dinajpur	36.51	30.77	74.84	45.77	36.64	77.62	25.5	25.19	39.81
Dakshin Dinajpur	54.28	50.3	78.55	52.34	46.41	78.52	61.33	61.25	82.04
Malda	41.25	38.41	73.85	45	39.03	74.46	38.68	38.14	68.46
Jalpaiguri	52.21	47.24	74.07	53.5	47.71	75.88	45.01	45.43	40.44
Darjeeling	62.94	55.39	78.52	63.67	55.51	78.85	37.92	30.89	54.68
Cooch Behar	56.12	53.56	79.77	58.79	55.8	81.64	47.11	46.72	57.87

Source: Census of India, 2001.

If we further look into the performance of backward sections of our population here, the task appears to be colossal. Thus Table 9 reveals that the rate of total female literacy among the SCs and STs is 46.90 and 29.15% respectively. This is a marginal improvement over the 1991 figures of 42.21% for SCs and 27.78 % for STs. District wise SC female literacy rate again points to the depressing state of affairs in Purulia (26.35%), Bankura (27.11%), Birbhum (33.05%), Uttar Dinajpur (35.71%), Malda (38.87%), Murshidabad (39.27%) and Burdwan (39.59%). So far as ST female literacy is concerned, the performance of Uttar Dinajpur (17.63%), Birbhum (18.17%), Malda (19.63%), Purulia (23.40%), Burdwan (28.19%), Nadia (29.20%) and South 24 Parganas (29.88%) is not satisfactory. It is a matter of serious concern that in many SC and ST villages in the state the female literacy is just near 20 per cent.

Finally, rural Muslim women also suffer from lower levels of literary achievement in the state. Table 10 evinces that as compared to the total state female literacy, Muslim women fall behind by at least 10 % in this crucial gender development aspect in 2001. And there are districts like Uttar Dinajpur (25.50%), Purulia (34.14%), Malda (38.68%), Murshidabad (42.76%) and Nadia (44.03%) where the total female literacy rate is way behind the over all percentage of 49.75. These statistics clearly suggest a major undercurrent of gender discrimination particularly among the backward communities. Such vulnerability exposes women to social and cultural evils like child marriage, dowry and trafficking. Let us now concentrate on the problem of gender violence in West Bengal.

VIOLENCE AGAINST WOMEN IN WEST BENGAL

Ever increasing incidences of crimes against women is a matter of serious concern for NGOs, women organizations and policy makers in the state today. National Crime Record Bureau data reveals that over the last one decade such crimes have increased in a much greater proportion as compared to total cognizable crimes committed under the Indian Penal Code in the state. Thus, incidences of crimes against women have increased from 6453 in 1996 to 12,785 in 2006 (98% increase) whereas total cognizable (IPC) crimes have got reduced from 69118 to 68052 during the same period in the state. In 2001, the number of cognizable crimes per 1 Lakh population in the state was only 70.7 which is less than half of the all India average of 172.3, with only Meghalaya and Mizoram reporting a lower rate. This implies that West Bengal is not otherwise affected by rising number of crimes even though crimes against women and particularly domestic violence & dowry related crimes have significantly augmented here over the last one-decade or so. West Bengal accounted for 7.8% of crimes against women (CAW) in the country in 2006 as against 7.6% in the preceding year. As a corollary, the state's ranking as per percentage share has remained fixed at 6th position in 2006 in the country. It is deleterious to note that in spite of certain positive steps taken by the government to improve the conditions of women, the state has experienced an increase of nearly 82% of crimes against women in between 2000-2006 (cases up from 7043 to 12785) as compared to the all India increase of only 17% (from 141373 to 164765) during the same period. Table 11 and 12 unveils the state of crimes against women in West Bengal. They clearly demonstrate that crimes like rape, dowry death, cruelty

Table 11
Crimes Against Women in West Bengal, 2000-2006

Crime Heads	*2000*	*2001*	*2002*	*2003*	*2004*	*2005*	*2006*
Rape	814	709	759	1002	1475	1686	1731
Molestation	1057	945	964	1186	1566	1572	1837
Sexual Assault	55	48	34	71	64	54	63
Dowry Death	284	265	273	329	396	446	445
Dowry Prohibition Act	5	6	6	17	36	18	25
Cruelty by Husband & Relatives	4025	3859	4069	4948	6334	6936	7414
Kidnapping &Abduction	749	695	694	801	1018	1039	1199
Importation of girls	00	3	01	01	12	61	01
Immoral Traffic (P) Act	49	31	42	152	121	74	66
Indecent Rep. of Women Act	05	00	00	01	25	01	04
Sati Prevention Act	00	00	00	00	00	00	00
Total Crimes against Women	7043	6570	6842	8508	11047	11887	12785
Percentage of CAW against Total IPC Crimes	10.70	10.67	11.60	13.91	15.93	17.90	18.79

Source: Compiled from NCRB.

Table 12
Selective Crimes against Women in West Bengal by Districts, 2005

Districts	Rape	Molestation	Sexual Harassment	Kidnapping & Abduction	Importation of Girls	Dowry Death	Cruelty	Total	% to Total
Burdwan	122	66	0	66	0	44	570	868	7.36
Birbhum	78	42	0	37	0	5	160	322	2.73
Bankura	43	54	0	27	0	22	149	295	2.50
E. Midnapur	54	28	0	53	0	34	325	494	4.19
W. Midnapur	93	60	0	44	0	21	300	518	4.39
Howrah	61	60	4	43	1	18	400	587	4.98
Hooghli	42	31	0	30	0	5	539	647	5.49
Purulia	34	37	0	8	0	8	108	195	1.65
24 Pargs (N)	217	151	5	153	0	71	886	1483	12.57
24 Pargs (S)	136	123	2	117	0	64	915	1357	11.51
Kolkata	16	153	35	70	0	7	236	517	4.38
Nadia	148	95	3	97	60	48	545	996	8.45
Murshidabad	236	223	1	110	0	35	696	1301	11.03
U. Dinajpur	53	47	0	24	0	17	158	299	2.54
D. Dinajpur	28	45	1	27	0	20	141	262	2.22
Malda	96	137	0	36	0	3	287	559	4.74
Jalpaiguri	108	103	1	48	0	15	237	512	4.34
Darjeeling	39	41	2	19	0	1	81	183	1.55
Cooch Behar	82	76	0	30	0	8	203	399	3.38
Total	1686	1572	54	1039	61	446	6936	11794	100.0

Source: NCRB, 2005.

by husband and relatives, and molestation particularly have increased in a much greater proportion than other types of crimes in recent times. As a result the rate of CAW in the state has aggravated stunningly from 8.9% in 2000 to 14.8% in 2006. Interestingly, the national rate of CAW has also increased marginally from 14.1 to 14.7% during the same period (see Chart 1).

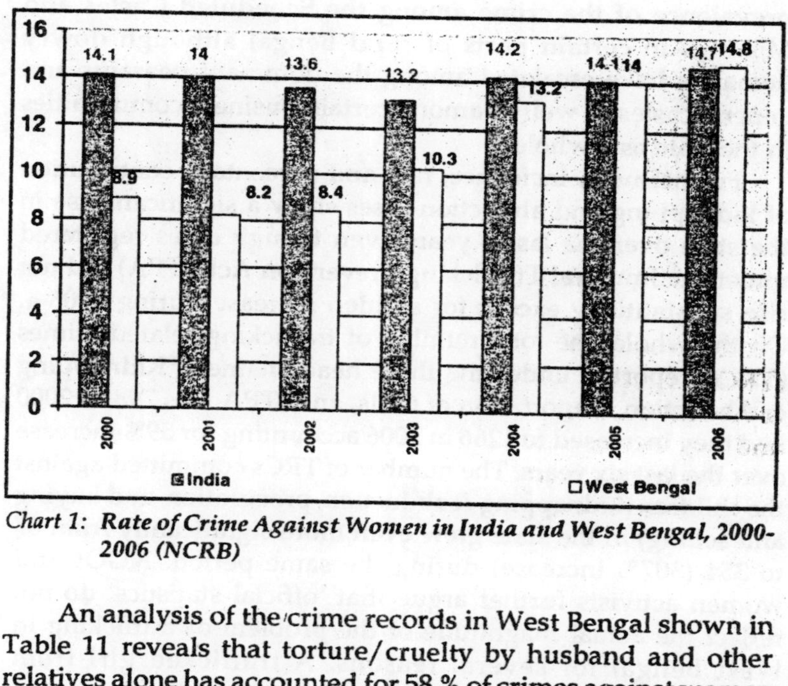

Chart 1: ***Rate of Crime Against Women in India and West Bengal, 2000-2006 (NCRB)***

An analysis of the crime records in West Bengal shown in Table 11 reveals that torture/cruelty by husband and other relatives alone has accounted for 58 % of crimes against women in 2006. Among others, rape (14%), molestation (14%) and kidnapping (9%) incidences have aggravated gender violence to a large extent. Collectively these four crimes have contributed to 95% of crimes against women here in 2006. Dowry death, another significant dimension of gender inequality, which is qualitatively different from other crimes, is constantly increasing in West Bengal and the state is sixth in the country in this respect in 2006 in terms of number of incidence.

As cruelty related to dowry is also reflected through domestic violence, the near universality of the phenomenon needs more serious treatment. District wise analysis of dowry deaths and other related post-marriage crimes shown in Table 12 reveal that they are more prominent in 24 Parganas (South & North), Nadia, Burdwan, Midnapur, Hooghli and Murshidabad[6]. Our field experience[7] also points to the prevalence of the crime among the Scheduled Castes and Muslims in certain parts of rural Bengal although dowry demands have escalated among the dominant peasants and general castes as well as among certain business communities in the state as a whole.

Furthermore, incidence, rate and percentage contribution of kidnapping and abduction cases show a significant rise in the state over the last 5 years even though cases registered under the Immoral Trafficking Prevention Act (ITPA) did not rise substantially except for sudden increase during 2003-4. On the whole, the total number of trafficking related crimes (TRCs) reported under the three heads namely, Kidnapping & Abduction, Importation of Girls, and ITPA was 798 in 2000 and they increased to 1266 in 2006 accounting for 59% increase over the last six years. The number of TRCs committed against the children (kidnapping & abduction, procuration, and buying and selling) in the state grew even more significantly from 87 to 354 (307% increase) during the same period. NGOs and women activists further argue that 'official statistics' do not reflect the actual magnitude of the problem of trafficking in West Bengal for several reasons. A trafficked girl from Bangladesh or Nepal enters West Bengal for distribution at different locations. It is estimated that nearly 10% of the prostitutes in Kolkata are from Bangladesh and Nepal (Sinha 1997). The geographical location of West Bengal therefore makes it a vulnerable place for trafficking. The porous border with Bangladesh is particularly a thorny problem as it covers 4155 Km in length, 71% of which is land area[8]. Moreover in North Bengal there are 14 entry points with Nepal. Hence it is often difficult for BSF to keep a close look and demarcate trafficked persons from other migrants and trespassers. Again, in majority of the instances trafficking takes place in cognizance of relatives or known persons[9]. Hence, the girl does not normally protest against any spatial movement unless otherwise faced with the ultimate reality. As a result trafficking within the state gets blurred with the normal processes of migration, immigration and mobility. Also the failure of the family members, neighbours and the civil society in general to maintain a strict surveillance, stand by the suffering of women and children and bring the matter to the notice of the police may be other strong reasons for trafficking being unknown and secretive. Often the traffickers are so powerful in a locality that the common man rather prefers to ignore the plight of trafficked young or minor girl. The case of Shyamali Sarkar, a sex worker from Kolkata, may be cited here. She was brutally killed by the people involved in trafficking due to her protest against the trafficking of minors (Gupta and Chattopadhyay, 2005: 124). It is worth mentioning here that West Bengal had a yearly average of 1304 cases of women and children under all the three trafficking related crimes (TRCs) in between 2000 and 2006. But the average (yearly) missing figures of adult female and children appear to be much higher than those of TRCs if we consider the fact that there are 1,763 women and 1,599 children found missing every year on an average from the city of Kolkata alone (Institute of Social Sciences 2005: 171). Interestingly such missing figures are almost uniform over a span of 7 years (1996-2001). In 2006, the state accounted for about 60% of minors who went missing in the country. Thus, out of 3,916 cases of missing persons below 18, Bengal led the list with 2,529 cases followed by Delhi, Himachal Pradesh and Assam. This again calls for a paradigm shift in police's approach to trafficking in West Bengal. To the police, a clear case of trafficking cannot be established just by any disappearance of any person. It is true that such disappearances may be linked to elopement. But to trace all missing stories as cases of elopement is equally suicidal. Reports and surveys have documented that some of West Bengal districts like 24 Parganas (North and South), Murshidabad, Darjeeling, Jalpaiguri, Uttar and Dakshin Dinajpur, Cooch

Behar, Nadia, Midnapur, Malda and Birbhum act as the major source areas of trafficking. It is not a mere coincidence that crimes against women of all varieties are comparatively higher in those districts where people belonging to backward and minority sections dominate. Thus, for instance, South 24 Parganas contain 30 per cent of Muslims and 32 per cent of SCs. Similarly Murshidabad has 61 per cent of Muslims and 12 per cent of SCs. This proves that vulnerability of women increases with social and economic backwardness of a community.

Finally, there appears to be a silent complicity to child marriage in the state; many rural and backward communities treat it as normal and routine. Parents know about the legal age of marriage and that there are laws to prevent and restrain child marriage and even punish the guilt for violating the law. Yet only 8, 2 and 6 cases were registered in the state under the Child Marriage Restraint Act, 1929 in 2004, 2005 and 2006 respectively. It may be noted here that in between 1994 and 2002, not a single case was registered under the CMRA in state and the 'drought' ended in 2003 with a single case being registered after a long time. Hence the issue remains one of major concerns in many parts of rural Bengal. Census data reveals that 37.16% of the girls in the state got married before 18 in between 1996-2001, while the corresponding figure for the country, as a whole was 32.10% only. The state is ranked 7th among 35 states and Union Territories in terms of percentage of child marriage in 2001. The rural areas of the state show a much higher percentage (43%) and in certain localities and communities the practice is almost 'normal'. Consequently the mean age at marriage for the currently married women during 1996-2001 is calculated to be 18.9 in West Bengal in contrast to the all India figure of 19.0 (0-33 age group). It should be noted here that the mean age at marriage in the state had remained well above the all India figure for both men and women during 1971-1991. The findings of the latest National Family Health Survey-III, carried out in 29 states during 2005-6, further reveals that West Bengal along with five other states have shown rise in under-18 marriages of women[10]. In the districts like

Murshidabad, Malda, North 24 Parganas, South Dinajpur, Birbhum, Nadia, Purulia, Cooch Behar and South 24 Parganas the problem is more acute. Among the rural Muslims, Scheduled Castes and Scheduled Tribes, child marriage has attained almost vigorous proportion. Undoubtedly, there is tremendous adverse impact of child marriage on the physical, psychological and emotional make up of the girl child. It is the principal reason, among others, for low literacy achievement, poor productivity, low economic contribution, high fertility and trafficking of minor girls.

Needless to say that the factors binding such violence are often poverty and low status of women. Poor, destitute and illiterate women who lack social security are the most vulnerable section and it is a pity that women belonging to minority and socially backward sections fall prey to trafficking easily. What is striking for us to note is that certain improvement in gender related index due to developmental activities in the state, which we have noted earlier, did not automatically check crimes against women. The situation therefore calls for introspection into those factors that are particularly responsible for gender violence in the state.

The growing incidences of crimes against women may however be attributed to greater awareness of rights among women in the state. While it is positive to note that violence against women do not go unnoticed in West Bengal, it cannot be the only explanation for rising incidences of gender violence in the state. Because in many instances such crimes are not reported to police due to social stigma attached to the life of women. We have noted earlier that cases against child marriage are hardly registered in the state even though they take place almost commonly with public knowledge. Contrarily, as compared to the national scenario, incidences of dowry deaths and domestic violence have increased steadily in the state during the last one-decade even though several women organizations and policy makers have campaigned against the heinous crimes. Hence, it cannot be very possessively argued that increasing CAW reflects only greater awareness owing to counter action by social and political organizations here.

Rather, it has been observed that police or civil society organizations intervene only when the matter turns worse or assumes new proportion. From this point of view, increasing incidences of child marriage, dowry deaths or trafficking in any region may also be due to lack of surveillance by the community, police or other concerned.

There are several other important causes, which also broadly explain the prevalence of all other types of CAW. Apart from socio-economic 'push' factors, the growing stress on poor people in post-liberalized India and heightening social inequality, rising consumerism, growing demand for women and girl in the flourishing sex industry, increasing migration and mobility of people due to demand for cheap labour outside etc., are cited as the 'pull' factors causing disturbances in our social fabric. Also delayed action by police or authority, lack of coordination among police and civil society organizations as well as very low conviction rate have dejected many. Table 13 reveals that the rates of chargesheeting and conviction in many crimes in West Bengal are not very encouraging as compared to the all India average. Women all over the world lose out by being women. Their capabilities and choices are

Table 13
Rates of Chargesheeting and Conviction in Crimes Against Women in India & West Bengal, 2005

	Chargesheeting Rate		*Conviction Rate*	
Crimes	*India*	*West Bengal*	*India*	*West Bengal*
Rape	95.5	95.6	25.5	13.5
Molestation	97.0	92.7	30.0	7.1
Sexual Harassment	98.6	82.5	53.5	9.4
Kidnapping & Abduction	77.5	81.9	25.3	17.1
Importation of Girls	86.9	66.7	34.8	00
ITPA	99.6	96.2	82.2	66.7
Dowry Death	95.2	96.3	33.4	26.0
Dowry Prohibition Act	92.1	100	25.5	35.3
Cruelty by Husband/Others	94.6	97.3	19.2	20.2
Total IPC	80.7	74.3	42.5	16.5
Total SLL*	94.5	89.6	84.5	64.1

* Special & Local Laws.
Source: NCRB, 2005.

commonly thwarted by so-called customs, traditions, and culture that are legitimized by a patriarchal social order. It is time now for all concerned to consider sex-based equality as an urgent issue of political justice and thereby pursue a holistic approach to combat gender violence more seriously. Over and above, Gender Development Index (GDI) and Gender Empowerment Index (GEI) should take into consideration incidence and rate of different crimes committed against women in any social space to measure the extent of Social Development of any country/state.

TACKLING GENDER INEQUALITY AND GENDER CRIMES

It is pertinent to note first that changing values, age-old institutions and socio-structural imbalances are uphill tasks and any success in this endeavour would produce a far greater impact in the existing social structure than just tackling some specific crimes only. The problem is not just economic backwardness. Domestic violence and other crimes against women have been shooting up in the country despite educational and economic advancement. Challenging the existing marriage practices and value patterns may call for fighting the powerful patriarchal system, its age-old institutions and culture of subordination of women and girl child. Achieving the goal of gender justice would require fundamental changes in our ideas and pattern of behaviour, as well as the establishment of mechanisms to frame, monitor and enforce the relevant laws. Civil society has a critical role to play in this respect. For formulating, implementing and evaluating necessary policies and action plans, an affective partnership between the government and non-government agencies is strongly recommended. More importantly people's participation in the whole process becomes extremely crucial. As social inequality is a major cause of economic inequality, we need an alternative strategy that treats people as participants, not as targets or beneficiaries.

We also recommend the formation of monitoring boards in all the districts and particularly in the most vulnerable pockets like backward areas of 24 Parganas (North and South), Murshidabad, Jalpaiguri, Uttar and Dakshin Dinajpur, Cooch Behar, Nadia, Midnapur, Malda and Birbhum with government, non-government, local elected leaders, teachers, social workers and professional participations. To break the nexus between gender and crime, a material upliftment of the socially and economically backward areas of the state with adequate income generating employment facilities for the women is required badly. It has been experienced that the fruits of socio-economic development in West Bengal did not percolate down particularly to women belonging to backward classes and minorities. There is therefore no substitute to social, economic and political empowering of women of concerned social groups and classes to combat the menace of child marriage, dowry, trafficking or other types of violence against them. The real inhibiting factor of 'powerlessness' of women can be tackled by such *holistic empowerment*. As social development is basic to raising the status of women and giving her a more equitable share of development benefits, we have to see how women are faring in this field. In this sense, 'development' and 'empowerment' becomes coterminous and overlapping. We should constantly make efforts to provide useful skills and information through a conscientisation strategy particularly to adult women belonging to disadvantaged groups as formal method of literacy may take a very long time, and thereby help them to become confident, motivated and aware. Simultaneously, we shall have to ensure that adolescent girls get education at least up to the high school level.

The process of strengthening SHGs should also be expedited through careful selection of sustainable schemes, sorting out marketing bottlenecks and providing training to women members. SHG members may fight against the imposed invisibility and silence of women in rural society. At the same time successful implementation of the anti-poverty programmes, strict surveillance and prompt action by police and judiciary, community policing, effective partnership between the police and NGOs, protection and rehabilitation of the victims are effective steps to prevent gender crimes. Furthermore, comprehensive legislations in the form of compulsory registration of marriage, recording the gifts given during marriage to girls, making ITPA and the recently introduced Protection of Women from Domestic Violence Act 2005[11] more effective, handling child trafficking separately may make our 'system of control' much more effective. Also, higher charge sheet and conviction rates, fast-track courts at district levels to deal with gender crimes, and increasing strength of welfare officers like Dowry Protection Officers in the districts could act as deterrents. Finally there is also need to build up awareness campaign at various levels about the rights of women. Women's right to good health and control over their body and fertility should become an important agenda of such campaign. Adolescent boys and girls should be compulsorily taught about certain basic values related to social, gender and health issues. A Compulsory Social Science subject at the secondary level of schools may be very handy to do such needful. The media, local bodies, women organizations, experts and SHGs should be effectively involved in the campaign. The democratic processes and structures that have been strengthened in West Bengal through local bodies and reservation for women, must relentlessly work in favour of a meaningful political will for this mission. Fighting gender injustice and crimes require an all-encompassing and continuous effort on the part of all concerned. Hence, one should not expect any immediate result in combating the crimes, but the steps suggested here would certainly make these goals more strong and cherished. In a world that stresses too much on 'market globalism' through liberalization, privatization and withdrawal of state initiative in the social sector, we need to specially look into gender based disparities for the emergence of a truly developmental state in active participation with the civil society organizations.

NOTES

1. This paper is based on the research that I have done in connection with the editing and compilation of a report on *Trafficking in*

Women & Children, Child Marriage and Dowry: A Study For Action Plan in West Bengal, published by UNICEF and Government of West Bengal, 2007. My colleague Mr. Ananda Mohan Kar has helped me in this endeavour.

2. Women constituted only 15.33% of the Main Workers and 55.20% of Marginal Workers in West Bengal in 2001. In 1991, the Female Work Participation Rate (FWPR) was 11.25% in the state. This could not be significantly improved during the last Census decade like Haryana (from 10.76 to 27.31%), or Tripura (from 13.76 to 21.02) or Punjab (from 4.40 to 18.68). The 55th Round of NSS data also show that in both rural and urban areas of the state, FWPR has declined for the 25 to 49 age groups.
3. The density of population for the country as a whole was only 324 in 2001. The Union Territories of Delhi (9294), Chandigarh (7903), Pondicherry (2029), Lakshadweep (1894) and Daman & Diu (1411) however had much higher density of population. But among the states, West Bengal is followed by Kerala (819), Bihar (880) and Uttar Pradesh (689).
4. According to Planning Commission 84% of the absolutely poor population of West Bengal lived in rural areas, compared to 74% in India as a whole. As a result difference between rural and urban per capita consumption is higher in the state than the all India pattern. The number of 'very backward' villages in the state according to government's assessment was 4602 as against a total of nearly 38,500 villages.
5. Birth (live), death and infant mortality rates for the country, as a whole in 2001 was 25.4, 8.4 and 66 respectively. It may however be noted here that the number of women and children suffering from anemia in West Bengal is quite high. Thus, the latest (2004-5) National Family Health Survey shows that 69% of children and 62% of pregnant women in the state are anemic. The comparative figures for the country as a whole are 79.2% (children) and 57.9% (pregnant women). This report further reveals that the benefits of growth are not reaching, not even trickling down to women and children in both rural and urban India.
6. District wise data for 2006 is yet not available.
7. We collected field data on *Child Marriage, Dowry and Trafficking Offences Against Women and Children* in the six districts of Southwest Bengal during June-December 2005 under a major

project sponsored by Unicef & the Department of Women and Child Development and Social Welfare, Govt. of West Bengal.

8. It is estimated that nearly 10 to 15 thousand women and children are trafficked to India every year from Bangladesh. Majority of such trafficking takes place from 30 Bangladesh districts adjacent to the Indo-Bangladesh border. The Southwestern Districts like Khulna, Jhenidah, Meherpur, Chuadanga, Satkhira, Jessor are mostly exposed to trafficking.

9. The study by the National Human Rights Commission found the following profile of the traffickers nearly half of whom were female: Friends (35%), Family members/relatives (20%), Brokers/pimps/agents/brothel owners/sex workers (29.4%), Police/politician (1.2%), Not mentioned (14.4%).

10. West Bengal reported 45.9% of under-18 marriages of women in the earlier NFHS-II survey conducted during 1998-99. But the figure moved up to 53.3% in the latest survey. The survey shows that more and more women in the states like Arunachal Pradesh, Punjab, Mizoram, Sikkim, Tripura and West Bengal are being married off while they are 15. On the whole, nearly 45% women in the country, aged between 20-24 years, were married off before they reached 18, the legal age to marry.

11. West Bengal has lagged behind many other Indian states in implementing this new law and only from the end of 2007, Social Welfare Officers of 18 Districts, who are given additional responsibility of serving as 'Protection Officers', started accepting cases. But just within 8 months 46 cases are filed with the Chief Judicial Magistrate, Burdwan. Even those who earlier did not get justice by filing cases under 498A are now turning to PWDVA for maintenance relief and other compensations.

REFERENCES

Agarwal, S. N. (1962), *Age at Marriage in India,* Kitab Mahal Private Ltd., Allahabad.

Ahuja, Ram (2000), *Violence Against Women,* Jaipur: Rawat Publication.

Bagchi, Jasodhara (ed). (2005), *The Changing Status of Women in West Bengal, 1970-2000–The Challenge Ahead.* Sage Publications, New Delhi.

Council For Social Development (2006), *India: Social Development Report,* New Delhi, Oxford University Press.

Dube, Leela (1997), *Comparative Perspective on Gender in South and South East Asia*, United Nations University Press.

Ghosh, Biswajit (ed). (2007), *Trafficking in Women & Children, Child Marriage and Dowry: A Study For Action Plan in West Bengal*. UNICEF & Govt. of West Bengal, Kolkata.

Government of India. *Census of India*. 1991 & 2001.

Government of West Bengal. *Statistical Abstract: West Bengal, 2003-04*. Bureau of Applied Economics and Statistics, Kolkata.

Government of West Bengal. 2004. *West Bengal Human Development Report 2004*. Development and Planning Department, Kolkata.

Gupta, M and R. Chattopadhyay (2005), 'Law and Violence against Women' in J. Bagchi (ed), *The Changing Status of Women in West Bengal, 1970-2000–The Challenge Ahead*, (111-129). Sage Publications, New Delhi.

Institute of Social Sciences (2005), *Trafficking in Women and Children in India*, Orient Longman, New Delhi.

International Institute For Population Sciences and ORC Marco (2000), *National Family Health Survey (NFHS-II) 1998-99 India*, IIPS, Mumbai.

International Institute For Population Sciences and ORC Marco (2007), *National Family Health Survey (NFHS-III) 2005-06 India*, IIPS, Mumbai.

——— (2001), *Reproductive and Child Health Programme*, (Rapid Household Survey-I & II), 1998-99. IIPS, Mumbai.

Kapadia, K. (2003), *The Violence of Development: The Politics of Identity, Gender and Social Inequalities in India*, Zubaan, New Delhi.

Krishnakumar and Rajalakshmi (2005), 'Child Brides of India', and 'The High Social Cost', in *Frontline*, July 5.

Mehta, Asha Kapur (1996), 'Recasting Indices for Developing Countries: A Gender Empowerment Measures', in *Economic and Political Weekly*, 26 October.

Mohanty, Debabati (2005), *Violence Against Women: An Analysis of Contemporary Reality*, New Delhi, Kanishka Publications.

National Crime Records Bureau (2000-2006), *Crime in India*. Ministry of Home Affairs, Govt. of India, New Delhi.

Premi, Mahendra K. (2001), 'The Missing Girl Child', in *Economic and Political Weekly*, 36 (21): 1875-80.

Sagade, J. (2005), *Child Marriage in India.* Oxford University Press, New Delhi.

Sanlaap. 2002. Human Trafficking. Kolkata: Sanlaap.

Sen, S. and P. M. Nair. (2005), *Trafficking in Women and Children in India.* Orient Longman, New Delhi.

Sharma, U. (2000), 'Dowry in North India: Its Consequences for Women' (in) Uberoi, P (ed), *Family, Kinship and Marriage in India,* Oxford University Press, New Delhi.

Sheel, R. (1999), *The Political Economy of Dowry: Institutionalisation and Expansion in North India,* Manohar Pub., New Delhi.

Sinha, Indira and Staff of Sanlaap (1997), 'The Velvet Blouse: A Study of Child Prostitution in West Bengal', *Sanlaap,* Kolkata.

Tilak, J. B. G. (2006), 'Education: A Saga of Spectacular Achievements and Conspicuous Failures' in *Social Development Report* (33-49). Council For Social Development, Oxford University Press, New Delhi.

UNICEF (2001), Trafficking of Women and Children in South Asia: Regional Strategy Framework for UNICEF's Work to Combat the Trafficking of Women and Children in South Asia. Katmandu: UNICEF.

Section Three

Women: Dual Identity

even before the completion of her eleven years. Early marriage was then customary in Bengal. Women of milkman class used to sale milk and curd in the market. So they used to go out of their residence. Of course mother-in-laws would not always allow housewives to go out side every now and then. Radha would cook various items for her husband Ihon (Bhattacharya 1999).

A few decades ago, when elderly women blessed others, they used to say 'be like Sita, Sabitri'. We may add a few names to this list like Damayanti, Behula etc. This proves that they were idols to the [illegible]. Since childhood, an Indian girl is taught to be an ideal house wife. Husbands are treated as the replica of God. A wife should follow her husband in every walk of life. Her first and foremost duty is to obey her husband, satisfy him even at the cost of her own self or life. If the husband is not [illegible], if he has attachment to other women, still wife should not desert him, dishearten him. If the husband tortures her physically it is her noble duty to bear with this torture whether it is physical or mental. In other words, a wife [illegible] in every [illegible] including self comfort, prestige, honour in spite of facing tremendous humiliation from her husband. She must not protest it. Such a wife is considered to be an ideal one. Such one is considered *Sati Sadhi*.

Tagore's *Mukti* (Salvation) is one of the important compositions of *Palataka*, the poetry collection. The speaker of the poem speaks herself. The poem is a frank confession of the speaker's long monotonous life of twenty two years. When she was only nine, she came to her husband's residence as his life partner. She earned appreciation from all quarters for her ideal qualities befitting a house wife. Every one praised her attributing *Sati*, *Lakshmi* etc. But according to the speaker, she had to materialize the desires of others. She had no freedom, no choice. Her routine life was full of monotony.

Randhanar pare Khaoa abar khaoar pare randha
Baish bachhar ek chakai [illegible]

After cooking, she had to take her meals and after taking the meals she had to be busy with cooking again. Thus she [illegible] in the cyclic order of the life

5

Problems of Working Mother: A Dilemma in Motherhood

SAMITA MANNA & BHASWATI SARKAR

Unlike father hood, mother hood invites many challenging responsibilities, particularly since the second half of the twentieth century when globalization has pervaded each society, the world of women has been changing very fast. In general there is a great debate between the naturist and the nurturist. It is true that there are physical and biological differences between men and women i.e. differences in physical features as well as sexual organs. As a result, women give birth to children and have a natural maternal instinct. On the other hand, men are physically stronger having the power of possessiveness. They play a dominating role, control others by their physical strength. Gradually, different institutions of societies are controlled by the dominant sex. In most primitive societies, when there was no such regulatory institutions like marriage, men and women used to share many rights and obligations jointly. They jointly shared the obligations of taking the burden of their children and family.

The institution of marriage gradually became a universal institution. Religious sanctity was also given for the institution. Generally marriage has its religious sanctity protecting the lifelong partnership jointly for performing duties which are *dharma* (duty), *artha* (material prosperity) and *kama* (pleasure).

> In modern terminology these are the three principal motivating forces or urges or drives around which the whole life and conduct of man could be comprehended.... and formulated in terms of these three, with reference to the ultimate end of life viz. moksha (Prabhu 1961).

In Indian society marriage is regarded as a religious sacrament for performing these functions. For this reason male and female unite, procreate children and live together. It is considered a tie, not between persons but between families in order to perform religious duties.

But the institution of family and marriage have also been dominated by the norms of patriarchy. Societies from the early stage to modern advanced democratic societies, women have all along occupied subordinate position. Patriarchy's chief institution has been the family.

As Firestone (1972) argues, unlike economic class, 'sex class' sprang directly from a biological reality. According to her view, true liberation will come only when women will be freed from uterus i.e., she is talking about artificial reproduction. So radical and revolutionary feminists often argue that women's subordination status originate from a biological reality that women are constrained by reproduction.

But this opinion does not reflect the thinking of most of women. Even educated women want family, husband and children. Moreover the working women desire to establish a harmonious relation between home and work place. As a result, they try their best to cope themselves with their family, children and work place. The real problem of working woman is that at the same time she has to perform the parallel role of a mother. This is really a complicated task of working woman. Even a professional woman also feels unhappy if she looses the attribute of motherhood and suffers from barreness. So in this context, we can not ignore the view of nurturists. Gender is socially constructed. Through the process of socialization, a society constructs a man as a man and a woman as a woman according to the norms, values and prescriptions of the society. Patriarchal society develops strong masculinity and weak feminity. In the man-made society, male dominance is institutionalized and considered as normal and accepted by the members of the society. Even many women accept it as natural. They do not cherish the idea of a boy in a feminish way and the girl in a boyish way.

Radical feminists often suggest a complete reallocation of power even at the cost of family ties, abolishing every form of gender division of labour in order to establish a gender-just society. Definitely their emphasis is on establishing multidimensional economic bond between women and the wider society, apart from the services to which they are assigned traditionally. Implicit in the idea is a disjunction between tradition and modernity in a sense that orientation to tradition enslaves them in what is called the 'province of women' (Finch 1996).

The problem starts here. The waves of modernization, and now globalization, not only inculcate new values pointing to qualitative changes in the relation between two sexes, but also create a need for recognition not as a subject but as a citizen. Western notion of equality is severely haunting the 'culture of hierarchy' which emphasizes on 'self denial' and 'sublimating the ego' (Chitnis 1988).' These new values can not act in 'vacuum' and need new institutions for their sustenance and expression' (Beteille 2000).

Women, who work outside their home for wage or salary, are known as working women (Anjana 1993). According to the 1991 census, the total number of working women in India was 278.35 million and one third of the labour-force of India consists of women (ibid 1993). In India, female work participation rates were 23.31, 27.93, 14.22 and 20.85 in the census of 1951, 1961, 1971 and 1981 respectively (Swarnalatha 1993). It has been recognized in the forty-eighth session of the International Labour Conference (1963) that women play a vital role in the economic and social life. In the world, as a whole, 27 out of every 100 women are economically active and about one third of the word's labour force is made up of women (Chakraborty 1978). But the problem arises from the conflict between tradition and the upcoming economic order. At the same time it is also true that the domestic activities of the women cannot provide the source of self-esteem as it is not regarded as prestigious. Agarwal (1988) writes,

> However important these activities may be a stigma of inferiority is attached to household work. The reason could be that it is considered unproductive and the labour is not valued in terms of cash.

Actually, in all patriarchal societies, the position of women in the family is clearly defined by men (Hareven 1977). McDowell and Pringle (1992) rightly assert that the masculinity and male behavior are always the reference points in defining the behavior of women in concrete situations. The emerging ideology of dual career family has recognized the special status of women but has not relieved them from their traditional responsibilities. Women are solely defined, even today, for all domestic activities. The dilemma of the married working women arises from this dialectic.

Irrespective of their educational levels, married working women confront dual responsibilities at home and in office. Sometimes it is thought that men are incapable of doing domestic activities. As Lewis (1992) shows,

> Men and women in many cultures and subcultures subscribe to the view that men are inept or incapable of domestic work and this serves to excuse men's non-participation in family work and to avoid confrontation.

Thus, the married working women overstrain themselves to manage both the domestic and workplace activities. The dual loyalties 'adversely influence a career woman by creating stress and strain, in her life' (Agarwal 1994). Motherhood of such women creates another problem. Working mothers often suffer from guilty complex arising from the feeling of neglecting their children and the family. So they always continue to strive harder to prove that no one will suffer because of their job engagement. Rowbotham (1992) shows,

> Women received less than one tenth of the world income, but do two thirds of the world's work. Although earning less than men, they work longer hours–2 to 5 hours more in developed countries, 5 to 6 hours more in Latin America and the Caribbean and as much as 12 to 13 hours more in Africa and Asia. When housework and child care are taken into account, women on average have a 60 to 70 hours week.

Women have to do more work than men but they have limited access to economic resources and benefits. Actually these are largely appropriated by men. Observations of the Humphrey Institute of Public Affairs are important in this respect.

> While women represent 50 per cent of the world population, they perform nearly two thirds of all working hours, receive one-tenth of world income and own less than one per cent of the world property. (cited in Sharma 2000).

The situation of the working women is more frustrating where they have no real economic independence at all. In many cases, married working women have to hand over their entire income to their husbands or in-laws. When a working woman lives with her in-laws, she has extra responsibility to take care of them. Such multiplicity of duties and responsibilities, create strain and role conflict. As Rani (1976) views,

> The dual responsibilities of a working wife not only overloads her but may be so incompatible that they cannot be performed properly. Having less time and more congruent demands of roles, she experiences more and more role conflict in modern situation.

Thus, it can be said that involvement in work for men folk is advantageous in respect to the mental health, whereas it is a source of overload and conflict for the women. Besides, still the society thinks that much devotion to the work and workplace on the part of women may make them irresponsible in their household duties. In this connection Mead's (1964) statement is very much appropriate.

> The more successful a man is in his job, the more certain everyone is that he will make a desirable husband; the more successful a woman is, the more most people are afraid, she may not be a successful wife.

Employment is a factor that draws women out of the family and domestic duties and which had hitherto made up their fate (Ramaswamy 1996). There is no doubt that women's access to paid job raises their status to a great extent. It also brings larger participation in decision-making and greater confidence in their capabilities. But they cannot enjoy themselves according to their own will. Very often, they avoid deliberately better career opportunities, because till today, the family considers the demands of the husbands, children and other relatives as women's responsibility and obligation. Thus they are totally overburdened both physically and mentally. Considering their home and outside activities, they work for fourteen to sixteen hours a day. In many families, husband and the other members of the family recognize their problems but they do not share the household responsibility.

> Maintaining cleanliness in the house, looking after the children's needs and listening to complaints against the servants as soon as women return from work are all instances of the persistence of the primacy of the family role for women (Desai 1996).

In spite of all these, legal attempts have been made to give access in education and employment in order to raise women's status and to raise their ability to protest against all kinds of oppressions. The position of women in general could not reach up to the level of expectation. This does not mean that working women gain no advantage in relation to those who do not engage themselves in paid work. Women's economic participation and close relation to outside world, help to erode many superstitions attached to the women's traditional role. But to remove an overall oppression and to alter the value system, a fundamental change in thinking and attitude is very much necessary where a woman should not be regarded only as a wife and a mother.

Contemporary feminist movements have been able to highlight women issue at the national and international levels. But till today, it has brought little respite in their life as patriarchy exists and controls the social system as such. It is not a question of mere economic self-sufficiency, mere inclusion of the 'excluded' rather it is a question of empowerment–a true redistribution of power. No doubt some western countries have made serious progress in this regard. Globalization has blurred the cultural boundaries of nation states, let the fresh air of western liberalism blow in our mind too.

The dilemma of the married working women arises from the dialectic between tradition and modernity in a wider sense. While the former demands more time in the domestic activities, the latter requires more devotion in official duties. Unlike many of the western countries, women in India, whether working or not, give priority to their role of housewife. They want to be the ideal wife in order to enjoy recognition from others including their neighbors. This recognition provides them more readily the necessary source to develop self-esteem than the admiration of successful performance by their office colleagues.

It is serious problem of course. The educated working women are, more often than not, caught between these two worlds. Their male counterpart, on the other hand, can concentrate more on their careers overlooking many of the domestic duties, overloading their working wives. The problem is complex, multidimensional and in many cases latent. Only the sufferer could realize its severity; the social scientist could only probe into their minds to guess its extent. Such an attempt has been made in this study.

II

To examine the above propositions from an empirical point of view, we conducted a study among working women in a particular area.

The main thrust of this work is to find out the nature and forms of dilemma confronted by the working women in their daily life. The origin of this dilemma is the dual responsibilities of the married working women. The study also highlights different coping strategies by which they adjust with these conflicting situations and the dilemma amidst the duality of domestic activities and official responsibilities. The study shows special emphasis on the married working women because the married women of our country have to take more domestic responsibilities in their in-laws' family. Concomitantly, they have to render their services in their workplaces. This is the dialectic-the married working women have to combat always. This study focuses on this issue.

The study is conducted among the married working women of Kalyani town[1] of Nadia District[2] (West Bengal, India). Kalyani is well known for its educational and industrial advancement. A good number of educational institutions and industries have given the town a distinct position in the map of West Bengal. Besides, being an urban area there is the explicit impact of radical thinking and modern ways of living. Naturally, the respondents of Kalyani have a wider worldview and strong inclination towards individualism.

Table 1

Distribution of the Sample

Area	*Block*	*No. of Working Women*
KALYANI	A	129 (33.50)
	B	230 (59.74)
	C	16 (4.16)
	Other Residential Areas	10 (2.60)
	Total	385 (100.00

N.B. Figures in the parentheses indicate percentages.

Service sector[3], at least in principle, is free from preferential discrimination so far as gender issue is concerned. That is to say that, except in a few cases, appointment in governmental or semi-governmental organizations is open to all irrespective of sex. Contemporary discourses on 'women in employment' sometimes bypass the issue of their real empowerment in true and wider sense emphasizing only the economic aspect of such participation. Women's employment to large extent, has given them self-sufficiency from the economic point of view. But if the question is their overall empowerment including the power of 'agenda setting' and 'thought manipulation', it is only a partial view. The common experience is that both in office and outside it, women, despite their economic self-sufficiency, are underestimated as 'second class members'. Their vocational profile follows a definite pattern in tune with the 'cultural psyche' of the existing society. The answers of the questions why do they prefer particular types of occupation or why do they avoid transfer sacrificing their professional career are that they belong to our Indian traditional society.

Though male-female equality is accepted from the theoretical point of view, female participation in work sphere is still considered from conservative outlook. Indian patriarchal society idealizes women only as housewives. The concept of working women is still now not encouraged. Today the changing values help to accept women's economic participation equally with the male and a good number of women are engaged in various remunerative jobs. Devendra (1996) in his study, Changing Status of Women in India, has shown that generally the employment of women was confined to unskilled jobs or occupations involving little skill. But Mukherjee (1957) has asserted that women's economic sphere was once limited to household chores or labour on the firm, has expanded considerably. He wrote in his book *Women in Ancient India* that there is scarcely any avenue of employment in which the women have not pronounced their presence. Similarly, in his work, Emancipation and Empowerment of Women, Giri (1998) has observed that women's economic independence is the first step of real empowerment of women. He also shows that statistics reveal that the number of women in employment has been increasing and they are accepting various jobs which were once considered as special domain of men. Background information of the sample have been shown in Table 2. In the

Table 2
Socio Economic Profile of the Sample

Age	*18-38 (Years)*	*39-59 (Years)*	*60 and above (Years)*	*Total*			
	81 (21.04)	302 (78.44)	2 (0.52)	385 (100.00)			
Education	Illiterate	Up to Class XII	Higher Secondary	Graduate	Postgraduate	Total	
	1(0.26%)	36(9.35%)	35(9.09%)	152(39.48%)	161(41.82%)	385(100.00%)	
Occupation	Sweeper	Peon & Group D Staff	Clerk	Officer	School Teacher	College, University Teacher	
	5(1.290)	90(23.37)	53 (13.77)	16 (4.16)	199 (51.69)	21 (5.72)	Total 385
Income	Rs. 1001-5000	Rs. 5001-10000	Rs. 10001-15000	Rs. 15001-20000	Rs. 20001 +	Total	(100.00)
	30(7.79)	207(53.77)	132(34.29)	14(3.64)	2(0.52)	385(100.00)	
Family Size	Small	Medium	Large	Total			
	1-3 Members 132 (34.29)	4-6 Members 231 (60.00)	7-10 Members 22 (5.71)	385 (100.00)			
Family Type	Simple	Extended	Total				
	234 (60.78)	151 (39.22)	385 (100.00)				

N.B. Figures in the parentheses indicated percentages.

present study, the respondents show the causes of their job engagement which are mainly economic in nature. More than half of the total respondents take the job for economic reasons (59.22%). Some of the respondents take their fathers' job after their death; some of them join the service sector to maintain their family as being an elder among the brothers and sisters. But there are others who join the remunerative job for social reasons (36.88%). Educated women today want to enhance their own status through economic self-sufficiency. No doubt women's job involvement increases their prestige in society. This study shows that economic needs are not the only reasons behind women's job involvement. Besides economic pressure, a good number of women of this area join the service sector for enhancing their position and prestige in the society. In doing so, they want to transform their traditional image, in which they were regarded as the burden of the society. Today women's economic self independence proves that they are no more the liabilities but also the assets of the society.

Out of 385 women studied, 68.31% joined the service sector before their marriage. So it can be said that the respondents are well aware about their need for economic self-sufficiency. The respondents are highly educated. Most of them are graduates or post graduates. Their advanced educational level provides more opportunities for them in the job market. Now, after completion of education, educated women do not waste time and try to join the service. There are many women who do not want to get married unless they are economically self-sufficient.

A few respondents move to their workplaces by foot and by rickshaw (8.31% and 9.09%). This signifies that these respondents' work places are situated in local and surrounding areas of the Kalyani town. But data depict that a good number of the working women use to go to their working places by bus and train (39.22% and 40.00% respectively). So this reveals that their workplaces are not within the township. Majority of them (60.78%) have opined that it takes thirty minutes or less to reach to their workplaces. Married working women because of their dual responsibilities always try to choose their job placement nearer to their home. They have to go to the offices after completing their household responsibilities and after returning from the office, they have to manage the household activities again. So traveling a long distance between the workplace and home is quite problematic for the married working women. But no respondent has been found whose workplace is situated at a distance that takes more than three hours to reach their work place.

As all the respondents are government employees or engaged in semi-government organizations, majority of them have to work five hours or less (62.59%) whereas 36.62% have to work for six to eight hours in their offices. Some respondents (nurse and medical officers) have to work for nine to eleven hours or twelve hours or more a day (0.5% and 0.28% respectively). These women have to work in their offices for such a long period, face tremendous problems in their home front, whereas long working hours do not create any such problem for the males.

Household responsibility of married women is perhaps the cause of their preference for non-transferable jobs. Home management is still considered as a female responsibility. A man can stay outside for his job leaving all the responsibilities to his wife but a woman can not do this. More than half of the total respondents (57.15%) have engaged themselves in non-transferable jobs. If the women are working in transferable jobs they often take their children with themselves or they manage their posting nearer their home. Out of a total 385 married working women, 42.85% respondents are engaged in transferable jobs.

In the present study the researchers have also observed an interesting feature regarding the nature of job of the respondents. Out of 385, 98.19% respondents are engaged in office duty and only 7 (1.81%) respondents who reside at Block-B have to do field duty (Table 3).

Most of the women desperately try to combine their workplace responsibilities with their household obligations. After marriage they have to take number of responsibilities in their family. The experience of motherhood normally delimits all kinds of personal desires of an Indian woman. Nicolson (1993) in her work on *Motherhood and Women's Lives,* observes that mothers need to be strong to cope with mothering and with the social conditions surrounding the roles : child rearing, managing child caring arrangements, maintaining relationships with parents, friends duties and formalities towards neighbors, the home etc. She also adds that the working mothers often suffer from guilt prompted by the continued blames that maternal deprivation arises when they go to their workplaces. For this reason, working women like to join occupations where the volume of work is limited (viz. teaching occupation) or sometimes they deliberately do not take promotion fearing more responsible office duties or transfer. It has been observed that out of a total of 385 respondents, 85.20% respondents have not accepted promotion though most of the working women's length of service is quite long i.e. fifteen years and above (75.85%). The educational qualifications of the married working women who have enjoyed promotion are below graduation (17.46%) and above graduation (12.42%).

Gender equality is perhaps much more prominent in work than in family surroundings. Male violence or male use of power in any from is not so common in the government or semi government organizations than in private workplaces. The respondents have opined that in work place, the environment is more or less suitable for their work. In most of the cases the offices are free from male violence; rather helping attitude and cooperation among the workers of both sexes characterize the healthy environment of the work place. As a result, out of a total of 385 married working women, 59.22% partially and 36.63% are fully satisfied with their own work environment. But 4.15% respondents have confessed that they are not satisfied at all. These respondents are mostly nurses and medical officers. They have complained that subordinate workers often spoil the environment of the hospitals and make the task of serving the patients very difficult. Some clerks in government offices have also opined that some of their male colleagues constantly irritate them in different ways.

It has already been pointed out that more than half of the respondents are engaged in school teaching in different girls' schools. So a good number of respondents (40.77%) have opined that their colleagues are mostly female. On the other hand, 35.86% respondents have said that the number of male and female colleagues is equal and 18.70% have told that their colleagues are mostly male. Out of the 385 respondents, 4.6% married working women have opined that they are the only female staff in their offices. 57.15% respondents think that colleagues should not be differentiated in terms of gender. But a few respondents (27.27%) prefer to have exclusively female colleagues in their offices. This signifies that there is still the influence of patriarchal conservatism which prompt women to think that to work with men is not congenial.

Relationship with the colleagues, subordinates and higher authority in most of the cases are satisfactory. They have opined that the colleagues, subordinates and higher authority are cooperative and have helpful attitude towards them. The health workers and field workers of agricultural department have opined that all colleagues irrespective of gender cooperate with each other. They have said that they work in healthy environment and all colleagues are more or less very much attentive to the official work. But there are also a few working women who have complained that the relationship with their colleagues, subordinates and higher authority are very much unsatisfactory (0.28%,1.31% and 0.80% respectively).

III

Industrialization, whether in capitalist or socialist countries, created employment opportunities in disproportionate ways. This 'technology-led economic growth' and its associated processes, which are generally termed as 'modernization', challenged the traditional values and liberated many women from their domestic roles. This process was strengthened during the last few decades of the twentieth century.

The shift in emphasis from capital and labour to knowledge and service in the economic sphere again attracted women for economic self-sufficiency particularly in urban areas. However, the increased involvement of women in economic activities has two important aspects. Firstly, though women are getting jobs in increasing rates, they are still in disadvantageous position as compared to men. Secondly, their household responsibilities are considered primary, therefore, duties and obligations associated with their employment are additional burden to them. Lewis and Cooper (1988) in their study on the *Stress in Dual–Earner Families* have shown women are increasingly sharing the breadearner role but in domestic sphere the responses from the male parts (in the form of sharing the domestic activities) are very low. In another study, Lewis (1992) points out that in many cultures or subcultures men and women subscribe to the view that men are inept or incapable of domestic work. In the study *Differential Socialisation of Boys and Girls in the Family : A Study of Lower Socio-Economics Households among Gujrati Castes and Communities in Ahmedabad,* Kanhare (1978) says that traditional patriarchal family system has restricted women's role mostly to the domestic sphere and has given them a subordinate status, authority and power compared to men. The contemporary discourses on role conflict of the women arising from their dual responsibilities have not been able to lessen their problems, but it has placed the issue to the fore. Behera and Padhi (1993), in their study on 126 mothers employed as school teachers in the town of Berhampore (South Orissa), have shown that the working women become overburdened with workloads in connection with their home and workplace. Often this dual burden creates the role conflict among the married working women. Rani (1976), dealing with the problems of working women, has opined that the dual responsibilities of a working woman not only overloads her but may be so incompatible that they are not able to perform those properly and experience more role conflict in their life.

It is widely acknowledged that western feminism is basically different from Indian feminism in its orientation and application. While western feminism is aggressive in nature, Indian women to a considerable extent accept male domination and their position, even sometimes in the name of religion. The problem of dual responsibilities of the women, particularly of the married working women, become complex when they themselves think that to render services to the members of their families are their prime and holy task. Sengupta (2000) in her study on *Socio-Cultural Dimensions Influencing Status of Rural Women* has said that from the very childhood, the specific roles which girls are supposed to play as wives are inculcated into them through the socialization process. They automatically accept the subordinate status because they are completely tuned psychologically to accept the position in a system of hierarchical relations within the family.

Peculiar value system, belief pattern and cultural practices existing in our country have made the task of empowering women through economic self-sufficiency, extremely difficult, if not impossible. The position of women or the attitude of patriarchy towards them is associated with so many cultural factors that only economic self-sufficiency brings marginal changes in their real life. Despite the formal duties in their offices, they have to take the total responsibilities of their families.

Out study shows that the educational qualifications of the respondents are considerably high and most of them hold different responsible positions in their offices. The teachers have to teach their students, the officers have to take important administrative decisions, the health workers have to render services to the people. Their responsibilities are not less significant than that of their male colleagues. But to their family members these are secondary, even unimportant. Primary is their household duties-to render services to their husbands, in-laws and children. Their husbands also expect that their working 'wives' should be their wives first.

As a result, the working women have to take all domestic responsibilities along with their official duties. In our study, in only 4 (1.04%) cases, out of 385, their husbands solely take these responsibilities. Normally, more than 66.00% working women of all occupational groups have to look after all household activities. The working husbands of these working women return home to enjoy family life. Another important finding is that only 32.21% husbands are sympathetic and frequently they share the responsibilities with their wives mainly in domestic activities and child rearing. It is slightly higher in case of health workers, schools teachers, clerks and officers (Table 4).

But at present the husbands have shown their liberal attitude towards working of their wives. Except a few (1.55%), they allow their wives to continue their job. This is perhaps motivated by the fact that 'wives' employment also enhances family income and helps to maintain family prestige in an emerging consumer culture. 83.90% respondents have opined that their husbands accept their job involvement to the extent that it does not disturb their family life.

Out of 385, only 4 (1.04%) respondents have opined about the negative ambivalent attitude of their husbands towards their wives and in extreme situation they may have to resign from their jobs. Interestingly they have said that even if they have to resign due to their husbands' objection, they will do it willingly. This is perhaps the unique feature of the Indian women who can sacrifice everything for the sake of their family. At the same time it is also important to note that women prefer those services which are not transferable and do not require field visits.

The working women not only have to do domestic works at home but sometimes they also have to finish some official work at home after completing all household responsibilities. Though their percentage is low, yet it is enough to understand the extent of burden of the married working women. Besides, the women who are particularly engaged in teaching profession, have to set up question papers, evaluate the answer sheets, prepare mark sheets and frequently they have to prepare themselves for the next day's teaching. The consequence is far reaching. It hampers their performance, lessens their professional devotion and affects their health. The cumulative effects of these have again weakened their position in different institutions. Despite their numerous obligations at home, women are sincere about their official work too. Though this puts much strain on them, they have to perform the official work at home regularly. It is also noticeable that in most of the cases the family members including their husbands and in-laws accept and permit such official works at home because these women are economically self sufficient and contribute financial assistance to the family.

58.70% respondents have said that they do not face any apparent problem in offices due to their domestic duties, but any careful analysis will show that heavy burden at home inevitably affects their role performances in office. However, there are some sector wise differences in opinion. 65.12% respondents in Block -A have confessed that they feel some problems in office as they have to work hard for their families. But 69.13% respondents in Block–B, 60.00% and 100.00% respondents in Other Residential Areas (ORA) and Block–C respectively have denied it.

As the working women have to spend most of the time outside their home, their children have to face some problems. It is found that most of the respondents live in nuclear families. During daytime their husbands also stay outside the home. So there remains no close family member to look after the children when their mothers are absent. In most of the cases the respondents employ maidservants for this purpose. The problem is less acute in extended families. But 74.12% children in the nuclear families grow up under the supervision of the maidservants. Though in extended families also, 44.44% children are kept under the maidservants, there are other family members who give them company. Most of the women living in nuclear families have reported that their children develop many bad habits from the maidservants. Besides, the maidservants often do not pay proper attention to the children. Some working mothers living in nuclear families keep their son or daughter under the supervision of their relatives or in-laws to avoid such problem (Table 5).

However, the respondents, in majority of the cases, have expressed their dissatisfaction in such arrangements. They have said that the mothers are the best providers of affection and care, and even the close relatives are not the substitutes.

Therefore, the working mothers under study try to spend time as much as possible with their children. But there are a few mothers (3.76%) who can not provide any time for their children. However, in 96.24% cases, mothers play with their children, tell story and take care of them whenever possible. But they think that they, as 'mothers', should give more time to their children. So sometimes they feel guilty for that. Only 11.02% mothers do not have such feelings. On the other hand, 70.97% mothers are not satisfied with the amount of time they spend for their children and they have said that they often feel guilty for depriving their children from their company. 18.01% mothers always feel guilty for their children.

Not only the mothers feel that they can not spend enough time for their children, their sons and daughters also demand more time from them. Often the children feel lonely and become aggressive and obstinate. Out of 372[5] respondents, only 21 (5.65%) have said that their children do not demand more time from them. But the majority of them (63.17%) want their mothers' company more and they feel that their mothers should spent more time for them. A good number of them grow up under the supervision of maidservants. They are deprived of their parents' company to a great extent. The feeling is more acute in 31.18% cases. According to the opinion of these respondents, their children strongly demand their company. Thus as a whole, it is observed that the children of the working women want their mothers' company much more than what they get at present. Different problems faced by their children are depicted in Table 4.

Along with the fulfillment of the expectations of their children, expectations of their husbands and in-laws, expectations of their office colleagues and superiors, the married working women often have to take partial or sole responsibilities of their parents . 64.42% respondents have said that they do not have to take the responsibilities of their parents as till now in our country the daughters are regarded as the property of their husbands' families after their marriage. Though the married women sometimes look after their old parents, they seldom take the economic responsibilities of them

Table 3
Occupational Profile

Essential factors for enjoyment in jobs	*Social*	*Economic*	*Others*		
385 (100.00)	142 (36.88)	228 (59.22)	15 (4.00)		
Time of joining	*Before marriage*	*After marriage*			
385 (100.00)	263 (68.31)	122 (36.69)			
Types of Conveyance for working place	*By foot*	*Rickshaw*	*Cal*	*Bus*	*Train*
385 (100.00)	32 (8.31)	35 (9.09)	13 (3.38)	151 (39.22)	154 (40.00)
Time taking for working places	*30 minutes*	*1 hour or less*	*3 hours or less*		
385 (100.00)	234 (60.78)	89 (23.12)	62 (16.10)		
Working Hours in office	*5 hours or less*	*6-8 hours*	*More than 9 hours*		
385 (100.00)	241 (62.59)	141 (36.62)	3 (.79)		
Nature of Job	*Transferable*	*Non Transferable*			
385 (100.00)	165 (42.85)	220 (57.15)			
Nature of Duty	*Field duty*	*Office duty*			
385 (100.00)	7 (1.81)	378 (98.19)			

N.B. Figures in the parentheses indicated percentages.

Table 4
Working Mothers Reaction Performing the Dual Roles

Responsibilities taken for household works	*Wife's responsibilities*	*Husband's responsibilities*	*Shared by both*
385 (100.00)	257 (66.75)	4 (1.04)	124 (32.21)
Problems faced due to performing dual roles	*Acute problem*	*Moderate problem*	*No problem*
385 (100.00)	6 (1.56)	153 (39.74)	226 (58.70)
Company to the Children	*Not given company*	*Moderate company*	** 13 mothers have no children s*
372 (100.00)	14 (3.76)	358 (96.24)	
Guilty feelings of the mothers	*Always*	*Occasional*	*Never*
372 (100.00)	67 (18.01)	264 (70.97)	41 (11.02)
Children's Demand	*Strong demand*	*Moderate demand*	*No demand*
372 (100.00)	116 (31.18)	235 (63.17)	21 (5.65)

N.B. Figures in the parentheses indicate percentages.

Table 5
Working Mothers and Problems of the Children

Problems of the Children	*Physical*	*Mental*	*Bad association*	*Educational*	*No problem*	*Total*	*Respondents having no children*
	46 (12.37)	161 (43.28)	12 (3.23)	22 (5.91)	131 (35.22)	372 (100.00)	13
Measures	*To give of the Job*	*Taking leave*	*Mentally depressed*	*No choice*			
	40 (10.75)	271 (72.85)	49 (13.17)	12 (3.23)	-	372 (100.00)	13

N. B. – Figures in the parentheses indicate percentages.

as the sons do. The parents also are not ready to accept their daughters' monetary assistance. So it can be said that married working women's job engagements do not bring any change in economic condition of their parents' families. They solely contribute, to their husbands family only.

But there are 28.31% respondents who bear moderate responsibilities of their parents. These responsibilities also include financial support. Most of them are happy that their husbands do not generally respond negatively. Out of 385 respondents, there are 28 (7.27%) working women who take full responsibilities of their parents. The respondents have said that as they are employed, their husbands can not resist them from looking after their parents. However, they all agree that otherwise it would be quite impossible for them. Perhaps this is a new trend in parent-daughter relationship. The traditional notion *'Kanya is paraya dhan'* (daughters are others' property), in this regard does not fully persist any more. But today many married women can take care of their parents. The husbands also have changed their attitude. In the present study 35.58% respondents take total or partial responsibilities of their parents.

As a working woman she has to involve herself in many new responsibilities and obligations outside the home and most of the time she is overburdened because she has to perform the traditional familial duties equally. To manage the situation, women have to compromise and adjust all the time. In the present study, the respondents were asked to evaluate their performance of the dual roles within and outside the family. The responses were categorized into three groups 'Good', 'Medium' and 'Bad'. 58.70% respondents perceived that they can manage their dual roles successfully. 35.58% respondents have opined that they manage their dual responsibilities moderately. These respondents try utmost to adjust themselves with the duality of their lives and try to manage both the activities. On the contrary, 5.72% respondents think that their dual roles hamper both their role in family and their role in office.

Almost all the respondents have opined that in future if their dual roles seriously affect their families, they will sacrifice their career for the sake of their children, husband and families. This is a significant feature of the attitude of the Indian women; and as well as a significant hindrance for the expansion of a true feminist movement here.

NOTES

This is the text of the UGC sponsored project sanctioned in the year 1999 and financed by the University Grants Commission. I express my deep sense of gratitude to the Secretary, UGC New Delhi for providing necessary financial support for this project.

1. Kalyani town is divided into three Blocks-Block A, Block B, Block C. Block A is purely residential. Block B is purely residential and industrial and Block C is comprised of housing complex. The University of Kalyani is also situated in Block C. Some residential areas like Majherchar, Simanta colony, Natunpally, Kanthaltala etc. are situated within the jurisdiction of Kalyani Municipality which have been referred to as Other Residental Areas, in the present study.

2. Nadia is one of the districts of West Bengal. It was acknowledged as a separate district in the year 1787. Before that Nadia was within Jessore Division. Later on, Nadia Division was formed and Krishnagar was its head quarter. In 1860, the quarter of this Division was shifted by the then British Govt. to Alipore. It was composed of four districts and Nadia district was one of them. But the present Nadia was formed in 1948 after the partition of Bengal.

   From the time of Lord Chaitanya i.e. fifteenth century, AD, the district Nadia has distinct cultural and spiritual environment. Its cultural ethos and ideological structure was strongly influenced by Vaishnavism. It is a district of glorious educational and cultural heritage and has a long and deep-rooted tradition of learning.

3. All the respondents are working in different Govt. and semi Govt. organizations and majority of them are teachers in different Schools, Colleges and Universities.

4. Majority of the married working women belong to the age group of 39 years to 59 years. More than 80% sample women are educated upto graduate and post graduate level. Among the

Government and semi- government employees, a good number of them are teachers (57.41%) and their income is good. 60.78% women live in nuclear families following 60% having 4-6 members family.

5. Out of 385 working mothers, 13 women had no children.

REFERENCES

Agarwal, K. (1988), 'Status and Role of Middle Class Educated Earning Women in the Indian Family', in T.M. Dak (ed.) : *Women and Work in Indian Society.* New Delhi: Discovery Publishing House.

Agarwal, V. (1994), 'Stress and Multiple Role Women', *Indian Journal of Social Science,* Vol. 7, No. 3 and 4 July–December.

Anjana, M. S. (1993), *Women in a Changing Society.* New Delhi: Ashis Publishing House.

Behra, D. K. and Padhi, I. (1993), 'Role Conflict of Working Mothers in Teaching Profession', *Indian Anthropologist,* 23 (1).

Beteille, A. (2000), *Antinomies of Society: Essays on Ideologies and Institutions.* New Delhi: Oxford University Press.

Chakroborty, K. (1978), *The Conflicting Worlds of Working Mothers.* Calcutta: Progressive Publishers.

Chitnis, S. (1988), 'Feminism: Indian Ethos and Indian Convictions', in R. Ghadially (ed). *Women in Indian Society.* New Delhi: Sage Publications.

Desai, N. (1996), 'Women's Employment and their Familial Role in India' in A.M. Shah et al (Eds.) *Social Structure and Change: Women in Indian Society,* Vol II. New Delhi: Sage Publications.

Devendra, K. (1996), *Changing Status of Women in India.* New Delhi: Vikas Publishing House Pvt. Ltd.

Finch, J. (1996), 'Women, the Family and Families', in T. Cosslett *et. al* (eds): *Women, Power and Resistance: An Introduction to Womens Studies, Buckingham:* Delhi: Open University Press.

Firistone, S. (1972), *The Dialectic of Sex.* London: Paladin.

Giri, V. M. (1998), *Emancipation and Empwerment of Women.* New Delhi: Gyan Publishing House.

Hareven, T. K. (1977), 'The Family and Gender Roles in Historical Perspective in Women and Men; Changing Roles, Relationships and Perceptions Workshop on Men and Women by, L. A. Cater, A. F. Scott, W. Martyna (eds).

Kanhare, U. S. (1978), *Differential Socialisation of Boys and Girls in the Family: A Study of Lower Socio-economic Households among Gujrati Castes and Communities in Ahemdabad*. New Delhi: Mittal Publication.

Lewis, S. and Cooper, C. (1988), 'Stress in Dual-Earners Families', in Gutek *et. al.* (eds.). *Women and Work: An Annual Review*, Vol-III. California: Sage Publications.

Lewis, S. (1992), 'Introduction: Dual-Earner Families in Context' in S. Lewis *et. al.* (Eds.). *Daul-Earner Families International Perspectives*. Sage Publication : London.

McDowell, L. T Pringle, R. (1992), 'Defining Work in Defining Women', in L. McDowell and R. Pringle (eds.). *Social Institution and Gender Division*. UK: Policy.

Mookerji, R. K. (1957), 'Women in Ancient India' in T. A. Baig (ed.). *Women of India*. Publication Division (Ministry of Information & Broad Casting): Government of India.

Nicolson, P. (1993), 'Motherhood and Womens Lives' in D. Rechrdson and V. Robinson (Eds.). *Introducing Womens Studies*. Macmillan: Houndmills.

Pringle, R. (1992), R. Pringle (eds.). *Defining Women, Social Institution and Gender Division*. UK: Polity Press.

Rani, K. (1976), Role Conflict in Working Women. Chetana Publications: New Delhi.

Rowbotham, S. (1992), *Women in Movement Feminism and Social Action*. New York: Routledge.

Sharma, S. L. (2000), 'Empowerment without Antagonism: A Case for Reformulation of Womens Empowerment Approach', *Sociological Bulletin* 49(1).

Sengupta, N. (2000), Women on the Move; *Socio-cultural Dimension Influencing Status of Rural Women*. Calcutta: Minerva Associates.

Swarnalatha, E. V. (1993), *Womens Education and Occupational Aspirations*. New Delhi: Discovery Publishing House.

Mead, M. (1964), *Male and Female*. Middle Sex: Penguin Books.

Prabhu, P. N. (1961), *Hindu Social Oganization*. Bombay: Poplar Prakashan.

6

Widowhood: A Crisis in Social Identity

Panchali Chakraborty & Samita Manna

In Indian society widowhood is really a curse. Specially it is a tragic event in women's life. The widows are the worst victims of the circumstances as they are denied the possibilities of healthy living by the imposition of artificial restraints on their normal life and livelihood.

Widowed women face some typical problems due to their distinctive socio-cultural background. The social prohibition on remarriage despite its legal sanction is not the only problem in the lives of Hindu widows, many other restrictions are imposed upon them, reflections of which are found in their daily lives. Now-a-days, the joint families with their various positive features have been weakly replaced by nuclear families in which the members are less committed to their duties and responsibilities. This along with social injustice, many deep-rooted prejudices and cultural obligations have created the entire situation more problematic.

Concise Oxford Dictionary (1982) defines a widow as a woman who has lost her husband by death and has not married again. Naturally, having lost her husband by death, a woman by whatever way she chooses to live, i.e., either with the other members of the family or alone, holds a distinct social position. It is true that the position of a widow varies from society to society since different cultures and societies have prescribed distinctive rules of conduct signifying very clearly her status, role and privileges in a particular society. Sometimes in many societies remarriage of a widow is permissible whereas elsewhere it is strictly prohibited. Whatever may be the case regarding her remarriage, the fact is that in general, previously married females are less likely to marry again than previously married males (Monahan, 1952:280). As a matter of fact, whether they are dependent or not, the widowed women being deprived of a secured shelter, in all conceivable sense, encounter tremendous hardship and miseries in their lives in this male chauvinistic world. A woman following the death of her husband experiences great trouble in getting the financial support for herself, her children and for other dependent members of the family, specially, if she has no alterative source of income. In most societies men generally perform the role of a major or sole bread-winner. Another major problem arises from the changes in her role and relationship with the members of family, relatives, friends and neighbors. The loss of husband also creates difficulties in taking care and providing many other supports besides the financial one, to her children. A widow also faces trouble in taking decision regarding various matters of her family. Except these, the most vital problem of a Hindu widow is to follow the restrictions of life based on hardship, austerity and sacrifices. Although, the death of either spouse is purely a normal and natural event, but the moment husband dies, a woman is asked to accept this new state of life through a host of formalities which are to be observed continuously as she lives. The real meaning of this ritual observation throughout widowhood is nothing but the banishment of the widows from the social life in a deceptive way. Loss of the company of husbands and various problems arising out of this single state of existence sometimes affect the state of mind of the widows and make them indifferent or dejected to life and surroundings.

Everywhere widows face more or less these various problems; the severity of the problems only vary from society to society, even within the same society depending on different factors.

In Indian society, the widowed women experience these various difficulties throughout their lives. The widowers suffer from no such serious problems; the sanction of remarriage and absence of any restriction to be followed by them have placed them in a most advantageous position. The problems which the widowers face in the absence of their wives are difficulties in house-keeping, caring and rearing of children; the roles are primarily assigned to women, everywhere. Altekar (1938:136) *observes:*

> Man, however, wielded supreme power in society almost everywhere and was not prepared to sanction a custom adverse to his own interest and comfort.

The life of an Indian widow is really a pathetic one; apart from her perpetual widowhood, she is socially marooned (Aradhya, 1987:3).

A widow gets much less respect than other women; she loses her honorable position in the family and society. Every one looks down on her with extreme contempt. She is considered as papi (sinner) and is excluded from auspicious ceremonies in fear of evil or misfortune (Dubois and Beauchamp, 1906:352).

In India, generally a woman's lot is calculated with her husband and it is a widespread custom to bless a married woman by the term *saubhagyabati bhava* (be fortunate woman), i.e., may you live with your husband and all signs of married life till the last day of your life. Widowhood, on the other hand, is considered by the Hindus as a consequence of evil or sin committed by a woman in her previous life and thereby she is looked down upon as a 'sinner' or an 'evil woman'. Therefore, owing to this notion of widowhood, in a family, kin group or society as a whole, her position or fate hangs in the balance. She is expected or even sometimes forced to abide by the various norms prescribed for her to be loyal to her dead husband and is debarred form joining to auspicious ceremonies. It is assumed that the relationship developed through marriage is everlasting and mere death of husband cannot dissolve it. The highest virtue of a married woman consists in complete devotion to her husband irrespective of whatever he may be. So, a woman losing her husband by death must be overtaken by grief. Whatever may be the reason behind the rigorous life of a widow, the primary reasons are to restrain her sex urge, to make her less attractive in the eyes of others and to reduce the cost of her maintenance.

II

In the Rig Vedic age, women as a group had an honourable position in the society. They were allowed to enjoy their lives, as free-individuals, taking the advantages of all sorts of rights and privileges due for them. The Vedic Aryans, though believed in patriarchal authority, were very liberal in outlook; hence, no injustice was done by them to women. During this period, the widowed women could enjoy their lives equally with other women, no restriction was imposed on them. Though monogamy was undoubtedly a prevalent form of marriage, polygamy in the form of polygyny or polyandry was also in vogue. Indra (1940:117) found in the Vedas.

'...marriage, as a union between man and woman before the nuptial fire, was held to be the most unbreakable and subsisting even after the death.'

But widowed women were not compelled to spend the rest of their lives remaining alone, rather, were allowed to take the advantage of any one of the two customs of the then Hindu tradition, like remarriage and *niyoga*. The most inhuman practice *like satidaha-pratha* or the custom of 'widow-burning' was practically unknown at that time but its symbolic performance was allowed. Altekar (1938), Kane (1941), Shastri (1952), Paul (1964), Chattopadhyay (1965) have observed some passages in the Rig Veda in support of niyoga and refer to the custom of producing a son by a sonless woman during the life time of her husband or after his death with the help of younger brother-in-law or any other nearest male relative in the absence of a brother-in-law. As symbolic practice widows were taken in procession with their dead husbands to the cremation ground for burning. Ultimately, they were taken back home with the hope of starting a new life. The brother-in-law had the first preference in remarriage or 'niyoga' custom. If, a widow wished to remain single, she was not forced to observe a stern life or condemned as inauspicious personality. Regarding the property inheritance, the Rig Vedic society showed justice to woman. She should get a share of the ancestral property following the financial crisis or death of her husband and could inherit her deceased husband's property in absence of a child as a matter of right (Tarafdar: 1936). Child marriage, in the Vedic age, was not considered justifiable among the Hindus. Therefore, there was no child widows during that period. Even marriage was not compulsory for a girl at that time which is evident from the word 'amajur' meaning an unmarried old woman or the presence of maidens at the Samana festival (festival of recreation) and the existence of unmarried female Rishis like Apala-Atreyi (Shastri 1952:11).

However, this healthy social situation continued until about 300 B.C which took within its fold the later Vedic age, Sutra period and the early Epic age. Thereafter, the position of women, especially widow, began to deteriorate. The Atharva Veda-XVII,2,1 has mentioned:

> It was still customary for the widow to lie by the side of her husband's corpse on the funeral pyre; she was, however, asked to come down, and a prayer was offered that she should lead a prosperous life enjoying the bliss of children and wealth (Altekar, 1938:138).

Again the support of remarriage has been observed by Altekar (1938), Indra (1940), Kane (1941) and Shastri (1952) in the Atharva Veda-IX, 5, 27-28. Panchadana offering (sacrifice of a goat with five rice dishes) for a remarried woman and *ajapanchadana* offering (a goat with five rice-dishes with the light of sacrificial gifts) by a man taking new wife were necessary in order to keep their relation intact even after their death.

During the Epic period, widows, due to their mature age, would prefer to undergo their lives through rigorous austerity.

They were neither compelled to become sati nor to decorate themselves very simply (Jayal: 1966). The custom of child marriage also did not gain much popularity, though Paul (1964) and Kapadia (1966) have asserted from the *Grihya Sutra* that a girl must be given in marriage when she is *nagnika*. Again Paul (1964:68) mentioned that the word *nagnika* includes 'a naked girl of six or seven playing in the dust and young adolescent of sweet sixteen'. In this connection, Kapadia (1966:253) asserted that nagnika meant 'a girl whose breasts are not developed'. As there was no hard and fast rule in favour of child marriage, marriage of the female, among the Hindus, generally took place in mature age. 'Widow remarriage' was allowed as *satidaha pratha* was not permissible at that time.

After 300 B.C., women began to lose their earlier rights and privileges because of hard and unsympathetic attitude of the society towards them. The development of male supremacy owing to the influence of various factors was mainly responsible for the changing position of women. The customs like child marriage, polygamy, sati, enforced widowhood, *kaulinya pratha*, etc., were gradually appearing on the social scenario. A great controversy also arose among the Hindu *Shastrakars* (author of scriptures) over the *niyoga;* the custom of 'widow remarriage', which had the sanction of the Veda was also questioned. Ultimately, after 6th century A.D., i.e., in the period of *Dharma Shastra,* the custom of *niyoga* and remarriage of mature widows went out of fashion, because the concept of *Patibrat,* i.e., devotion of wife to husband earned distinctive prominence by this time. Manu argued that there is no declaration regarding her remarriage in the procedure of marriage. Only, *Vagdatta* (betrothed girl) was allowed by him for *niyoga* custom. Parasara Smriti supported by Narada and Agnipurna allowed the remarriage of a woman in the following five cases such as missing, death, impotence, degradation or sannyas of her husband (Altekar, 1938:180; Indra, 1940:124; Kane, 1941:610-611). Gradually the remarriage of child widows also went out of vogue completely from 1100 A.D. Aditya Purana declares:

> Widow remarriage is not to be performed in the Kali age (Altekar, 1938:181-182).

Tarafdar (1936:24) has asserted from the *Smritis* :

> A marriageable daughter, who without being married remains in the father's house, becomes a sudra, and the father who did not get her married at the proper time, commits a great sin.

The infant marriage, at the age of 8 years, was popularly known as *Gouridan* indicating a means of earning merit and salvation.

The Brahma Purana echoed that girls should be given in marriage between the age of four and ten; a girl of eight is know as Gouri (Paul, 1964:226).

Altekar (1938) and Kuppuswamy (1972) have observed that some social factors made the marriage of women, especially in their child hood, obligatory. The marriage of the Aryans was, at first, not confined to their own group. The non-Aryan women, who got married with the Aryan men, could not take part actively in religious ceremonies owing to lack of their vedic knowledge. Gradually, the restriction was extended to Aryan wives also. In course of time, the ascetic ideals of Buddhism, which influenced a large number of women to join the monasteries, was another factor behind the prevalence of child marriage. Later on, probably, the Muslim invasion in the country gave impetus to the custom of child marriage.

Besides infant marriage, many other evil practices like *Kaulinya Pratha, polygyny,* which were once out of fashion, began to take place in the society by this time. A typical *Kulin* status used to be ascribed to man of noble birth. Perhaps, the introduction of child marriage, endogamous caste system were at the root of *Kaulinya Pratha*. A typical *Kaulinya Pratha* is a practice where a man, kulin Brahmin by caste, would take many girls of his own caste as wives. The father of a girl child (*Kulin* Brahmin by caste), afraid of going to hell or casting out of society started giving his infant daughters (age not more than 10 years) in marriage to a person, who was much older or even at the point of death but belonging to his own caste group.

Prohibition on widow-marriage and *niyoga,* which had solved many problems of widows at the beginning of history, made the condition of widows, specially, child widows much more tragic. During this period, a widowed woman was compelled either to observe asceticism or to become sati. However, in the early period of *Dharma Shastra,* instead of *sati,* a hard life of renunciation was prescribed for widows leading to austerity as asserted by the law-givers, namely, Manu, Yajnavalkya, Vishnu Sharma, etc. The concept of *Patibrata,* i.e., being devoted to her husband alone was sanctioned and gradually popularized by them. The prime duty of a faithful wife was to give unstinted services to the husband. It was reiterated that the death of the husband could not break their tie of unity, i.e., undivided, eternal relation (Kapadia: 1966).

> Manu, the ancient Law-Giver, recommended and prescribed: ...a wife should lead the life like the shadow of her husband. The widow will regard her dead husband by sacrificing many things. She should not take meal in two times, she should take only fruits during the Ekadasi (i.e. eleventh day of the moon, both in brighter and darker halves) or on full moon days, she should never utter the name of any man who is considered 'Parpurus' or a paramour. ...a woman has become a widow owing to the evil activities or unchaste life of her earlier birth. She should, therefore, be mindful of her responsibilities and should strictly perform the religious duties in order to get rid of evil effects of the sins she committed (Sengupta, 1970:173).

Indra (1940), Kane (1941), Das (1962) have observed that after leading a chaste life a widow, even a childless widow, can be sure of her abode in heaven.

Such practices led to a peculiar *sati* custom. On the funeral pyre of the husband, the widow was sacrificed forcibly, performing some formalities, with a deafening cries and the sound of beating of drum under which her lamentation and groaning would be drowned out. Of course in Vishnu Smriti this custom of sati was mentioned (Kapadia: 1966).

At first, it was confined to the Kshatriyas only and gradually widows of other castes started to take recourse to this practice. Because, the later authors of *Smritis* and *Puranas* like *Sankha, Angira, Harita, Venavyas,* began to approve of the custom of Sati with praise. Vedavyas prescribed *sahamarana pratha* even for Brahmin widows while others kept them out of this custom.

Similarly, the *Padma Purana* also did not allow the Brahmin widows to become sati. According to the authors of Padma Purana, as Altekar (1938 : 150-151) and Paul (1964:231) have noticed, any person, who helps a Brahmin widow to die with her husband, will commit the sin of *brahmahatya* (murder of Brahmana).

In course of time, opposition to widow remarriage and *niyoga* was synchronised with question of the widows right of inheritance. While some of the authors of the Hindu scriptures recognized the widows' right to their late husbands' property, most of the authoritative law givers like Manu, Apastamba, Baudhayana vehemently opposed their rights on the property left by their deceased husbands in the absence of their sons. The law giver Vishnu expressed his view in favour of widows' right of succession in their deceased husbands' property by these words:

> Mothers should be receivers of shares according to the portion allowed to the sons (Roy, 1987:74). On the other hand, Das (1962), Chattopadhyay (1965) found that Vishnu argued even for the sonless widows' right to their late husbands' property.

Gradually, widows' right on their late husbands' property began to get more prominence; Yajnavalkya, Vrihaspati and others also gave opinion in favour of their (widows) rights of inheritance to late husbands' property. Jimutavahana, a law-giver of the early twelfth century A.D. strongly recommended widows' claim on the property of their dead husbands by saying–

> There is no authority to hold that the ownership in the husband's property, which the wife acquires at the time of marriage, terminates with the husband's death (Das, 1962:237).

None the less, all over India, except Bengal, only the widowed mothers of male children were given the right to look after the property (in case of minor sons) left by their deceased husbands in the joint family. They were only entitled to get maintenance. This restriction on the inheritance of property of late husbands left the widows in the *lurch*.

The childless widowed women, who were living in joint family at time of their husbands' death, had to depend on the mercy of the survivors of their families for their maintenance. This existence of the widows, wholly dependent on others, transformed them into nothing but domestic servants and thereby a typical treatment was meted out to them. In Bengal, widows were somewhat in a better position regarding the inheritance right; prevalence of *Dayabhaga* law helped even the childless (sonless) widowed women to become heiress of the property left by their departed husbands in the joint family. As Altekar writes (1938:164):

> The Dayabhaga law, which permitted even the childless widow to become an heir to her husband, was thus not an unmixed blessing to the weak-minded section of the women of Bengal.

In this way it continued for a prolonged period, until the beginning of the 19th century. People, in general, due to their ignorance, superstition and fanaticism accepted all these inhuman practices without any question. The low-caste people, who were not compelled to follow the ruling of the *shastras*, followed these practices in order to raise their social position. During the medieval period, i.e. , from 1200 A.D to 1800 A.D., the attitude of the society towards widows became much more severe. The custom of *widow-burning* gained much popularity afterwards. Regarding the custom of *sati*, Jean Baptiste Tavernier, Baron d'Aubonne, a French traveler who came to India in the seventeenth century remarked :

> They make scruple about killing a serpent, and even a bug, yet they regard it as a highly meritorious action to cause a living woman to be burnt in the fire together with the body of her deceased husband (*Ray*, 1985: 8-9).

Another custom of the medieval period was tonsuring of widows. Previously, widows were not allowed to comb their hair and to use hair oil; but during the later periods of Smritis and Puranas the custom of tonsuring began to appear in the society and gained much popularity afterwards. Vyasa describes the duties of widows in this way :

> With altered complexion and dejected face....Reduces herself with little food. Holding the dead husband, the Brahamani plunges in to the fire. If the widow be Brahmani (or if the widow be alive) she, with hair removed, reduces her body by austerities *(Subramanyam, 1909:34)*.

At first, only the Brahmin widows were allowed to shave their hair but gradually widows of other caste groups started to follow this practice.

Early nineteenth century witnessed a violent protest against various injustices of the Hindu society. The establishment of the British Raj at the end of the 18th century ushered in new education, thoughts and values. A new generation with new set of humanitarian values came forward with a missionary zeal to reform the Hindu society by removing various evil practices. Some attempts were made earlier by some Muslim rulers, Portuguese traders and Christian missionaries to stop burning of alive widows, but ended without any success. Renowned native social reformers, like Raja Rammohan Roy, Pundit Iswar Chandra Vidyasagar, in order to convince the orthodox Hindus that the customs of '*enforced widowhood*', sati, etc., and others had no sanction of the scriptures and had not been mentioned in any text as compulsory duty to follow, used the precepts of the scriptures as weapons of reform movement. Raja Rammohan Roy examined the Shastras, page after page, that showed almost all the scriptures, except very few law books of little importance, were silent about *sati* or had referred to it as a less commendable act. Pundit Mrityunjay Vidyalankar; another scholar of the age, also held the same opinion regarding the custom of widow burning. Similarly, Pundit Iswar Chandra

Vidyasagar (1881) an erudite scholar of the age, and Kacker (1830) with their profound knowledge of the scriptures challenged the renunciation of widow remarriage.

Gradually with the untiring efforts of the reformers, amidst country-wide protests, *sati* restraint Act (1829), widow-remarriage Act (1856), Child-marriage restraint Act (1929), etc., were passed by the then British Government.

While the constitutional position of the widowed women underwent a change in the last century, these laws failed to improve their position much in reality. It is true, the practice of widow-burning was abandoned by the Hindus few years after the passing of the law but the marriage of the widowed women took place rarely. At long last, Hindu widows of upper caste group irrespective of their age had to face a lot of trouble along with social ostracism.

III

At present, the condition of the widowed women is not at all satisfactory. Widowhood is still accompanied by the prevalence of various types of restrictions in our society. The widow-remarriage Act (1856) has remained only on paper even at the beginning of twenty-first century. The incidence of widow-remarriage is found only among a few castes and subgroups (Goode: 1963; Dubey: 1965). But deep rooted prejudices against remarriage and some other practical reasons stand in the way.

Moreover, the nuclear or semi-nuclear families are now-a-days taking the place of joint or extended families which once had provided food, shelter and met some other needs for the members in the family with a cluster of kinswomen. In the absence of such protection provided by joint family, widows, irrespective of their age, caste and class have been suffering from many acute problems even at present.

Widowhood continues to be a dark and gloomy aspect of women's lives. Everywhere it leaves the women in a situation full of sorrows and sufferings. In India various cultural and social taboos are strongly prevalent, nuclear or semi joint families are taking the place of traditional joint or extended families and along with inadequate security measures for the protection of widows, the problems of widowhood have become much more complicated. Several studies on the position of Hindu women reveal that in a patriarchal society like that in India women have never been accorded their due honour, respect and prestige even after performing their duties and responsibilities. They have always been stripped of enjoying their rights and privileges as free individuals and have to remain dependent on others for their existence at all stages of life. Only the Vedic age, specially the Rig Vedic age, provided them ample opportunities to enjoy their lives equally with men. All these things have now made their position very insecure. The sufferings of women go on increasing with the passing of their lives from one phase to another.

Widowhood turns their lives in a completely new direction which is totally unwanted. The widows are to live alone the rest of their lives and to abide by some typical social practices which the other single women need not follow. Apart from these, many other problems are faced by them; severity of the problems depend on their age, caste, class, family type, etc.

Amongst the other problems of the widows, financial difficulty is the major one. The death of husbands makes women, particularly of nuclear families, financially handicapped because they have always been taught to keep themselves confined at home and to be efficient in managing the domestic affairs while remaining under the control of the patriarch. Now-a-days, though women are also engaged in different types of occupation, yet, earning of money is considered as men's prime responsibility by both men and women. Majority of the women are still engaged in household activities. Dasgupta (1978:70) observes:

> A large number of women in our country still expect shelter, security and support from husbands not merely because they are not trained for any other occupation and have very restricted job opportunities, but also for the reason that they have been taught to depend on menfolk.

Moreover, the joint families which once served as an umbrella to these unfortunate women are going to be out of fashion now; the families which seem to live jointly, are not joint in real sense in most cases because except roof, nothing is common there. In the words of Baig (1990:106) :

> ... illness, loneliness, loss of parents, widowhood, handicaps and old age were no longer problems of the same magnitude in a group as in the single family unit. The joint family, however imperfectly, gave shelter and protection. Relations always had a home to go to in times of distress, the old never felt useless and abandoned, and living expenses were greatly reduced by the economic factors of common roof and kitchen.

Naturally, in these nuclear families, especially where husbands are chief or sole earning members, financial insecurity is felt much by the women in supporting themselves and other dependent members of their families when they become widow. The appearance of nuclear families has made the condition of aged widows miserable, especially for those who have to live alone under some compelling circumstances. Although the present day nuclear families provide food and shelter for the widowed mothers or sometimes unmarried brothers and sisters but the provision of food and shelter can not solve their problems fully. In the joint family also their condition is not satisfactory because the fulfillment of bare necessities of life can not solve their financial problem. Sometimes a widow and her children experience difficulty in meeting other demands of their lives. Besides financial hardship, some other problems which a widow faces in her life are: rearing and caring of children, participation in the decision-making process of the family, performance of domestic work, ill treatment of her family-members, observance of some special rituals, etc.

Looking after of children becomes a great problem to a woman in case of the death of her husband. A widow can not attend the needs of her children or cannot watch over the activities, friend circle, etc., of her children always due to her confinement at home and involvement in household chores. The problem is really acute when she is to go out for work besides household chores. Availability of little time and opportunities for coming closer to children also create difficulty in looking after her children carefully. Mothers are generally affectionate to their children. Deprivation of love from father and her departure from home for earning bread or dependence on children in absence of husband make her much more affectionate to them. This excessive love often creates obstacle in guiding her children. Sometimes a widow faces trouble in taking care of education of her children, in procuring job or in looking for suitable match for them due to her little education, limited contact with outer world, lack of experience or preoccupation with domestic and economic affairs.

A widow also experiences trouble in performing the domestic work. This problem is highly felt by a working widow of nuclear family, especially if she becomes unable to appoint a maid-servant owing to her poor economic condition created by the death of husband or has none at home to assist her. This burdensome situation also becomes acute in the case of widows belonging to joint families especially where they solely depend for food on others.

> As soon as the husband passes away, the wife loses her status in the family. If it is a joint family, she becomes more or less a slave of all the members. She is considered inauspicious and usually elders taunt her as woman bringing bad luck to the family (Hate, 1948:50-51).

The trouble is also felt by a widow in taking decisions regarding different matters of her family independently. It becomes more difficult to the widows who were not allowed to take decisions earlier or gave up everything on their late husbands or used to consult with their husbands always. After the death of husbands they suffer from lack of confidence in this case. Sometimes a widow is not permitted to participate in the decision-making process of the family or is not allowed to show curiosity or to express her opinion over any matter. She has only to comply with the decision of the family, even in her personal matters. Naturally, it causes a problem to her.

Their cups of miseries are not filled only with these problems. The Hindu widow, particularly of Bengal, suffer from some typical problems also in their daily lives which are found nowhere on earth. The death of husbands makes the women unacceptable to their families and society in most cases. Although the death of an individual is purely a natural event still they are accused and treated badly for the death of their husbands. It becomes more pronounced if their husbands die in young ages. Apart from this, many social and cultural taboos isolate them from the main stream of society throughout the rest period of their lives. These constantly haunt them in their lonely existence. The imposed sense of guilt together with social and mental isolation makes their lives more complicated.

IV

SOCIAL TRAGEDY: AN EMPIRICAL WORK

Early Vedic period was glorious and enriched as men and women were ensured equal rights and opportunities. But since the later Vedic period many new laws and restrictions were imposed to curtail the freedoms of women. As a result, in due course, they remained within the combines of four walls. Male supremacy and the norms of patriarchy make them victims of many social tragedies. Though the changing out look of British, new wave of globalization and impact of modernity have brought a tremendous impact on the life and society of the Indian women, but till now, in many cases majority of the women have to live either on the mercy of God or under the subordination of the rule of patriarchy.

It is an accepted phenomenon that in all societies, there exist a dual relation between superordination and subordination of different groups. Dominating groups always try to legitimatize the social norms for their favour and as a result, the subordinate groups will be under their control. With this practice, gradually the women are considered as a subjugated section of the society keeping them under the power of male folk. Different social factors have been imposed and gradually these are practised and accepted as social rules. Many such social causes make the condition of the women vulnerable in general and widows in particular.

Keeping all these social factors in mind, attempts were made by the present authors to collect field level data on the condition of widows in today's changing society. Naihati, an urban, industrial town of the district of North 24 Paraganas in West Bengal was selected for the present study. The data have been collected from 300 Bengali Hindu widows through random sampling (Table 1).

Table 1
Sample Distribution

Ward No	*No. of holdings having widows in each and every ward*	*No. of families having widows in each and every holding*	*Total No. of widows*	*No. of widows chosen for interview*	*No of widows interviewed*
1	127	149	160	35	23
6	152	204	209	46	44
7	155	180	183	40	34
8	208	262	273	60	56
9	125	146	157	35	30
16	116	129	137	30	24
19	432	447	470	104	89
Total	1315	1517	1589	350	300

Table 1depicts the details of sample selection from the areas under study.

The background information of the widows have been depicted in Table 2.

Table 2
Socio-economic Profile

2a. Widows by Age

Age (in years)	*No. of respondents*	*%*
29-25	11	3.67
36-42	16	5.33
43-49	34	11.33
50-56	44	14.66
57-63	62	20.67
64-70	62	20.67
71-77	41	13.67
78-84	22	7.33
85-91	8	2.67
Total	300	300

Contd...

2b. Widows by Educational Qualification

Level of education	*No. of respondents*	%
Illiterate	115	38.33
Literate without formal education	35	11.67
Primary (I-IV)	60	20.00
Upper Primary (V-VIII)	67	22.33
High (IX-X)	15	5.00
Higher (XI-I.A./XII)	6	2.00
Graduate	2	0.67
Total	300	100

2c. Widows by their Age at Marriage

Age (in years)	*No. of respondents*	%
5-9	28	9.33
10-14	128	42.67
15-19	120	40.00
20-24	21	7.00
25-29	1	0.33
30-34	-	-
35-39	2	0.67
Total	300	100

2d. Widows by the Type of Family

Types	*Sub Type*	*No. of respondents*	%
Nuclear base family	Nuclear family	-	-
	Supplemented nuclear family	116	38.67
	Sub nuclear family	92	30.67
	Supplemented sub nuclear family	35	11.67
Residentially joint units of various kinds	Lineal joint family	-	-
	Supplemented lineal joint family	2	0.66
	Collateral joint family	-	-
	Supplemented collateral joint family	20	6.67
	Lineal collateral joint family	-	-
	Supplemented lineal collateral joint family	3	1.00
Irregular family units	Single person	30	10.0
	Others	2	0.66
Total	300	100.00	

2e. Widows by the Size of their Families

Size	*No. of respondents*	%
Small (1-3 members)	119	39.67
Medium (4-6) members)	136	45.33
Large (7-9 members)	31	10.33
Very Large (10 and above members)	14	4.67
Total	300	100

Age at marriage of the spouse and the age gap between husband and wife play an important aspect of widowhood. In Indian society it is very common and accepted practice that the age at marriage of the bride will be lower than his groom. Table 3 depicts the age differences of the bride and groom during the time of marriage. This factor is responsible for persisting widowhood for a longer time. Early age at marriage makes a great difference of age gap between husband and wife. This long age gap is considered another important factor for widow hood. (Table 3).

Table 3
Widows and Widow hood

Widows by Age Difference with their Deceased Hosbands		
Age difference (in years)	*No. of respondents*	*%*
1-5	14	4.67
6-10	105	35.00
11-15	113	37.67
16-20	46	15.33
21-25	13	4.33
26-30	9	3.00
Total	300	100
Widows by Age at Widowhood		
Age (in years)	*No.. of respondents*	*%*
11-20	14	4.67
21-30	39	13.00
31-40	58	19.33
41-50	84	28.00
51-60	75	25.00
61-70	25	8.33
71-80	5	1.67
Total	300	100
Widows by their Length of Widowhood		
Length (in years)	*No. of respondents*	*%*
1-10	120	40.00
11-20	90	30.00
21-30	43	14.33
31-40	23	7.67
41-50	18	6.00
51-60	4	1.33
61-70	1	0.33
71-80	1	0.33
Total	300	100

Kamat (1963:18) has identified mortality as a prime demographic factor of widowhood and also added that the factors like age at marriage, age difference between the couple, incidence of remarriage, rate of population growth, etc, have their impact on this unhappy ending of married life.

Goldman and Lord (1983), Mathews (1987) have considered the differences in mortality rates, age at marriage between male and female, as causes of increasing number of widows. Females, generally, live much longer period of life than males and their (females) marriages also take place with persons older than themselves. The rate of remarriage for female is also lower than male.

Nagesh, (1987). Aradhya (1987), Chen (1998), Maribhat (1998) and Gulati (1998) found that considerable age gap exists between the spouses. Also, differences both in the expectation of life and the differential pattern of remarriage among males and females are the reasons for a large number of widows in India. The reasons may also be attributed to the prevalence of child marriage, polygamy, universality of marriage, etc.

The age of the respondents and their age at the time of death of their husbands are observed in Table 4. It is seen from the Table that 195 (65.00%) widows are aged or nearing old age (57 years to 91 years) . The age of the widows varies from 29 years to 49 years in 61 (20.33%) cases and the remaining 44 (14.67%) widows belong to 50 years to 56 years age group.

Women have to face a great financial hardship during their widowhood as, generally, many of them are not educated and employed like their deceased husbands. As a result, this financial crisis makes their life full of stress and strain. Not only this but also they are tortured and exploited by other family members.

Some information on demographic and socio-economic characteristics of the widowed persons of Rajasthan are found in the work of Bose and Sen (1966). Saraswati (1985) studied widowhood from a completely different point of view. He focused on the widows' longing for living in Kashi-a holy place of the Hindu. Nagesh (1987) and Aradhya (1987) studied various socio-economic problems faced by the Hindu widowed

Table 4
Widows by their Age and Age at Widowhood

Age at widowhood (in years)								
Age (in years)	*11-20*	*21-30*	*31-40*	*45-50*	*51-60*	*61-70*	*71-80*	*Total*
29-35	1	9	1	-	-	-	-	11
	(9.09)	(81.82)	(9.09)					(100.00)
36-42	1	9	6	-	-	-	-	16
	(6.25)	(56.25)	(37.50)					(100.00)
43-49	1	3	16	14	-	-	-	34
	(2.94)	(8.82)	(47.06)	(41.18)				(100.00)
50-56	1	4	10	22	7	-	-	44
	(2.27)	(9.09)	(22.73)	(50.00)	(15.91)			(100.00)
57-63	1	4	8	21	27	1	-	62
	(1.61)	(6.45)	(12.90)	(33.87)	(43.55)	(1.61)		(99.99)
64-70	7	6	7	15	20	7	-	62
	(11.29)	(9.68)	(11.29)	(24.19)	(32.26)	(11.29)		(100.00)
71-77	1	2	5	7	15	9	2	41
	(2.44)	(4.88)	(12.19)	(17.07)	(36.59)	(21.95)	(4.88)	(100.00)
78-84	-	1	4	4	5	6	2	22
		(4.55)	(18.18)	(18.18)	(22.73)	(27.27)	(9.09)	(100.00)
85-91	1	1	1	1	1	2	1	8
	(12.50)	(12.50)	(12.50)	(12.50)	(12.50)	(25.00)	(12.50)	(100.00)
Total	14	39	58	84	75	25	5	300
%	4.67	13.00	19.33	28.00	25.00	8.33	1.67	100

N.B. Figures in the parentheses indicate percentages.

women in India. They also took into account the demographic aspect of widowhood. Krishna Kumari (1987) conducted a study on the status of single women in India. In this study the scholar has shown various socio-economic problems of the working and non-working widows living in Bangalore city. Chakraborti (1990) made a comparative analysis of the pattern of widowhood in West Bengal as a whole with the same in Purulia-a district of West Bengal. He also throws light on the variation of the incidence of widowhood in Purulia by different factors like religion, caste, class, education etc. and also with some socio-economic characteristics of the widows, viz., the families they live in, their age, occupation and status, etc.

The widows are not only subject to harsh treatment, but also they outnumber the widowers everywhere. Thus the increasing number of widows has been revealed by the demographic scenario of the widowed people belonging to different countries of the world. In the United States, Goldman an Lord (1983:177) observed that the number of widows was 10.4 million in the year 1979 and the ratio of widows to widowers was over 5:1. Similarly, Matthews (1987:344) recorded 11.5 million widowed persons from Canada in 1981 and the ratio of widows to widowers was almost 5:1. In 1971, the ratio was nearly 4:1. Table 5 shows the year-wise distribution of the widowed population: 1981 and 1991 where the ratio of widows is higher than widows.

V

In the Hindu society a widow is looked on as a papi (sinner) and widowhood is assumed as the result of evils done or sins committed by her in present life or in previous lives. Widowed women also try to follow these various rituals in their daily lives. They have been brought up in families where these practices are maintained and they have also been socialized in this fashion.

In short, widows are not supposed to enjoy the worldly pleasure, luxury and comfort and are expected to dedicate themselves in the service of God till their death for absolving them from the supposed sin committed and for finally reaching

Table 5

Year-wise Distribution of the Widowed Population: 1981 & 1991

Year	*State/District*	*Total Population*		*Total Widowed*		*Ratio Widower: Widow*	
		Male	*Female*	*Male*	*Female*	*Male*	*Female*
1981	West Bengal	2,85,60,907	2,60,19,746	3,98,527	23,87,201	1	6
	24 - Parganas	56,42,438	50,97,001	60,642	4,41,381	1	7
1991	West Bengal	3,55,10,63	3,25,67,332	4,20,104	25,42,864	1	6
	North 24 - Parganas	38,18,197	34,63,684	37,967	2,65,275	1	7
	South 24 - Parganas	29,62214	27,52,816	29,584	1,99,478	1	7

N.B.: 24 Parganas District, situated in West Bengal, India was divided into two parts namely North Parganas and South Parganas on March 1986.

Source: Census of India, 1981 and 1991.

salvation. It has already been studied that in India widows are accused for outliving their husbands especially if the husbands die in early age. On the contrary, they are extolled if they die before their lords (husbands). The widows also think that they themselves are guilty of this unhappy incident. The moment the husbands die they feel very unhappy and consider themselves as 'papi' (sinner) since they have grown and have been socialized in a family or society where the traditional beliefs, superstitions, usages in favour of that notion are strongly maintained. The direct role of the 'caste system'–a typical feature of the Hindu society cannot be denied in this case. The degree of severity of different restrictions inflicted depend on the position of their caste, i.e., the higher the caste, the greater the restrictions and the lower the caste, restrictions are less.

The argument in favour of the perpetual widowhood and harsh living of widows is that the relationship developed between a man and a woman by marriage is permanent and never ends with the death of any one of them. Therefore, they are required to live in such way as to satisfy their husbands in heaven. The rituals reflect their eternal relation or love with their husbands and chastity, loyalty, devotion to them. At the same time these are indicative of their sorrow or unhappiness for the loss of their husbands (Marris, 1958: Saraswati, 1985). According to the same logic, widowers are required to observe the same rituals but they do not suffer from any discomfort due to their predominance in the society. Another argument is that the death of their husbands occur because of evils or wrong committed by them in this or earlier lives, so they must always strive to get relief from the evils and to reunite with their husbands in heaven.

In India, Hindu women who outlive their husbands are not only forbidden to marry again, but also forced to live without any social existence. They are required to live the rest of their lives observing some austere and rigorous discipline and to refrain from using or doing many more things in their day-to-day lives. The rituals of widowhood start from the very moment of their husbands' death. In Bengal, after the cremation of the dead husband, vermilion mark (*Sindoor*) is erased from their forehead and from the parting of hair; conch shell, red coral and iron bangles are taken off from their hands and thrown in water forever. All these activities are performed only with the help of other widowed women; the married or unmarried women are even forbidden to see these proceedings. In this connection, it is to be noted that the things mentioned earlier are given to the married women on the occasion of marriage and they are supposed to wear these things during their married lives as symbols of their marriage.

Besides these rituals, restrictions are also imposed on their food, dress, participation in auspicious ceremonies, etc. Some special days are also observed ritually by them. The widows (Bengali Hindu) as per the traditional custom are not allowed to wear any coloured garments especially of red colour.

As those are generally worn by the married or unmarried women. A white piece of cloth without any border which is known as 'than' is prescribed for the widowed woman. In our study we have found that different types of white sarees have been used by 77.33 per cent widows having lost their husbands either in early age or in old age. Out of this 77.33 per cent, only among 36.67 percent widows' narrow bordered white sarees are predominant; 14.00 per cent widows wear coloured saree, excepting red, and both white and coloured sarees are worn by a few widows (6.67%). (Table 6).

It is to be mentioned that the use of various metallic ornaments, particularly of gold, is prevalent fashion among the Bengali Hindu women. The married women are generally expected to be decorated by different types of gold ornaments, apart form conch shell, red coral and iron bangles. Gold ornaments indicate the healthy economic condition of the women. But the widows of the Bengali Hindu society are not allowed to wear any ornament; especially, ear-ring and nose-pin. Table 6 shows that restriction on wearing of ornaments is not strictly followed by 71.00 per cent widows (213); majority of these respondents (193) became widowed in childhood or in early age and very few (20) in old age. The highest percentage (36.00) of widows wear only bangles followed by

Table 6
Life of the Widows with Special Attributes

Wearing Apparel									
Age at widowhood (in years)	White Piece (Than)	Male's Dhoti	White Piece/ Male's Dhoti	White with narrow border	White with wide border	Coloured (excepting) red	White/ Coloured (excepting) red	Without restriction	Total
11-20	4 (28.57)	3 (21.42)	-	3 (21.43)	1 (7.14)	2 (14.29)	-	1 (7.14)	14 (99.99)
21-30	6 (15.38)	1 (2.56)	-	9 (23.08)	1 (2.56)	18 (46.15)	-	4 (10.26)	39 (99.99)
31-40	6 (10.34)	3 (5.17)	3 (5.17)	16 (27.59)	10 (17.24)	14 (24.14)	5 (8.62)	1 (1.72)	58 (99.99)
41-50	11 (13.10)	6 (7.14)	1 (1.19)	26 (30.95)	23 (27.38)	6 (7.14)	11 (13.10)	-	84 (100.00)
51-60	9 (12.00)	10 (13.33)	-	39 (52.00)	12 (16.00)	1 (1.33)	4 (5.33)	-	75 (99.99)
61-70	5 (20.00)	1 (4.00)	-	16 (64.00)	3 (12.00)	-	-	-	25 (100.00)
71-80	2 (40.00)	-	-	1 (20.00)	1 (20.00)	1 (20.00)	-	-	5 (100.00)
Total	43	24	4	110	51	42	20	6	300
%	14.33	8.00	1.33	36.67	17.00	14.00	6.67	2.00	100

N.B. Figures in the parentheses indicate percentages.

Contd...

Variety of Ornaments							
Age at widowhood (in years)	*Necklace*	*Bangle*	*Necklace, Bangle*	*Ear-ring, Bangle*	*Necklace, Ear-ring, Bangle*	*Nothing*	*Total*
11-20	-	3	1	1	2	7	14
		(21.43)	(7.14)	(7.14)	(14.29)	(50.00)	(100.00)
21-30	-	8	2	6	13	10	39
		(20.51)	(5.13)	(15.38)	(33.33)	(25.64)	(99.99)
31-40	-	23	7	7	6	15	58
		(39.66)	(12.07)	(12.07)	(10.34)	(25.86)	(100.00)
41-50	5	31	5	10	7	26	84
	(5.95)	(36.90)	(5.95)	(11.90)	(8.33)	(30.95)	(99.98)
51-60	2	37	9	3	5	19	75
	(2.67)	(49.33)	(12.00)	(4.00)	(6.67)	(25.33)	(100.00)
61-70	1	6	9	-	-	9	25
	(4.00)	(24.00)	(36.00)			(36.00)	(100.00)
71-80	2	-	-	2	-	1	5
	(40.00)			(40.00)		(20.00)	(100.00)
Total	10	108	33	29	33	87	300
%	3.33	36.00	11.00	9.67	11.00	29.00	(100.00)

N.B. Figures in the parentheses indicate percentages.

20.67 per cent widows wearing earring, besides necklace, bangle, etc., though earning is strictly forbidden for them. Only 29.00 per cent widows do not wear any ornament and they have been maintaining it since the death of their husbands. (Table 6).

The custom of *tonsuring or shaving of hair* by the widows belonging to different caste groups is another prevalent practice among the widows. In the caste-ridden Hindu society restriction was imposed on the caring or dressing of hair of the widowed women. The upper caste Hindu widows were not permitted to use hair oil, to part their hair, to comb and plait or put up their hair in bun. In fact, the custom of tonsuring, the symbol of austerity, was introduced in the society since the medieval period, but it did not gain much popularity and the custom is now almost extinct.

The Table also shows that 5.00 per cent widows have shaved their head; only 1.67 per cent widows shaved their head just after their widowhood merely as a convention of the society. The shaving of hair has been done by the remaining 3.33 per cent widows long after the death of their husbands and that has been done primarily due to their ailment in most cases. These respondents said at the time of interrogation that since it was not customary to keep and dress hair, they shaved hair at their old age just to avoid all kinds of trouble arising out of long hair. (Table 7).

It was also found that 62.33% widows do not follow the restriction relating to food. The non-vegetarian item, mainly fish, is taken by many of them. The remaining 37.67 per cent widows are purely vegetarian; 30.00 per cent widows take only vegetables with boiled rice before the sunset. Sundried rice (A type which is prescribed for the widows is taken once before the sunset by 7.67 per cent respondents of the vegetarian category and the norms relating to food are observed by them meticulously in 6.67 per cent cases, i.e., their food is prepared in separate kitchens. (Table 7).

At the time of cooking, regarding the use of crockery and spices, the widows of the traditional Indian society are to follow some restrictions. Traditionally, the Hindu widows are

Table 7
Widows of Different Castes by Hair Shaving/Tonsuring and Food Habites
(Hair Shaving/Tonsuring)

Caste	Just after	Present	Never	Total
Highest	1	4	45	50
	(2.00)	(8.00)	(90.00)	(100.00)
Higher	3	2	86	91
	(3.30)	(2.20)	(94.50)	(100.00)
High	-	3	103	106
		(2.83)	(97.17)	(100.00)
Low	1	1	47	49
	(2.04)	(2.04)	(95.92)	(100.00)
Others	-	-	4	4
			(100.00)	(100.00)
Total	5	10	285	300
%	1.67	3.33	95	(100.00)

N.B. Figures in the parentheses indicate percentages.

Contd...

Caste	Food Habit					
	Veg. with sun dried fice from the separate kitchen	*Veg. with sun dired rice from the same kitchen*	*Veg. with boiled rice from the separate kitchen*	*Veg with boiled rice from the same kitchen*	*Non veg.*	*Total*
Highest	8 (16.00)	1 (2.00)	9 (12.00)	24 (48.00)	8 (16.00)	50 (100.00)
Higher	10 (10.99)	2 (2.20)	8 (8.79)	29 31.87)	42 (46.15)	91 (100.00)
High	1 (0.94)	-	2 (1.89)	11 (10.38)	92 (86.79)	106 (100.00)
Low	1 (2.04)	-	-	7 (14.29)	41 (83.67)	49 (100.00)
Others	-	-	-	-.	4 (100.00)	4 (100.00)
Total	20	3	19	71	.187	300
%	6.67	1.00	6.33	23.67	62.33	(100)

N.B. Figures in the parentheses indicate percentages.

required to cook their food in separate kitchen using the utensils (made of stone, brass or bell-metal) which are not taken for the preparation of non-vegetarian items. They are also allowed to eat in special plates made of stone or bell-metal. It is necessary to mention in this regard that the widows of 'highest' caste group are not allowed to accept the food prepared by a person other than their own caste group. Very few employed widows (1.27%) and 17.19 per cent unemployed widows of vegetarian category follow meticulously the prevailing forms of separate kitchen, utensils, etc. In respect of cooking and taking of meal 11.39 per cent widows are vegetarian but they prepare their food in the same kitchen and with the same crockery which are also used for making non-vegetarian item, they just clean the kitchen and utensils before cooking. Evidently, the employed widows differ from unemployed widows in observing the said rules; probably their engagement in job is one major reason for this apart from many other reasons. In this connection it is to be mentioned here that five vegetarian widows who are now taking food from the common kitchen said that they followed the restriction rigidly for a long period earlier. Only eight widows eat at present in the plates made of brass or bell-metal. Both employed and unemployed widows living with their offspring (own family) or parents and siblings are non-vegetarian in most cases. Widows living in parental families enjoy more liberty in this case and it may be due to sympathy of their parents and brothers and other family-members.

In the Hindu society widowed women have to perform some rituals on some particular days like 'Ekadashi tithi' (the eleventh day of the lunar fortnight), 'Purnima' (the full moon day), Ambubachi (three consecutive days usually in the month Ashara, i.e., July), etc. During these days they are required to observe fast or to take restricted foods like fruits, milk, sweets, etc.

It is observed from the study that majority of the widows of both unemployed and employed categories abide by these traditional practices but their number is much higher among the widows confined within households only *(80.09%)* than the employed widows *(53.16%)*. The respondents, particularly the illiterates believe that taking rice during 'Ekadashi tithi' is tantamount to swallowing worm.

Besides various restrictions they are to perform many other rituals through which religiosity is expressed. Different rituals are performed by the respondents, 58.00 per cent widows are initiated from their preceptors (Guru) : everyday they sit and offer prayer to God with a murmuring sound of chanting, sometimes using a typical bead necklace or string of beads of rosary or the stem of sacred basil plant. They also participate in or attend religious discourses and or devotional songs. Some widows of this group also observe the death anniversary of their husbands in various ways like contributing to charitable funds of different religious organizations or social welfare, arranging devotional songs in their houses, etc., or offering pujas to their husbands daily. 42.00 per cent respondents do not perform these rituals, as they have no time or money or have no faith.

It has been noted earlier that the widows of Hindu society are required to spend the rest of their lives piously participating in or attending religious discourses or devotional songs or visiting different holy places where many sacred centres in the form of temples exist. Earlier widows preferred to live in Varanasi or Kashi, Mathura, Vridavana which are known as holy places among the Hindús. Still now many of them would like to go and settle in these holy places to gain 'moksa' or salvation.

VI

The attitudes and opinions of the widows regarding various formalities which are observed by them and the prevailing beliefs relating to occurrence of widowhood are mentioned in this section. A liberal attitude is seen among 55.33 per cent widows who have no faith in *'pup'*, *'punya'*, *dharma'*, *'adharma'*, *'janma'*, etc. They believe that death is purely a natural event, and each and every individual has to die according to the law of nature. So widowhood is also a natural phenomenon. Naturally these respondents do not think or support the view that a widow should spend her days only performing rituals and religious activities. A good number of widows also hold a favourable attitude towards widow remarriage. The percentage of widows having liberal attitude is higher both in early age group and old age group: only the aged widows between 64 years to 70 years and 78 years to 84 years are exception of it. (Table 8).

Table 8

Opinion of the Widows about Ways of Lives of Widows: Age-wise

Age (in years)	*Opinion*		
	Conservative	*Liberal*	*Total*
29-35	2 (18.18)	9 (81.82)	11 (100.00)
36-42	6 (37.50)	10 (62.50)	16 (100.00)
43-49	13 (38.24)	21 (61.76)	34 (100.00)
50-56	19 (43.18)	25 (56.82)	44 (100.00)
57-63	25 (40.32)	37 (59.68)	62 (100.00)
64-70	32 (51.61)	30 (48.39)	62 (100.00)
71-77	20 (48.78)	21 (51.22)	41 (100.00)
78-84	15 (68.18)	7 (31.82)	22 (100.00)
85-91	2 (25.00)	6 (75.00)	8 (100.00)
Total	134 (44.67)	166 (55.33)	300 (100.00)

N.B. Figures in the parentheses indicate percentages.

Majority of the widows of all caste groups have no faith in prevailing and traditional practices relating to widowhood. They expressed a liberal opinion regarding the life style of widows especially of young widows. Only the remarriage of widows, particularly of aged widows was not preferred by some of them. But most of these respondents believed that widowhood was a consequence of sin committed or evils done in the previous life or it was predestined. (Table 9).

Table 9
Opinion of the Widows about Ways of Lives: Caste-wise

Caste	Opinion		
	Conservative	*Liberal*	*Total*
Higher	21 (42.00)	29 (58.00)	50 (100.00)
Higher	35 (38.46)	56 (61.54)	91 (100.00)
High	52 (49.06)	54 (50.94)	106 (100.00)
Low	23 (46.94)	26 (53.06)	49 (100.00)
Others	3 (75.00)	1 (25.00)	4 (100.00)
Total	134	166	300

N.B. Figures in the parentheses indicate percentages.

Illiterate widows are conservative in most cases (62.61%). Generally these respondents believe that widowhood is the consequence of sinful acts and widows should observe the restrictions or rituals prescribed for them. They think that wearing of special dresses and ornaments, taking of special food items and performing certain religious activities should be maintained by each and every widow as the custom of the society, otherwise something (unusual) may happen. They strongly disapprove of the remarriage of widows.

Finally, it is to be mentioned that the opinions of the widows have no significant association with their age, educational level, caste and occupations and it may be owing to the strong influence of the custom or tradition of the society.

However, having lost their husbands by death women feel depressed; deprivation of love, company and all kinds of support of husbands on the one hand and social banishment on the other hand always remind them that they are alone. Loneliness, socially imposed guilt-complex affect them very much, they become mentally upset severely (15%). Besides these, many other problems arising out of loneliness adversely affect their interest to life. 75% of respondents are indifferent about their personal happiness or sorrows.

12.00 per cent respondents said that they had taken the death of their husbands easily though, at the time of death they were terribly upset but gradually they became adjusted with the situation. Some of the respondents of this group even reported that they had been relieved by the death of their husbands as they were of short temperament or many had other faults or regularly tortured by them. They thought that they were not alone, there are many other widows like them; they also added that they wanted to live for their children.

In Hindu society the life of widows is very problematic. The prevalent social customs, practices and attitude of the people often create a gloomy and segregated situation for the widows Though the situation has changed considerably in recent times but the widows are still experiencing a sub woman existence as per the dictum of the society.

NOTE

This article is a part of the Ph.D work done by *Smt. Panchali Chakraborty* under the supervision of *Prof. Samita Manna.*

1. Naihati–an urban, industrial town is situated in the north-west - direction of the district of North 24 Parganas under the Barrackpur sub-division of West Bengal. Earlier Garifa, Kanthalpara and Naihati were three separate villages with sparse population but now they are within the municipal limits of the town (Naihati).

   In the year 1869, Naihati was declared as a municipal town. Naihati is famous for its past glorious and rich cultural heritages. Once it was a centre of Sanskrit studies and many great Sanskrit scholars were then in the charges of many tolls (Sanskrit schools). As Naihati was situated on the bank of river Ganga naturally once it was a centre for trade and commerce of India. From the sixteenth century, the European traders like the Portuguese, Dutch, English and others began to come in Bengal and the town Hooghly become an important port of the river.

2. Naihati is divided into 19 (nineteen) wards of which 10 (ten) are residential and commercial areas, 7 (seven) are only residential and two are residential and industrial areas. The inhabitants of all these wards are mainly Hindu. The researcher has selected only 7 (seven) residential wards consisting of 4440 holdings. Finally through random sampling 300 widows have been collected which has been shown in Table–1.

3. In Table–2, the total number of widows are classified by their age, education, the year of 'age at marriage' types of family and family members.
4. In Table 3, the widows have been classified by Age difference with their deceased Husbands, age at widowhood and length of widowhood.
5. Out of 300, 221 (73.67%) widows are not engaged in any work. Only 12 (4%) are engaged in service and 10 (3.33%) are in small business and the rests are worked as labour.

REFERENCE

Altekar, A. S. (1938), *The Position of Women in Hindu Civilisation–From Prehistoric Times to the Present Day*. Benares: Benares Hindu University Press.

Aradhya, B. M. M. (1987), 'What it Means to be a Widow', *Social Welfare*, XXXIV (9).

Chattopadhyay, S. (1965), *Sicial Life in Ancient India (In the Background of the Yajnavalkya Smriti)* Calcutta: Academic Publication.

Chen, M. A. (1998), 'Introduction'. In *Widows in India: Social Neglect and Public Action*. Martha Alter Chen (Ed). New Delhi: Sage Publication.

Fowler, H. W. and Fowler, F. G. (1982), *The Concise Oxford Dictionary*. Bombay: Oxford University Press.

Das, R. M. (1962), *Women in Manu and his Seven Commentators*. Varanasi: Kanchana Publication.

Goldman, N. and Lord, G. (1983), 'Sex Differences in Life Cycle Measures of Widowhood, *Demography*, 20 (2).

Gulati, L. (1998), 'Widowhood and Aging in India' In *Widows in India: Social Neglect and Public Action*. Martha Alter Chen (Ed). New Delhi: Sage Publications.

Indra (1940), *The Status of Women in Ancient India*. Lahore: Minerva Book Shop.

Jayal, S. (1966), *The Status of Women in the Epics*. Delhi: Motilal Banarsidass.

Kacker, M. (1830), *Hindu Shastras on Marriage of Widows*. Part I (Virgin Widows). Allahabad.

Kamat, A. R. (1963), 'The Decline in Death Rate and Its Effect on the Extent of Widowhood', *Sociological Bulletin* 12 (1).

Kane, P. V. (1941), *History of Dharmasastra*: Vol. II, Part–I (Cncient and Medieval Religious and Civil Law) Poona : Bhandarkar Oriental Research Institute.

Kapadia, K. M. (1966), *Marriage and Family in India*. Bombay: Oxford University Press.

Kuppuswamy, B. (1972), *Social Change in India*, Delhi: Vikas Publishing House Pvt. Ltd.

Monahan, T. P. (1952), 'How Stable are Remarriages'? *American Journal of Sociology*, 58 (3).

Maribhat, P. N. (1998), 'Widowhood and Mortality in India'. In *Widows in India : Social Neglect and Public Action*. Martha Alter Chen (Ed). New Delhi: Saga Publication.

Ray, A. K. (1985), *Widows are not for Burning*. New Delhi: ABC Publication House.

Ray, B. B. (1987), *Socio Economic Impact of Sati in Bengal and the Role of Raja RamMohun Roy*. Calcutta: Naya Prakash.

Nagesh, H. V. (1987), 'The Plight of Widowhood in India', *Social Welfare*, XXXIV (4).

Shastri, S. R. (1952), *Women in the Vedic Age*. Bombay: Bharatiya Vidya Bhavan.

Sengupta, S. (1970), *A Study of Women of Bengal*. Calcutta: Indian Publications.

Subramanyam, M. (1909), *The Tonsure of Hindu Widows*. Madras: G. A. Natesan and Co.

Tarafdar, R. L. (1936), *Womanhood in Hindu Society, Ancient and Modern*. Dacca: Universal Press.

7

Awareness of Tribal Mothers Towards Child Health: An Enlightening Motherhood

Samita Manna

Perhaps the most impoverished and underprivileged communities of our country are the tribals, who suffer from a number of poverty related problems particularly the problems of malnutrition and consequent poor health. To study the impact of modern ways of living and of modern medicine upon a migrant tribal community, a study of a tribal group settled in the district of Nadia in West Bengal, was undertaken. A good number of tribal communities came to Nadia district and gradually settled themselves in different villages (Das : 1985). In the natural process of adjustment, they accommodated themselves with the local socio-environmental system. Basically, they are the children of nature because nature used to fulfil their basic needs, desires and help them to maintain a happy and peaceful life. But due to deforestation and impact of urbanization and industrialization the forests are gradually replaced by different rural and urban human habitation (Pal : 1995). In this new situation, the tribals have failed to cope with the new scenario and faced many new problems which have created many constraints in their day-to-day life.

As they are primitive, their tool and technologies used to be crude in nature which are still noticed among some Primitive Tribal Groups (PTG) in their gathering and distributing processes. So, the nature of their food and the process of consumption are also distinctive. They also use different indigenous medicines collected from nature. Sometimes these are prepared by their community medicine men for their treatment. But, in course of time these traditional ways of life have been mostly changed by the process of modernization. Implementation of many new strategies for their rehabilitation as well as uplift has also affected their life. Besides this, starting from the 1980's, the Government has implemented special and intensive welfare programmes like ICDS and IPP for poor and illiterate people in rural and urban areas respectively. These are very much important for the tribal people because being considerably poor, backward and ignorant they often could not avail the medical facilities either from the hospitals or from other health centers. These aggravate their health problems to a significant extent (Chowdhuri: 1986).

Many people believe that it is not right to look at the problems of the tribal community through the eyes of non-tribal social scientists and administrators. They felt that the old world of these people is going to be destroyed, therefore, they should be given support from outside. And in this way they want to integrate the tribal people with the mainstream of the population. We accept the fact that the tribal people have their own method of treatment and they have their own traditional medicine men. But in new localities where they are forced to migrate and settle the availability of the natural resources are often scarce to continue their age-old practices dealing with the health problems. It is of great sociological interest to see how these tribal people are accepting modern methods of treatment.

The conflict between their traditional mentality and modern view points can also be noticed in the tribals' definition of diseases and in their treatment. Every tribal community believes that an individual suffers from diseases when an evil spirit becomes angry. Therefore, they perform certain magical practices to appease it along with the measure taken to cure the disease with the help of traditional medicine men. Naturally, when the Government implements a new scheme to make available the minimum facilities of modern treatment to the tribal and other backward sections of the population, they do not accept it readily.

To look into the nature of change occurring among tribals regarding their health practices and their attitude to modern medicine, a survey was conducted among three tribal communities of Nadia District[1] of West Bengal living in different rural and urban areas. In some of these villages Integrated Child Development Services have been implemented by the Government of India in order to improve the health situation of the people. This study shows how the major tribal people of Nadia District namely–the Santal, Munda and Oraon have responded to this programme and moved a step forward towards integration with the mainstream.

In this study, the Santal community of Nadia District has been completely enumerated[2]. They are mainly concentrated in three Blocks of Nadia District. These are Haringhata Block, Chakdaha Block and Nakashipara Block. A good number of Santal families have been settled in different urban areas under the three municipalities. These are Kalyani Township, Gayeshpur township and Chakdaha Township. Thus in this study a comparative analysis has been done between the Santals living in rural areas and the Santals living in urban areas.

Besides the health situation of the Santals, the other two major tribal communities, the Munda and Oraon of Nadia District (Chakdaha Block) have also been studied. In the other two Blocks viz. Haringhata and Nakashipara, there is no significant concentration of these two communities. So all the villages of Chakdaha Block, which consist of a good number of the Mundas and Orans[3] have been completely enumerated to evaluate the functioning of the mother and child health care programmes as a whole.

These tribal people of Nadia District are not the original people of this area. During the different stages of historical upheavals, they have migrated to this region to have a secured socio-economic shelter. Most of them had come during the British period for indigo plantation and railway construction. The British administration expoiled this huge labour force at a very cheap rate. In course of time, however, they have been settled in different remote villages of Nadia District and have accepted agriculture as their occupation. In almost all the cases, they cleared the jungles and established their own villages. Sometimes their courage, physical strength and honesty were used by the Zamindars and well–to–do families who employed them as security forces. Often they were encouraged by Zamindars to settle in the outskirts of the villages.

Most of the Santal families have migrated from the state of Orissa whereas maximum number of the Munda and Oraon families have migrated from Murshidabad and Birbhum Districts of West Bengal. Thus among the Santals inter state migration and among the Mundas and Orans inter district migration is found in maximum cases. A good number of Munda and Oraon families have also come to Nadia from the state of Bihar and a few Munda families have flocked to this district from Bangladesh.

For this study the lists of the villages where the Santals, Mundas and Oraons are available have been collected from the panchayat offices. All the mothers who have children up to 5 years of age and all the pregnant mothers of the Santal, Munda and Oraon communities have been selected for the study from three Blocks which are already mentioned. (Table 1).

II

The rate of illiteracy is very high among these trbal people. It is observed that in all Municipalities and Blocks the rate of female illiteracy is much higher than of the male illiteracy. Another important feature is that in Kalyani Township the rates of male and female illiteracy are lower than the rate of male and female illiteracty in other Municipalities viz. Gayeshpur and Chakdaha. The educational attainment of the Santals in Kalyani is also more satisfactory than that of the Santals in other two Municipalities. Though no female graduate in the

Table 1
Block and Panchayat wise Distribution of Sample

Tribe	*Area*	*Municipality/ Block*	*Panchayat*	*Village*	*No. of Respondents*	*Total*
Santal	Urban	Kalyani Municipality	-	-	143	
		Gayeshpur Municipality	-	-	44	
		Chakdaha Municipality	-	-	23	
	Total	3	-	-	210	210
		Haringhata Block	Haringhata I	Balindi	10	38
				Ganguria	10	
				Subarnapur	9	
				Laupala	5	
				Dighapara	4	
Santal	Rural		Haringhata II	Haringhata (Farm)	35	76
				Mohanpur	24	
				Kapileswar	17	
			Fatehpur	Fatehpur	19	46
				Brahmapur	15	
				Bihariapara	12	
			Mollabelia	Mollabelia	33	56
				Nischindipur	23	
			Birohi	Birohi	6	6
		Total	5	14	222	

Contd...

Tribe	*Area*	*Municipality/ Block*	*Panchayat*	*Village*	*No. of Respondents*	*Total*
		Chakdaha Block	Madanpur I	Teghari	16	44
				Junglegram	9	
				Narapatipara	8	
				Jibannagar	7	
				Koutukpur	4	
Santal	Rural		Madanpur II	Basantapur	9	9
			Ghetugachi	Jaykrishnapur	6	16
				Chotojaguli	5	
				Gobindapur	5	
			Rautari	Rautari	17	17
		Total	4	10	86	86
		Nakashipara Block	Bikrampur	Bamandanga	16	16
		Total	1	1	102	16
	Total	3	10	25	324	

**Total Santal Population (Municipality + Block) 534 = 324 (Block) + 210 (Municipality)

Table 1.2
Block and Panchayat wise Distribution of Sample: Munda & Oraon

Tribe	*Area*	*Municipality/ Block*	*Panchayat*	*Village*	*No. of Respondents*	*Total*
MUNDA	RURAL	Chakdaha Block	Dubra	Bagdob	53	
				Jagannathpur	22	
				Bishnupur	12	
			Tatla I	Dhanicha	28	
			Ghetugachi	Ghetugachi	26	
			Silinda	Amdanga	57	
			Rautari	Enayatpur	23	
				Rautari	11	
	Total	1	5	8	232	
Total						232
ORAON	RURAL	Chakdaha Block	Silinda	Pitulitala	63	
			Ghetugachi	Banamalipara	15	
			Madanpur II	Kestopur	11	
			Tatla I	Ichhapur	55	
				Sutra	36	
				Ghola	15	
	Total	1	4	6	195	
Total						195

Santal community is found in this town but there are a few graduate males.

Among these three tribal communities, the Santals are little bit advanced than the Mundas and Oraons in educational attainment. But till now the rate of illiteracy is very high among them. In fact for a long period of time these Santals, Mundas and Oraons were out side of the educational institution and they did not realize the importance of education. But today the situation has changed and the boys and girls of the present generation are interested to go to school. Regarding occupation, no new trend is observed. Majority of the tribal people, young and old, are engaged in agricultural work as they have no skilled training. This trend is observed among all the three groups of tribal people.

Thus the principal occupation of the Santal, Munda and Oraon males and females is agriculture, though in most of the cases they do not have their own land and work as agriculture labourers. However, it is hopeful that at present a few males in these tribal communities are taking the opportunity of reservation of seats and participating in different service sectors.

It is found that the major portion of their income is spent for food. So they can not save money for future and when some crisis appears they have to take loan from their friends or relatives. The amount of money they take as loan is not very large, as they know that it will be very difficult for them to make repayment of it.

The rate of interest in rural areas is the same as in the urban areas i.e., 5% to 10% per month. The poor tribal often can not repay the money in due time, so in most of the time, they have to pay good amount of interest to the lender. But when they take loan from their friends or relatives, they often do not claim interest. But this does not mean that they have no poverty. Those poor tribal people sometimes want to take loan but find hardly any one who can lend them money. The money lenders are doubtful about their capacity to repay and do not entertain them.

Due to their poor economic condition, the respondents can not build brick-built house and the condition of the Mundas is worst in this regard. On the other hand, among the three tribal communities, maximum number of brick-built houses has been found among the Santals. As most of the Santal, Munda and Oraon families live in Kuncha houses, they cook their food in one corner of the verandah.

More than 57.00% Munda and Oraon families cook their food in verandah. Unfortunately, no Munda family was found to have separate room for cooking purpose. 42.67% Munda families cook their food in open courtyard. However, 3.59% Oraon families have kitchen of their own. In this tribal community also a good number of families (38.46%) cook their food in open courtyard. (Table 2).

The study shows that the number of families having a separate kitchen is higher among the Santal than the Mundas and Oraonas. In fact Mundas and Oraons are economically backward than the Santals. They also do not have essential sufficient utensils and other necessary things required for cooking.

In course of time the tribal mothers have developed some awareness of the necessity of clean drinking water. So now-a-days they do not go to the nearby ponds for it. Instead they use water from tubewell or tap for this purpose. Besides, the municipalities and the local panchayats in this regard also have played an important role by installing tubewells even in the remote villages.

The Santals, Mundas and Oraons still prefer to use open field than the latrines for excretion. It should be mentioned here that in some villages the local panchyats have made up a few community latrines. But, in most of the cases, these are not cleared properly and after some days some of these are abandoned. In the Munda and Oraon villages also the Government through the local panchayats has made a few community latrines. But majority of the Munda and Oraon respondents do not use these. Some of those are very dirty. During the time of fieldwork even it is found that the Oraons of Suntra village have stored straws for their domestic cattle

Table 2
Some Facilities and Practices Related to Health

Items	*Tribes*	*Open place*	*Verandah*	*Kitchen*	*Total*
Cooking facility	Santal	65 (12.17)	385 (72.10)	84 (15.73)	534
	Munda	99 (42.67)	133 (57.33)	-	232
	Oraon	75 (38.46)	113 (57.95)	7 (3.59)	195
Drinking water facility		Tube well	Tap	Others	
	Santal	284 (53.18)	250 (46.82)	-	534
	Munda	223 (96.12)	9 (3088)	-	232
	Oraon	170 (97.18)	9 (4.62)	16 (8.21)	195
Sanitary facility		Open field	Latrine	Others	
	Santal	469 (87.83)	65 (12.17)	-	534
	Munda	209 (90.09)	23 (9.91)	-	232
	Oraon	173 (88.72)	22 (11.28)	-	195
Practice of drinking Hadia		Never drink	Regularly drink	Occasionally drink	
	Santal	30 (5.62)	497 (93.08)	7 (1.31)	534
	Munda	8 (3.45)	222 (95.69)	2 (0.86)	232
	Oraon	5 (2056)	186 (95.38)	4 (2.05)	195
Practice of drinking milk during pregnancy		Never drink	Regularly drink	Occasionally drink	
	Santal	499 (93.45)	30 (5.62)	5 (0.94)	534
	Munda	231 (99.57)	1 (0.43)	-	232
	Oraon	192 (98.46)	1 (0.51)	2 (1.03)	195

N.B. Figures in the parentheses indicate percentages.

in a latrine. Thus the study shows that there is no difference among the three tribal communities regarding the habit of going to the field for natural excretion. In fact the Santal, Munda and Oraon mothers under study live in very poor socio-economic condition. They lead a very traditional life and struggle all the time for their minimum subsistence. The habit of these tribal people to go to the field for natural excretion is very much associated with their early ways of simple social life.

The practice of drinking country liquor is prevalent among the tribal people. They prepare it from putrefied rice, store in a big earthen pot and drink every day. The children, however, are not allowed to drink. The country liquor, popularly known as Handia or Hanri, in fact, has become a part of tribal life and tribal culture and they do not find any wrong in drinking Handia. And perhaps, in the past, when they prepared Handia from various forest products, it was not so harmful to their health. But now the process in which they prepare Handia and the material they use are not, by any means, good for health. The addiction of Handia is acute during the dull agricultural season, when their level of income comes down to a minimum; they prepare and drink Handia regularly, even when they fail to collect their full meal.

The same thing has been found among the Munda and Oraon communities. In these two tribal communities 95.69% and 95.38% women drink Handia almost everyday. They prepare Handia in the same process, which has been followed by the Santal as such. In these three tribal communities, the expectant mothers also drink Handia. This practice sometimes directly affects the financial condition of the family and makes them lazy and dull and prevents them from participating in normal life.

Regarding taking food, the pregnant mothers do not get special attention from the elders or their husbands due to their impoverished condition. Normally they take usual foods, which are available to them. Special drinks like milk or other health drinks are not available for them. Only in few cases, they drink milk which is available from their own community.

The number of mothers in all the places, irrespective of communities, who take milk to maintain their health during their pregnancy period is few. The percentages of mothers who take milk during their pregnancy is much lower among the Munda and Oraon communities than that among the Santals. Only 0.43% mothers in the Munda community and 0.51% mothers in the Oraon community get milk during pregnancy to maintain their health.

This does not mean that the tribals do not know about the necessity of extra protein during the pregnancy period. In fact, they are, in most of the cases, so poor that they can not afford extra food for the expectant mother. Generally, the tribal people take meal thrice a day–at morning, at late noon and at night. The items are also very simple–rice and vegetable curry, occasionally if they can hunt rat or rabbit, they relish the meat. Sometimes they also catch fish from the nearby ponds and prepare a fish curry. Thus they normally eat the rat and rabbit but on festive occasions they prefer chicken or pig. Not only the pregnant women but also the children after 10 months–12 months of their age become habituated with this type of food. So it can be said that the pregnant mothers and the children do not get sufficient amount of food by which they can maintain good health.

III

The health problems of the tribals are aggravated in many cases, due to their migration from the forests in different periods of history and the consequent retaining of many of their old habits. Also, due to this displacement, the tribals are unable to use their traditional methods of treatment during illness. Besides, as they had lost their rights on the forest products that had nourished their health for thousands of years, but now they have been suffering from the problems of malnutrition, poor health etc. Gradually they are compelled to take the help of modern methods of treatment.

The health problems of the mothers and their children in the tribal societies are many and related with their poor socio-economic conditions; but in most cases they do not pay much

Table 3
Child Care: Prenatal and Post natal

Items	*Tribes*	*Took help*	*No help*	*Total*
Doctor's help for pregnancy	Santal	20 (3.75)	514 (96.25	534
	Munda	-	232 (100.00)	232
	Oraon	-	195 (100.00)	195
Place of birth (0-5 years of children		*Home*	*Hospital/PHC*	
	Santal	326 (62.45)	196 (37.55)	522
	Munda	189 (92.20)	16 (7.80)	205
	Oraon	151 (82.07)	33 (17.93)	184
Immunization of the children (0-5 years)		*Taken*	*Not taken*	
	Santal	363 (69.54)	159 (43.80)	522
	Munda	118 (57.56)	87 (42.44)	205
	Oraon	106 (57.61)	78 (42.39)	184
Child Death		*Living*	*Dead*	
	Santal	522 (90.16)	57 (9.48)	-
	Munda	205 (94.04)	13 (5.96)	-
	Oraon	184 (94.85)	10 (5.15)	-

N.B. Figures in the parentheses indicate percentages.

attention to these (Doyal: 1995; Gupta: 1998).

The tribals are the sons of the soil and hence they are very close to nature. They also accept pregnancy as a normal phenomenon like other physiological process. Naturally they neither pay much attention to it nor become much anxious for it. Except a few, in most of the cases, they do not take any help from the doctors for becoming pregnant. Only 3.75% Santal Women in Kalyani have sought the help from the doctors for their pregnancy. (Table 3).

There are two most important reasons for which the tribal people generally avoid to go to the doctors during their illness. Firstly, they are very simple and are less aware of and indifferent to their health problems. Secondly, the tribal people are very poor and often can not afford money for their modern treatment. Only in some extreme cases they take help of the doctors. Unlike the educated urban non-tribal people, they do not, in most of the cases, feel any need to take doctor's advice during their pregnancy to maintain good health for safe delivery.

Most of the respondents who have taken doctor's advice usually go to the public government health centers during pregnancy. The urban-rural differentiation in this regard is noticed clearly. The percentage of Santal respondents, who have visited doctor's place for medical checkup during their pregnancy, is much higher in urban areas than in rural areas. In fact, in the villages there are practically very few qualified doctors in comparison to the town areas. Therefore, the villagers have to depend on the government health centres or hospitals. The percentages of women, who have not remained under doctors' supervision during their pregnancy are much higher in the Munda and Oraon communities than that among the Santal community. In fact no Munda and Oraon woman has taken advice from the doctors during their pregnancy for safe delivery. There are a few reasons for this. Generally the tribal people, being extremely traditional, do not give much importance to their pregnancy and do not feel any need to take help from the doctor. Though during the pregnancy they maintain certain customs and taboos, they do not keep themselves away from all sorts of household works. Even they go to the fields regularly in order to earn money except for a few days in the advanced stage. Their reluctance to go to doctor is reinforced by the fact that in almost all the cases they face no difficulty during the time of delivery, which, instead of the skilled doctors, is done with the help of Daima or village mid-wife.

Normally when labour pain starts, a mid-wife or Daima is informed to help the expectant mother for delivery. Every tribal community has its own Daima, who is not only aged but also experienced in this profession. She is given some money and sometimes a new saree. In most of the cases delivery takes place in her in-laws' house. For delivery purposes generally a corner of the covered verandah is preferred and the male members are not allowed in that particular place. Usually there is only one Daima in each village. Sometimes some problems also arise during the time of delivery. One Munda respondent in Bagdob village has reported that at the time of her delivery the Daima of her community was out of the village. She gave birth to her daughter at about 6 in the evening but there was no one to cut the umbilical cord and in such a situation the baby was kept by her side attached with the umbilical cord. In the next morning the Daima came and separated the baby from her mother by cutting the umbilical cord.

But in general during the time of delivery or after it, these tribal mothers do not face any major problem. So they do not want to go to hospital or health centre for delivery. Even a good number of women, who have sought doctors' supervision during their pregnancy, have decided not to go to the hospital for delivery. Except in Kalyani town, most of the children in Gayeshpur and Chakdaha town were born at home. As a whole, majority of the Santal, Munda and Oraon children were born at home despite the fact that in all those towns and Blocks there are government run health centres.

Thus it is clear that the tribal mothers generally consider delivery at home under the supervision of Daima as safe. For quite obvious reasons the mother do not go to doctors after delivery for their treatment or for their new born babies, except those few, who go to hospital or P.H.C., for delivery. Even if after delivery bleeding continues, they take suggestions from the senior female members of their community. It has, however, been found that bleeding after delivery is automatically stopped within 1 month after delivery in case of most of the tribal women.

Even a good number of respondents in urban and rural areas could not say about the nature of bleeding after delivery. They, in fact, have considered it as natural phenomenon and accepted it a part of normal life. One point to be mentioned here is that the tribal women are so simple that they hardly feel any hesitation to answer the most intriguing questions ever to an unknown person. Except a few in Haringhata, Chakdaha and Nakashipara Blocks, all the Santal respondents in rural areas feed breast milk to their children within 3 to 8 hours after the delivery. No Munda or Oraon mother under study feeds breast milk immediately after the delivery (within 2 hours of birth). Like the Munda community most of the respondents provide their children with breast milk within 3 to 5 hours of delivery. A good number of Munda women give breast milk to their children after 8 hours or more. Like the Mundas, the Oraon mothers, who give breast milk to their babies within 3 to 5 hours after delivery, are in the majority.

The Government of India, with a view to extend the minimum medical facilities to every person, has been trying to strengthen its infrastructure, since independence. No doubt, the advancement in the knowledge of medical science in the developed countries has influenced the health care technology of our country, but a vast majority of its population till now depend on indigenous methods and quack treatments. The hospitals, health centres and subcentres established by the Government to offer people free medical treatment, are not only inadequate in number but in many cases these centres suffer from the problem of the shortage of medicines. Even there are instances of the shortage of medical officers. Lack of communication facilities in the rural areas again aggravates the problem.

In Nadia there are 14 Governmental hospitals, 66 health centres (including Blocks, and Primary Health Centres) and 494 Subsidiary Health Centres. (Table 4).

Table 4
Available Medical Facilities: Nadia

		Health Centre		
Subdivision	*Hospital*	*Block Primary Health Centre*	*Primary Health Centre*	*Subsidiary Health Centre*
Kalyani	5	2	7	72
Krishnanagar	6	10	28	298
Ranaghat	3	4	15	124
Total	14	16	50	494

In these health centres there are altogether 4847 beds in which the patients can take admission during their illness. But this district also faces acute shortage of medical practitioners which hampers the total system. Besides, the district is in acute shortage of saline which is essential for diarrhoea and gastro-enteritis. The Annual Administrative Report of Nadia District (1993-94) writes:

Sporadic cases of gastroenteritis are being admitted, but the district is in acute shortage of saline, solutions etc. and not also is in a position to place purchase orders for technical reasons.

There is acute crisis of Injection A.R.V. for Dog bite cases (weekly requirements 2000 vials in a month but getting 300 doses). Such inadequacies affect the poor people to a considerable extent as they are not in a position to avail the medical facilities from the nursing homes or private doctors.

There are other problems too. The mass approach to the solution of the health problems as such is essential but this is to be balanced by the individual approach that includes supervision at the individual and family levels. This is particularly true in case of the rural people who are mostly illiterate, ignorant and less aware of the modern medical technology.

In order to control this problem, the Government through Social Welfare Directorates has implemented Integrated Child Development Service popularly known as ICDS, with significant emphasis on the health of the mother and the children. The Integrated Child Development Service, which has become an important programme to extend medical facilities to the poor people at the grass root level, has some specific objectives:

(1) To improve the nutritional and health status of the children in the age group of 0-5 years;

(2) To lay the foundations for proper psychological, physical and social development of the children;

(3) To reduce the incidence of mortality, morbidity, malnutrition and drop-out of the school-going children;

(4) To develop effective co-ordination of policy and implementation amongst the various department to promote child development; and

(5) To increase the capabilities of the mother to take the care of the general health and nutritional needs of the child through proper nutrition and health education.

With these objectives Integrated Child Development Service had been launched in the rural areas of Nadia during 1980–81. A group of voluntary workers, *Anganwadi* workers and helpers are working silently at the grass root level in the villages, overcoming many difficulties and hurdles including tremendous financial hardship. It is true that the major thrust of this scheme is to look after the health of the mother and child but the *Anganwadi* workers have also to take the responsibility of the non-formal pre-school education of the boys and girls belonging to the age group '3 years to 6 years'. Though the *Anganwadi* workers are supported by the supervisors and Project Officers, the Integrated Child Development Service mainly depends on the Anganwadi workers for the implementation of its **six package of Services** at the individual level. These services are:

1. Supplementary Nutrition.
2. Health Check Up.
3. Primary Health Care/Referral Service.
4. Immunisation.
5. Nutrition and Health Education.
6. Non-formal Pre-school Education.

Supplementary Nutrition is provided 300 days in a year not only to the children belonging to the age group '0 – 6 years', but also to the nursing (up to 6 months after delivery) and expectant mothers for their nourishment.

> The aim is to supplement intake by about 200 calories and 8–10 gms. of protein for children below 1 year, about 300 calories and 15 gms. of protein for children between 1 year and 5 + year of age and about 500 calories and 25 gms. of protein for pregnant women and nursing workers (Annual Administrative Report, Nadia, 1993-94).

Besides regular health check up of the children and mothers in the *Anganwadi* centres, the *Anganwadi* workers take a crucial role in the immunization of the chidren against some deadly diseases like diphtheria, tetanus, whooping cough, polio, tuberculosis, measles and in the immunization of the pregnant women against tetanus. These are aimed to be done in the *Anganwadi* centers but due to the lack of suitable infrastructure, at present, in many cases, the *Anganwadi* workers insist the mother of the children and the pregnant women to go to the nearest health centers for immunization. From these centers the children are given vitamins and the mothers are given iron tablets and folic acid tablets, free of cost.

Another important aspect of this Integrated Child Development Service is that through various *Anganwadi* centers the Government is trying to inculcate a favourable attitude towards education among the boys and girls belonging to the age group '3 – 6 years'. Generally the parens in the rural areas are less educated and less aware of the necessity of education to change the existing conditions and to build a prosperous future. As a result, the students in the rural areas feel little attraction to formal education. The Government, thereby, through the Anganwadi workers, has been trying to cultivate the reading habit among the children belonging to the age group ' 3years to 6 years' and to motivate them to formal school-education. The *Anganwadi* workers, whose educational qualification is at least Madhyamik, everyday, except on Sundays and other Government holidays, teach the boys and girls with utmost care. It is, however, not a very comfortable task for them. In most of the cases, the *Anganwadi* centers have no permanent building. The *Anganwadi* workers, under the problematic situation, teach the students in open courtyards, month after month, in sun and rain. Often they have to travel a long distance to come to the centers from their houses. It is unfortunate that a large number of educated women, who have taken the responsibilities of extending such important services to the poor grass root people as the *Anganwadi* workers, are being deprived of a minimum financial return. At present, though they are getting more than what they used to got earlier, the salary is quite low as compared to their heavy work load.

For obvious reasons the rate of infant mortality is high among the poor and backward communities who have little health awareness, inadequate medical facilities and large-scale malnutrition. The study shows that altogether 24 Santal children (0 to 5 years) out of 260, died in various diseases in the urban areas, whereas the number is, to some extent high in rural areas. 33 cases of child death (out of 309) have been recorded in Haringhata and Chakdaha Blocks. Every incidence of child death in the Santal community has occurred within 1 month to 1 year of age. Another important finding is that in all urban and rural areas the percentage of child death is higher in the age group '1 month to 1 year than in the age group '1 month or less'. 66.67% children (out of 12 death cases) in Kalyani town and 66.67% children (out of 9 death cases) in Chakdaha town died within 1 year of their age. On the other hand, in Haringhata and Chakdaha Blocks 70.83% children (out of 22 death cases) and 59.10% children (out of 11 death cases) died within 1 year of their age respectively.

On the basis of the responses of the parents the three most important diseases found to cause child death are fever, diarrhoea and jaundice. In Kalyani township 16.67% Santal children died in fever and jaundice. A good number of Santal children in Geyeshpur municipality area (55.56%) died in jaundice. In Haringhata Block 40.19% Santal children died in diarrhoea. Here 9.09% children died in severe fever and another 9.09% children died in jaundice. In Chakdaha Block, more than 50.00% Santal children died in fever. In other two tribal communities viz. Munda and Oraon, the number of child death is much lower than that among the urban Santal and rural Santal children. More than 53.00% children (out of 13 death cases) in the Munda community died within 1 month of their birth. But in the Oraon community 60.00% children (out of 10 death cases) died within 1 year of their age. In this tribal community 40.00% children (out of 10 death cases) died within one month of their birth. Like the Santal children, three major diseases, by which the Munda and Oraon children had been attacked and which became the cause of their death were fever, diarrhoea and jaundice. Among the Mundas in 23.08% cases, diarrhoea was the cause of child death. But this disease did not afflict any child in the Oraon community. Majority of the Oraon mothers did not know the cause of the death of their children. 10.00% of them said that child had been attacked by fever and another 10.00% Oraon mother pointed out jaundice as the cause of the child death.

Another common disease, according to the Munda respondents, whch causes death for many children in the Munda community is popularly known as *Pancha Penchi* (though no case has been recorded in the present study). In this disease, the Mundas believe that the spirit of a dead person enters into the body of the child and the child behaves abnormally. As a result, he or she before abnormally eats abnormal amount of food. The Mundas believe that *Pancha Penchi* is a curse and has no treatment.

Generally, in these tribal communities the dead body of the child, unlike that of the adult members, is buried in the nearest cremation ground. Various beliefs and death rituals are associated with the death of a child. One interesting custom found in the Munda community is worth mentioning. If a Munda mother gives birth to a dead child consecutively two or three times, the father cuts the right hand of his dead child by a knife and then it is buried. The Mundas believe that when some evil spirits become angry the mother gives birth to dead child consecutively and so they cut the hand of the dead child to identify the child, whether the same child is born again, by taking scarmarks on his or her right hand.

IV

Tribal women are mostly illiterate, ignorant and to a great extent superstitious. For a quite long period of time, and even today, they consider illness as a result of a curse of supernatural powers–gods, spirits, ghosts and others. They identify various gods and goddesses or different kind of spirits behind diseases which frequently or occasionally affect them. Naturally, they try to appease these supernatural powers by propitiating them in strict ritualistic ways. This sort of belief system, prevalent among the tribals, is the most perpetuating hinderance to develop health awareness among them.

In some cases as a result of their greater exposure to the larger society and to various mass media, health awareness among the tribal women are being developed. But till today tribal mothers do not take care to keep their children clean or to develop hygienic practices among their children. Even a good number of mothers in all the tribal communities under study do not clean their mouth and teeth in the morning and do not take bath regularly. They rarely wash their clothes, comb their hair and cut their nails. Even the adult male and female members in the tribal society do not hesitate to urinate in the courtyard by the side of their house and to spit here and there. The children in these societies are born and brought up in such an extremely filthy and unhygienic environment, which an outsider can hardly imagine.

Most of the mothers in the Santal, Munda and Oraon communities go to nearby fields, early in the morning, for excretion. In fact they are habituated with this practice right from their early childhood. But at present, owing to increase in population some times they face difficulties for finding a proper place for such practice. Thus, negatively speaking an compulsion is being developed, which in future, may help to stop such an unhygenic practice.

At present the tribal mothers have developed a favourable attitude towards small family. It is true that, as most of them are agricultural labourers, they know that after certain age, their children (both male and female) have to go to the field for helping the family financially. But some of them are so poor that they can hardly maintain more than 2 or 3 children at present. Secondly, the parents of the younger generation are gradually realizing the necessity of the education of their children so they want to restrict the number of children and give attention to a few. This attitude is not result of any concern for their reproductive health. The preference for small family, is a product of their existing economic condition. (Table 5).

Most of the Santal mothers want to use massage oil for their children. Generally they apply mustard oil to the body of their children and keep them in the direct exposure to sun for a few hours. These tribal mothers believe that this gives

Table 5
Tribal Mothers: Opinions and Attitudes

Opinions	*Tribes*	*1 Child*	*2-3 Children*	*3+ Children*	*Total*
Preferred no. of children	Santal	153 (28.65)	285 (53.37)	96 (17.98)	534
	Munda	67 (28.88)	132 (65.90)	33 (14.22)	232
	Oraon	58 (29.74)	117 (60.00)	20 (10.26)	195
Need for massage oil for children		*No need*	*Necessary*	*Do not know*	
	Santal	100 (18.73)	379 (70.97)	55 (1030)	534
	Munda	86 (37.07)	100 (52.59	24 (10.34)	232
	Oraon	45 (23.08)	150 (76.92)	-	195
Need for boiled water for children		*No need*	*Necessary*	*Do not know*	
	Santal	299 (55.99)	180 (33.71)	55 (10.30)	534
	Munda	160 (68.97)	48 (20.69)	24 (10.34)	232
	Oraon	149 (76.41)	19 (9.74)	27 (13.85)	195
ORS as primary treatment		*No need*	*Necessary*	*Do not know*	
	Santal	213 (39.89)	321 (60.11)	-	534
	Munda	90 (38.79)	133 (57.33)	9 (3.88)	232
	Oraon	80 (41.03)	115(58.97)	-	195

N.B. Figures in the parentheses indicate percentages.

their babies extra strength and helps them to combat cough and cold. 30% of the respondent mothers in Kalyani, 53.66% of them in Gayeshpur and 23.81% mothers in Chakdaha town have reported that they do not apply any brand of massage oil on the body of their baby. The habit of use of massage oil for the children is more common among the Oraons than among the Mundas. In the former group, 52.59% of the respondent mothers use massage oil for their children whereas in the latter group more than 76% of them use it to maintain good health for their children. Thus most of the mothers have developed a positive awareness, in this regard, to make their children healthy. But these tribal mothers, as such, are not much anxious about the other aspects of health of their children and so, they hardly take any other special care for their baby. The children in the Santal, Munda and Oraon communities are not provided with, in most of these cases, extra food or vitamins. Even most of them, at their very early age are not given boiled water for drinking, which is often suggested by the medical practitioners. This is an important aspect of health awareness because water diseases are very common among children. Among the urban areas the percentage of Santal mothers, who give boiled water to their children is highest in Kalyani (37.69%) and lowest in Chakdaha town area (9.52%).

So the Santal, Munda and Oraon mothers, in majority of the cases, are not aware of the usefulness of boiled water for drinking purpose. Even those who give boiled water to their children do not drink boiled water for their own health. Generally, they drink water from tubewells, which the Government has installed in the villages. One important finding is that these tribal people do not store drinking water in clean pots and pitchers by which they could maintain their good health everyday. During the time of fieldwork, it has been observed that they do not always cover the pots and pitchers in which they store water. Besides they often drink water in unclean glasses and pots. Such practices are not, definitely an indicator of their health awareness.

Perhaps due to the fact that these tribal people have little hygienic sense as to what sort of food items are to be given to the child, what sort of cleanliness is to be maintained during the time of eating and drinking etc diarrhoea, which is popularly known as Antrik, is very common among the children particularly during the summer and rainy seasons. ORS or home-made saline (made up of water, salt and sugar) is very much effective as a primary treatment of this disease and the Government through various mass media and through the health workers has been trying to propagate its importance. As a result, most of the Santal, Munda and Oraon mothers today know the usefulness of ORS and they frequently give their sons and daughters this solution. But paradoxically, in Kalyani urban area most of the Santal mothers have opined that they do not know what is ORS.

One thing to be mentioned here is that as these tribal people live along with their kin groups and there is a strong community feeling among them, during the time of illness of the children or other adult members, the relatives and friends take care of the affected individuals equally with the family members. Even in some cases the senior members of the kin group take more initiative and give advice to the affected family.

It has been observed that the young mothers are often less aware of their children's health or of their own health. Another important aspect of health awareness, in the present day context, is the awareness of arsenic pollution. It has been stated already that these tribal people mainly depend on tubewells for drinking water, which have been installed by the State Government through the local panchayats. Recently, in many villages (other than those under study) of this district arsenic has been found in the water of tubewells beyond the permissible limit which causes severe skin diseases and other health problems. But most of the respondents of the present study are unaware of this problem. Actually campaigning for the problem of arsenic has not been done in these villages, as till today in the villages under study arsenic has not been found beyond the permissible limit from the ground water.

The respondent are now-a-days influenced by different mass media mainly from radio news. It has already been pointed out that most of the respondents are illiterate. Even those who can read, do not read newspaper. Radio, therefore, plays a vital role to increase their level of awareness regarding various issues including health. As a result, the level of awareness has been slowly increasing among the tribal mothers. It should be mentioned here that these tribal mothers do not try in most of the cases, to develop health awareness of their sons and daughters right from their childhood. Naturally the children do not develop good habits which might help them to prevent many diseases. Yet the tribal mothers and children do not fall in illness frequently because perhaps they have a natural immunity.

Another point is that all Santal, Munda and Oraon mothers have opined that they prefer allopathic treatment whenever necessary. Besides these, particularly in case of their son's or daughter's illness, they worship various gods and goddesses for recovery. During this time, all family members take sincere care of child. No discrimination in this regard is made between male or female child. In fact only in a few aspects of their life such discrimination is made. The attitude of the tribals towards male and female child becomes evident from the opinion of the pregnant women who have not indicated any special preference either for a boy or for a girl. Due to poor socio-economic condition the tribal mothers often do not get sufficient amount of food during their pregnancy. The children also become habituated with the same type of food items that are prepared for the adults.

These mothers are also less aware about the necessity of medicines during their pregnancy. The ICDS workers visit every household and try to motivate them to go to the nearest health centres for iron tables, TT etc. Sometimes they also give these. But in many cases it has been found that they stop the course immediately. At the same time it is also to be mentioned that as a result of the implementation of ICDS, the health awareness of the tribal people has increased.

Table 6
Villages Having no ICDS Centre

Tribe	*Block*	*Panchayat*		*Villages*
SANTAL	Nakashipara	Bikrampur		Bamandanga
	Chakdaha	Madanpur I		Narapatipara
		Madanpur II		Basantapur
		Ghetugachi		Jaykrishnapur
	Haringhata	Fatehpur	(i)	Brahmapur
			(ii)	Fatehpur
		Haringhata I	(i)	Subarnapur
			(ii)	Laopala
			(iii)	Ganguria
		Haringhata II	(i)	Kapileswar
			(ii)	Dighapara
			(iii)	Santoshpur
MUNDA	Chakdaha	Dubra		Bishnupur
		Silinda		Amdanga
		Rautari		Enayatpur
ORAON	Chakdaha	Tatla I	(i)	Ichhapur
			(ii)	Ghola
			(iii)	Sutra
		Ghetugachi		Banamalipara
		Madanpur II		Kestopur

All over the country the impact of ICDS on rural people has been felt. Individual supervision and monitoring have some positive results in awareness building. Several studies have also pointed this out. Chakladar et al (1984) have clearly mentioned how this project has changed the life style of the people under different *Anganwadi* centers. Similarly Chandra et al (1985) have shown that implementation of ICDS has led to the reduction of infant mortality rate and child mortality rate. National Institute of Public Cooperation and Child Development conducted a study on the impact of ICDS in 1992 and recommended its implementation in all non-ICDS blocks.

In all the villages where ICDS centres have been opened, the tribal mothers have accepted it readily. All pregnant mothers and all children have been immunized though in a few cases they have stopped immunization. The rate of admission in ICDS schools is also very satisfactory. The Santals are more advanced in this regard. One major cause of this is the fact that in Santal villages the ICDS had been implemented earlier than in the Munda and Oraon village.

NOTES

This article is based on the study carried out at Nadia District under a project entitled "An Evaluative Study of Mother and Child Health care Programme Among thr Tribals: Awareness and Participation (Nadia District)". It was financed by the Ministry of Social Justice and Empowerment (Tribal Development Division), Government of India. The author expresses her thanks to all the members of the sanctioning authority for their financial support.

1. Nadia is one of the districts of West Bengal. It was acknowledged as a separate district later. Before 1854 it was within the Jessore Division. Later on, Nadia Division was formed and Krishnanagar became its head quarter. After the partition of Bengal in 1948 Nadia was acclaimed as a separate District.

   From the time of Lord Chaitanya i.e. fifteenth century, AD. the District had its distinct cultural and spiritual environment. Till now it is influenced by Vaishnavism- a deep religious and cultural ethos of Lord Chaitanya.

2. Altogether 534 Santal mothers have been selected from three municipal areas (urban) and three blocks (rural). These three

municipalities are Kalyani, Gayeshpur and Chakdaha from which 210 Santal mothers (including pregnant mothers) have been selected.

In Hringhata Block, there are 5 Panchayats having 14 villages consisting of 222 sample Santal mothers and in Chakdaha Block there are 5 Panchayats of which 10 villages consisting of 86 Santal mothers. Only in Nakashipara Block there is one village under Bikrampur Panchayat having 16 families. In this way total 324 rural mothers have been selected.

3. Munda and Oraon sample mothers are only available in Chakdaha Block. 232 Munda mothers and 195 Oraon mothers from different villages under different Panchayats have been studied.

REFERENCES

Chakladar, B. *et. al.* (1984), *Assessment of Impact of ICDS Scheme on Pre-School Children*. Karnatak: Kasturba Medical College.

Chandra, H. R. *et. al.* (1985), *Impact of ICDS on Mortality and Morbidity*. Bangalore: Bangalore Medical College.

Chowdhuri, B. (1986), 'Medical Anthropology in India with Special Reference to Tribal Population'. In B Chawdhuri (ed.): *Tribal Health: Socio-Cultutal Dimension*. New Delhi: Inter India Publications.

Das, B. (1985), *Educational Choice and Occupational Aspiration of the Mixed Tribal Students: A Sociological Study*. Unpublished Dissertation.

Doyal, L. (1995), *What makes Women Sick-Gender and Political Economy of Health*. Houndmills: Mcmillan Press.

Gupta, R. (1998), 'Socio- economic Status of Tribal Women in West Bengal, *Bulletine of the Cultural Research Institute*, Vol. XX, No. 1 (60-63).

Pal, A. N. (1995), 'The Political Economy of Migration Among the Oraon', *Man in India*, Vol. 75, No. 1.

8

Islamic Law of Marriage and Divorce: Subjugated Womanhood

S.A.H. MOINUDDIN

In Islam, marriage is a civil contract made by mutual consent between man and woman. Justice Mahmood (Rashid 1999:51) argues that though Muslim marriage is solemnized generally with recitation of certain verses from the Quran, yet the Mohammedan law does not positively prescribe any service peculiar to the occasion. That it is a civil contract is manifest from the various ways and circumstances in and under which marriages are contracted or presumed to have been contracted. And though a civil contract, it is not positively prescribed to be reduced to writing, but the validity and operation of the whole are made to depend upon the declaration or proposal of the one, and the acceptance or consent of the other of the contracting parties, or of their natural and legal guardians before competent and sufficient witnesses; as also upon the restrictions imposed, and certain of the conditions required to be abided by according to the peculiarity of the case.

Justice Mahmood has been accused of holding the view that the Muslim marriage is nothing but purely a civil contract. But this is not the fact. Justice Mahmood himself highlighted another aspect of marriage that is its social aspect. He argues that marriage is a contract which has for its design or object the right of enjoyment for the solace of life, and is one of the prime or original necessities of man. It is therefore lawful in extreme old age after hope of offspring has ceased, and even in the case of death or illness. The pillars of marriage, as of other contracts, are Ejab-o-kubool, or declaration of acceptance. The first speech, from whichever side it may proceed, is the declaration, and the other the acceptance.

If we take note of Muslim marriage from a religious angle, it is considered as lbadat (devotional act). The prophet Muhammad is reported to have said that Marriage is essential for every physically fit Muslim who can afford it. Moreover, the following traditions may also be considered.

> "He who marries completes half of his religion; it now rests with him to complete the other half by leading a virtuous life in constant fear of God."
>
> "There are thee persons whom the Almighty Himself has undertaken to help-first, he who seeks to buy his freedom; second, he who marries with a view to secure his chastity; and third, he who fights in the cause of God."
>
> "....whoever marries a woman in order that he may retain his eyes–Allah putteth blessedness in her for him and in him for her."

The prophet Muhammad is further reported by some writers to say that marriage is equal to Jehad (holy war); it is sinful not to contract a marriage; it is a Sunnah; and it is obligatory on those who are physically fit.

If we go through all these traditions carefully then we may rightly observe that it is not merely a civil contract. Marriage is for the solace of life...it is therefore lawful in extreme old age after hope of offspring has ceased, and even in the case of death or illness. In the words of Ameer Ali (ibid:54) marriage is "for the protection of society, and in order that human beings may guard themselves from foulness and unchastity."

According to Mulla's principles of Mohammedan Law, conditions for Muslim marriage are as follcws:

(1) Every Mohammedan of sound mind, who has attained puberty, may enter into a contract of marriage.

(2) Lunatics and minors who have not attained puberty may be validly contracted in marriage by their respective guardians.

(3) A marriage of a Mohammedan, who is of sound mind and has attained puberty, is void, if it is brought about without his consent.

A Muslim marriage has fixed and rigid rules which were laid down and practised by the prophet. It is essential for the validity of a marriage that there should be a proposal made by or on behalf of one of the parties to the marriage and an acceptance of the proposal by or on behalf of the other, in the presence and hearing of two males or one male and two female witnesses, who must be sane and adult Muslims.

Shushtery (1972:397) opines:

A woman who has reached the age of puberty is free to choose, to accept or to refuse an offer, although such conduct may be against the declared wishes of her parents or guardians. If a woman was married in her infancy, she may renounce and dissolve the contract on reaching her maturity. Her consent in any case is necessary, though parents are allowed to find a suitable match and even in some cases to force her to give her consent, which however, is not legal. She can make her own terms before the marriage, as to the amount of the dowry to be paid to her, the dissolution of marriage in case if her husband leaves the place and goes to some other country or in regard to any other matter. All terms and conditions agreed to mutually would be binding on the husband. Freedom, age and health are the conditions for a marriage.

FORMALITIES OF A VALID MARRIAGE

Formalities of a valid Muslim marriage are as follows:

Marriage may be constituted without any ceremonial; there are no special rites, no officiants, no irksome formalities (Fyzee:

1963). Neither writing nor any religious ceremony is essential (Hidayatullah: 1972). Nevertheless, following conditions are necessary:

(i) Offer on the part of one party to the marriage.

(ii) Acceptance by the other party.

Here we must note that the offer and acceptance may be made by the parties, or by their agents, if both are competent. In case of legal incompetency, like minority or unsoundness of mind, the guardians may validly enter into a contract of marriage on behalf of their wards.

(iii) Presence of two witnesses where the parties are Hanafis ; no witness is required if parties are Shia.

(iv) The words with which the marriage is contracted must be clear and unambiguous.

(v) The proposal and acceptance must both be expressed in one and the same meeting.

In this regard Hidayatullah (ibid :256) argues that the proposal and acceptance must both be expressed at one meeting; a proposal made at one meeting and an acceptance made at another meeting do not constitute a valid marriage.

In certain cases where man and woman are living as husband and wife, the question may arise whether they are presumed to be married. The most recognized and accepted view is that, if the cohabitation is continuous and prolonged, the man and woman may be treated as husband and wife. The same presumption will also be there in the case where the man acknowledges the woman as his wife, or the child born of the union as legitimate.

But where the woman is non-Kitabiya, related to the man within prohibited degrees of relationship, the wife of another person, and so on, she cannot be presumed to be the wife. In a case where a Buddhist Burmese lady cohabited with a Muslim male for some time, the Privy Council observed that no presumption of marriage in such a case could arise (Aga Mohammed 1893: 56). Similarly, cohabitation with prostitute cannot give rise to the presumption of marriage.

From the above discussion the essential conditions of a valid marriage may be categorized by Ameer Ali as follows:

Ijab (offer), qubul (acceptance), baligh (adult age or puberty), Rashid (sound mind not majnum or non-compos mentis) parties i.e. groom and bride, or when minor their guardians, two witnesses (in Hanafi law, not Shia law), and same meeting (that is at one session complete). The completion of this contract which commences with proposal or demand in marriage and ends with is called 'aqd' (Rasid 1999: 57).

Now the question is what are the legal effects of a valid marriage? There are nine legal effects of a valid marriage:

(i) Sexual intercourse becomes lawful and the children born of the union are legitimate.

(ii) The wife becomes entitled to her dower.

(iii) The wife becomes entitled to maintenance.

(iv) The husband becomes entitled to restrain the wife's movements in a reasonable manner.

(v) Mutual rights of inheritance are established.

(vi) The prohibitions regarding marriage due to the rules of affinity come into operation.

(vii) The wife is not entitled to remarry after the death of her husband, or after dissolution of her marriage, without observing iddat.

(viii) Where there is an agreement between the parties, entered into either at the time of the marriage or subsequent to it, its stipulations will be enforced, insofar as they are consistent with the provisions or the policy of the law.

(ix) Neither the husband nor the wife acquires any interest in the property of the other by reason of marriage.

Along with these there are some typical valid conditions attached with a marriage contract.

(i) The condition agreed upon by the guardians of minors whose marriage has been so contracted, that the wife could divorce the husband in case he takes a second wife without her consent (Zahedunnissa 1941: 657).

(ii) If the man is forsaken in the Malak-O-Badar community or is expelled from it by the spiritual head, his wife may get a divorce from him as pronounced by a person appointed by her which divorce he will accept as valid (Sanai Badar 1923: 262).

(iii) It can validly be agreed upon that the wife shall live in her parent's house and shall not be removed elsewhere; and in the case of dissension with the husband, he would pay a monthly allowance to her as maintenance and will allow her to remain in her parent's house.

(iv) The wife may validly be allowed to leave her husband's house in case of his misbehavior or cruelty.

(v) The husband allows the wife to seek divorce in the event he mistreats her, her parents or her relations. In one such instance, it was found that the husband instituted a criminal proceeding against his wife and her parents. The complaint proved frivolous. The wife exercised her right to seek divorce and sent a notice to this effect to her husband though the husband did not receive the notice it was held that the fact whether husband received notice or not is immaterial. The eventuality in which he has allowed his wife to seek divorce is present and she is not affected in any way by the non-service of the notice (Abdul Samad 1926: 1144).

(vi) It is the obligation of the husband to maintain his wife. On his failure in doing so, the wife may seek divorce (Mumtaj Begam 1936: 1716).

CLASSIFICATION OF MARRIAGES

If we go through the writings of Fyzee and Tyabji, the legal experts of Islamic law, then we can classify Muslim marriages into three categories. These are:

(i) Valid,

(ii Void and

(iii) Irregular.

Valid Marriage: A valid marriage is one which conforms in all respects with the legal requirements, and there should be no prohibition affecting the parties. When the legal conditions are fulfilled, the marriage is called Sahih or correct (Rashid 1999:61) that is , a marriage in which no prohibition affect is the parties. Prohibitions may be either permanent or temporary. If they are permanent, the marriage is void, if temporary, it is irregular.

Void: A marriage which has no legal results is termed as void. A marriage forbidden by the rules of the blood relationship, affinity or fosterage is void. Similarly, a marriage with the wife of another, or remarriage with the divorced wife, without observing the strict rules set for this occasion, is void.

Now the question is what are the legal effects of a void marriage. A void marriage is an unlawful connection which creates no mutual rights and obligations between the parties. As Fyzee observes, it is a semblance of marriage without reality. Being no marriage at all, the Muslim woman can have it declared void at any time and the man can create no hindrance against her action. The woman gets no right to dower. If either party dies during the period of this union, the other acquires no right of inheritance. Neither can enforce any marital obligations against the other, e.g. the man can not compel the woman to submit to his company. The children of such marriage are not legitimate. But according to Radd-ul Muhtar, if they have consummated the marriage, the woman would be entitled to her dower (mahr-ul-misl).

Irregular: A marriage may be either lawful or unlawful. Unlawfulness may be either absolute or relative. If the unlawfulness is absolute, the marriage is void. If it is relative, it is an irregular marriage.

The following are the types of irregular marriage:

(a) A marriage without witness.

(b) A marriage with a woman undergoing iddat.

(c) A marriage prohibited by reason of difference of religion.

(d) A marriage with two sisters at the same time.

(e) A marriage with a fifth wife.

In Shia law, all the above irregular marriages are treated as void, because Shia law does not recognize the distinction irregular and void marriage. A marriage is, according to that system, either valid or void.

Now the question is how the irregular marriage be made regular? There are some provisions for it in Islamic law. But we must keep in mind that the irregular marriage may be made regular by removing the impeding irregularity, which must not be of a permanent nature. Some marriages can not be validated at all. Marriage contracted within the relationship of consanguinity, affinity and fosterage cannot be validated. Then also, marriage with a woman whose husband is living would not become valid even after the death of the first husband, because the marriage is void ab initio.

Other types of marriages may of course, be validated by removing the temporary irregularity. Thus, a marriage in the absence of witnesses becomes regular on consummation; marriage without free consent; by ratification with free consent; marriage with a non-Muslim, by conversion to a religion which could make the marriage valid; marriage by a person who has already four wives, by death or divorce of any wife reducing number to four; marriage prohibited by unlawful conjunction, by terminating the marriage which creates this prohibition.

MUTA MARRIAGE

There is another form of marriage in Islam, which is known as Muta marriage. "It is lawful among Shias", says Wilson, "to enter into contract of (so-called) marriage for a limited period, which may be a terms of year, a month, a day or even a part of a day"(Rashid 1999:61). But it is not always the case. Fyzee says that among the Shias themselves, only Ithna Ashari School recognizes it, and it is rejected by every other Muslim School. The practice is not common in India, and in Lucknow, Rampur and other places where there is a Shiite population; ladies of better class do not accept Muta marriage. In case of Muta marriage, the marriage dissolves of itself, on the expiration of the term of marriage. If no time limit is expressed, the marriage is presumed to be permanent. The number of wives that can be taken into marriage is unlimited. The ceiling of four wives does not apply here. A Shia male may contract Muta with a Muslim, Christian, jewish or parsi (fire-worshipper) woman, but not with a woman following any other religion. A woman may not contract Muta with a non-Muslim. The amount of dower must be specified in the contract of Muta otherwise the agreement is void. The child born of a Muta marriage is legitimate and capable of inheriting from the father. But, in the absence of an express agreement, neither party to a Muta is entitled to inherit from other. Maintenance is not due for the Muta wife unless it has expressly been agreed upon.

There are some essential requirements of Muta. These are (a) period and (b) dower. Muta being a temporary marriage in essence, it is necessary that the Muta contract must specify the period of enjoyment. The fixed period can again be extended by a new contract. It can also be presumed to be extended unless disproved. Now the question is if the contract is for—

(i) Unspecified time–that is mention of period is omitted, intentionally or unintentionally, or

(ii) Specified for lifetime–will such contract result into Muta or Nikah ? There is a difference of opinion among Muslim jurists. According to a decision by the Hyderabad High court (Fakher Jung 1953), in both cases a permanent Nikah will result. Fyzee (1987: 120) does not agree with this view. As to the second he says that fixation of a period in marriage contract destroys the concept of Nikah as understood in Islamic law. As the first, in his opinion the deciding factor should be intention of the parties rather than the form of the words.

PROHIBITIONS TO MARRY CERTAIN CASES

Tyabji gives the following nine grounds on which Muslims are prohibited from intermarrying with each other.

(i) *Consanguinity*–A Muslim is prohibited to marry-

   (a) his ascendants or descendants;

   (b) his father's mother's descendants; and

   (c) The sister or brother of any ascendant.

(ii) *Affinity*–It is unlawful for a Muslim to marry

   (a) ascendant or descendant of his wife; and

   (b) The wife of any ascendant or descendant.

(iii) *Fosterage*–A child is called the "foster-child" of the woman, who not being the child's mother, has nursed the child whilst it was under two years of age. The woman is called the "foster-mother".

   Muslim law prohibits marriage within certain limits of foster-age. A man may not, for instance, marry his foster-mother or his foster-sister.

(iv) *Unlawful conjunction*–it may be because of two things:

   (a) *Number*-Muslim male may marry any number if wives do not exceed four; but a Muslim woman can marry only one husband; if she marries with a second husband, she may be punished under Section 494 Indian Penal Code.

   (b) *Relationship between co-wives*–A man is forbidden to have two at the same time, so related with each other by consanguinity, affinity or fosterage that they could not have lawfully intermarried with each other if they had been of different sexes.

From the above argument it comes out clearly, for instance, that it is unlawful to marry two sisters at the same time, or to marry the sister of the wife during the wife's lifetime. In the leading case of Azizunnissa V. Karimunnissa (1895) the Calcutta High court held that such union are void. But, the High Court of Bombay, Madras and Lahore, and the chief court of Oudh considered them to be merely irregular (Fyzee 1987 : 113).

(v) *Iddat*–A widow, a divorced woman or a woman who is pregnant by illicit intercourse is prohibited from remarrying or marrying during the period of iddat. The object of iddat is to ascertain whether the woman is pregnant or not and to ascertain the paternity of the child.

The period of Iddat in case of (a) the marriage dissolved by death is 4 months and 10 days or if the woman is pregnant, till delivery, whichever is longer; (b) the marriage is consummated and dissolved by divorce, it is three courses, or till delivery in case of pregnancy.

(vi) *Divorce*–After the husband has pronounced three talaqs against his wife, their marriage is irrevocably dissolved, and they are prohibited from remaining with each other unless and until:

(a) The woman is lawfully married to a second husband.

(b) Her marriage with her second husband is actually consummated,

(c) It has been lawfully dissolved, and

(d) The woman observes iddat.

(vii) *Difference of religion*–Under Hanafi law, a man may marry a Muslim woman or a Kitabiya, but a Muslim woman can not marry anyone except a Muslim.

A Muslim, therefore, can not marry idolatress or a fire-worshipper; and a Muslim woman can not even marry a Kitabi. Among the Shias, however, no one can marry a non-Muslim in the Nikah form, but the male can contract a Muta marriage with a Kitabiya (including a fire-worshipper).

[A Kitabi is a man, and a Kitabiya a woman who believes in a revealed religion possessing a Divine book. In India, these terms apply only to jews and to Christians, each of whom posses a revealed book (Kitab).

(viii) *Supervening illegality*–If one of the parties to a marriage becomes a fire-worshipper or an idolator, or the husband becomes Chirstian, then the marriage becomes invalid by what is known as supervenient prohibition.

(ix) *Pilgrimage*–Under the Ithna Ashari and Shafii law, a man who has gone to perform Haj (pilgrimage) and has entered the sacred enclave of Kaba after putting on the pilgrim's dress (ahram), may not enter into a contract of marriage. Under Shia law, a deliberate breach of this rule debars that man and woman from ever becoming husband and wife.

MAHR OR DOWER

Another important aspect of Muslim marriage is Mahr or Dower. As soon as Nikah has been read, the bridegroom's father is required to fix the mahr. Mahr, which is also known as sadaq is an essential part of Islamic marriage. Without Mahr-nikah can not be said to have been properly solemnized. A man asks for the hand of a woman from a man, pays sadaq (dower money) and marries her. Its origin is pre-Islamic and tribal and it is essentially a bride price, but Islam elevated it from being merely a bride-price to being a token of love, truthfulness and sincerity.

Most of the Quarashites and other tribes followed similar customs. In pre-Islamic Arabia, it was given to the family of the woman for offering her hand in marriage. There was a basic difference between mahr and sadaq. The former was paid to the marriage guardian (i.c.wali) and the latter to the bride herself (Hanfi 1954: 151).

Mahr, or dower, is a sum of money or other property which the wife is entitled to receive from husband in consideration of marriage (Hidyatullah 1972:277). It is to be paid or fixed before the solemnization of marriage and it is the exclusive preserve of the bride to determine the amount. The mahr amount paid to her is her own. Neither her father nor her husband can claim it. She alone owns it in her own right (Engineer 1992:55). The Quran repeatedly exhorts men to give mahr to the woman they intend to marry. It says (Shrah 4,4):

> And give women their dowries as a free gift. But if they of themselves be pleased to give you a portion thereof, consume it with enjoyment and pleasure.

It means, mahr should be a free gift and the husband can enjoy it only if the wife permits it, not otherwise (Moinuddin 2000:111).

According to Abdur Rahim (Rashid 1999:82) it is either a sum of money or other form of property to which the wife becomes entitled by marriage....It is an obligation imposed by law on the husband as a mark of respect for the wife....

(Tyabji :82-83) defines it in the following way :

Mahr or dower is a sum that becomes payable by the husband to the wife on marriage, either by agreement between the parties, or by operation of law.

Kind of Mahr or Dower

Broadly speaking, there are two kinds of dower in Islam : (i) specified, and (ii) unspecified. The specified dower has been further divided into-prompt, and deferred.

(i) *Specified dower*–An amount settled by the parties at the time of marriage or after is called specified dower. If the bridegroom is minor, his father may settle the amount of dower. Hanafi law says that the father is not personally liable for the dower, but according to Shia law, he will be so liable.

The husband is bound to pay the amount of the specified dower, however, excessive or beyond reach it may be. In Oudh, however, the excessive amount may be curtailed to a reasonable amount.

Prompt and Deferred Mahr or Dower

Prompt dower is payable on demand, and deferred dower is payable on the dissolution of marriage by death or divorce. The prompt portion of the dower may be realized by the wife at any time before or after consummation, but the deferred dower could not be so demanded.

In the case where it is settled how much of the dower is prompt and what part of it is deferred, the Shia law holds that the whole of dower is prompt; the Sunni law, however, holds that only a part is prompt. This part is to be fixed with reference to:

(i) Custom

(ii) The status of the parties

(iii) The amount of settled dower

There are two aspects of the prompt dower or mahr (mahr-i-muajjal)–the time factor and the quantum factor. Prompt in theory means immediately on demand or at the time of marriage, or at any time before consummation, or after consummation. In practice however, it is seldom paid promptly at the time of marriage or even when demanded; or equally tardily demanded. The fear of annoying the husband; of his pronouncing talaq in retaliation of vengeful ouster by him–factors like these choke the demand.

(ii) *Unspecified mahr or dower*–In such cases where mahr is settled at the time of the marriage or after, it is fixed with reference to the social position of the wife's family and her own personal qualifications. Help would be taken by taking into account the amount of the Hedaya, the wife's age, beauty, intellect and virtue will also be considered. Such mahr's are called mahr-ul-misl.

One aspect of the mahr beneficial to the Muslim woman is that even where the parties to the marriage have not stipulated any mahr the husband remains under an obligation to pay it. Only under the Ithna Ashari law an adult wife can waive the requirement of mahr. Under other schools of Muslim law, even where the wife stipulates that she will not demand any mahr, she remains entitled to it and the rule of estoppel with not apply to her. This implied mahr is called proper mahr or customary mahr (mahr-i-misl).

Minimum and Maximum Amounts of Mahr

Minimum–According to Hanafis it is 10 dirhams where as according to Malikis it is 3dirhams. But among Shafiis and Shias there is no minimum amount of mahr. The amount of money fixed for mahr varies from 11/4 surkh dinar to any amount 11/4 surkh dinar is the sharai mahr or the mahr which is adjusted as the ideal amount fixed by the prophet.

Maximum–Among the sunnis there is no maximum; any amount may be fixed. Fyzee cities an example based on his personal knowledge, of a mahr amount of Rs. 2,20,00,000. But normally the amount of mahr depends on the girl's family status. The more financially well established and renowned the family is more is the amount of mahr fixed (Moinuddin 2000:112). Some people consider it as security for woman and fix large sum of money as mahr. "Dower is often high among Mohammedans, to prevent the husband from divorcing his wife, in which case he would have to pay the amount stipulated [Zakeri Begum V. Sakina Begum (1982) 191. A. 157,165,19 Cal. 689]. Yet bargaining is very much there over the amount of mahr. Sometimes, such bargaining leads to unpleasant occurrences and cancellation of marriage. The girl's parents always desire to fix a high amount which ought to be beyond the means of the bridegroom so that daughter will not have to face the threat of divorce from her husband in future. Among some of the sects of Shias, however, there is a tendency not to stipulate for a sum higher than the minimum fixed by the Prophet for his favorite daughter Fatima, the wife of Ali, namely 500 dirhams (Rs. 100 approximately).

From the above discussion, we may say that in Islam, marriage is nothing but a contract. Islamic law permits a man to take as many as four wives at any given time, subject only to the proviso that he must treat all of them equally and justly. Woman's legal rights in respect of marriage and divorce are not only inferior to those of men, but are completely out of harmony with the demands of the modern time. Religion makes the husband, the family head and expects the wife to obey and serve him.

THE QURAN (SURAH 4:3) SAYS

And if have reason to fear that you might not act equitably towards orphans, then marry from among (other) women such as are lawful to you–two, or three, or four; but if you have reason to fear that you might not be able to treat them with equal fairness, then (only) one–or (from among) those whom you rightfully possess. This will make it more likely that you will not deviate from the right course.

All these provisions ensure the predominance of men over women and this is sanctified by religion. Bhatty (1976), a sociologist says, a Muslim man can have up to four wives, with no legal protection to the woman against the exercise of this privilege. The law does not admit polygamy as a cause for seeking divorce by Muslim woman. Of course, the corresponding right of a woman to have more than one husband in any circumstances is inconceivable, much less is granted under law....A man can divorce at will just by uttering the words 'I divorce you' three times, anywhere, at anytime without any witness. He is also not required by law to give any maintanence to the wife beyond the period of Iddat, which are three months and a few days after divorce. If a man divorces his wife, he is obliged to pay mahr, a sum of money agreed upon at the time of marriage. This provision is also taken as a security for Muslim women against easy divorce. But as long as the right to have four wives continues to be enjoyed by a man ,he need not divorce his wife if he does not wish to pay mahr he can simply discard her, or ill treat her, while taking another wife... so as to every stage Muslim law is fettered with inequalities, with the woman in every case being less equal.

MUSLIM LAW OF DIVORCE

The Muslim law of divorce is found upon expressed injunctions contained in the Quran, as well as in the traditions. Islam permits dissolution or rather break of relations between husband and wife. The Arabic word, talak is usually rendered as 'repudiation', it comes from root tollaqa, which means to release (an animal) from a letter; hence, to repudiate the wife or free her from the bondage of marriage. Divorce among Muslim is a complex subject where aspects of Islamic jurisprudence, customary regulations of gender roles, prescriptions of Qur'anic verses and related aspects of everyday living are inextricably intertwined. The event of divorce in the fields of biography, society and history scarcely offer easy determinants and designs.

When we discuss divorce in Muslim communities, the tendency quite often is to place theology and law at the centre. Of course, to say so the intention is not to suggest that the theological and legal perspectives on divorce in Muslim communities in India are not in themselves important or relevant. Divorce is fundamentally a legal process. A marriage can be terminated by desertion or even dissolved informally, but a couple is not considered divorced unless the dissolution of their marriage has been sanctioned by law. However, law is only one of the variables that comes into interplay and contributes to the incidence of divorce. Other more potent factors are social attitudes towards marriage, the personal commitment of the spouses to sustaining their marriage, the presence of social support necessary for a marriage to continue and the factors that affect possibilities of conflict resolution that lead to marital breakdown. Phillips (Ahmad 2003:29) rightly comments:

Divorce is not an isolated legal event that is unrelated to other personal, familial and social actions and circumstances, but is the final stage of a marital process. In crude and schematic terms the main stages of the process are marriage, marital tensions, and the decision by one or both spouses to terminate the marriage, and finally its legal dissolution by divorce. Some, however, might go the point of breakdown without any manifestation of it in social or legal terms. Yet other broken marriages are terminated socially, the spouses living apart independently without the intervention of law. At each stage of the process, then, proportion of the total population of marriages goes no further.

Professor Ahmed (ibid: 13) has also expressed the same view. To him divorce in Muslim community entails substantial theological and legal dimensions, but takes as its point of departure the view that it is only by placing divorce in the social and cultural context that meaningful conclusions can be arrived at. So in our understanding of Muslim divorce, first we try to analyze or discuss the legal aspects and then we observe the practice of divorce in Muslim society.

The teaching of the subject is as follows:

The Cow

Surah 2,226

Those who swear to keep away from their wives (with intent of divorcing them) have four months to grace; then if they reconcile (during this period), surely Allah is forgiving and kind.

Surah 2, 227

And if they are bent on divorce, Allah heeds all and knows everything.

Surah 2, 228

Women, who are divorced, have to wait for three monthly periods, and if they believe in Allah and the Last day must not hide unlawfully what Allah has formed within their wombs. Their husbands would do well to take them back in that case, if they wished to be reconciled. Women also have recognized rights as men have through men had an advantage over them. But Allah is almighty and all-wise.

Surah 2, 229

Divorce is (revocable) two times (after pronouncement), after which (there are two ways open for husband), either (to) keep (the wives) honorably, or part with them in a decent way. You are not allowed to take away the least of what you have given your wives, unless both of you fear that you would not be able to keep within the limits set by Allah. If you fear you can not maintain the bond fixed by Allah, there will be no blame on either if the woman redeems herself. Do not exceed the limits of Allah, for those who exceed the bond set by Allah are transgressors.

Surah 2,230

If a man divorces her again (a third time), she becomes unlawful for him (and he can not marry her) until she has married another man. Then if he divorces her there is no harm if the two utite again if they think they will keep within the bonds set by Allah and made clear for those who understand.

Surah 2, 231

When you have divorced your wives, and they reached the end of the period of waiting, then keep them honorably (by revoking the divorce), or let them go with honor, and do not detain them with the intent of harassing lest you should transgress. He who does so will wrong himself. Do not mock the decrees of Allah, and remember the favors Allah has bestowed on you of the consequences of doing wrong. Have fear of Allah and remember, Allah is cognizant of everything.

Surah 2, 232

When you have divorced your wives and they have completed the fixed term (of waiting), do not stop them from marrying other men if it is agreed between them honorably. This warning is for those among you who belief in Allah and the Last Day. This is for those among you who believe in Allah and Last Day. This is both proper and right for you, for Allah Knows and you do not know.

Surah 2, 236

There is no sin in divorcing your wives before the consummation of marriage or setting the dowry; but then provide adequately for them, the affluent according to their means, the poor in accordance with theirs as is befitting. This is surely the duty of those who do good.

Surah 2, 237

And if you divorce them before the consummation of marriage, but after setting the dowry; then half settled dowry must be paid, unless the woman forgoes it, or the person who holds the bond of marriage pays the full amount. And if the man pays the whole, it is never to piety. But do not forget to be good to each other, and remember that Allah sees all that you do.

Surah 2,241

Making a fair provision for women who are divorced is the duty of those who are Allah–fearing and pious.

Surah 2,242

So does Allah pronounce His decrees that you may understand.

In the Shah Bano Case (1986), the main problem arose with the interpretation of the two aiyats (verses), 241 and 242 of Surah 2 of the Quran, which argue that is an obligation on Muslim husbands to provide for their divorced wives. The Arabic version of those aiyats and their English translations are as follows.

Arabic Version	*English Version*
aiyat 241	
wa lil motallaqatay	for divorced woman
mataun	maintenance (should be provided)
bil maaroofay	on a reasonable scale
haqqan	this is a duty
alal muttaqeena	on the righteous
aiyat 242	
Kazaleka yubaiyyanullaho	thus doth Allah
lakum ayatehee la allakum	make clear His signs
taqeloon	to you, in order that you may understand.

To some, the main problems arise with the word, Mata, in aiyat 241 which means 'provision' and not 'maintenance'. For having some clear idea of these two aiyats we can quote some translation done by some learned scholars on the subject.

The translation of aiyats 240 to 242 in the meaning of the Quran reads thus:

Those of you, who shall die and leave wives behind them, should make a will to the effect that they should be provided with a year's maintenance and should not be turned out of their homes. But if they leave their homes of their own accord, you shall not be answerable for whatever they choose for themselves in a fair way; Allah is All powerful, All-wise. (Likewise, the divorced women should also be given something.

This is an obligation upon the Allah fearing people.)

Surah 2, 242

Thus Allah makes clear His commandments for you; it is expected that you will use your common sense.

Allama Abdulla Yusuf Ali's translation (1982) runs as follows:

For divorce women maintenance would be provided on a reasonable scale. Thus is a duty on the righteous.

Pickthall (1930) reads it as:

Surah 2, 241

For divorce women a provision in Kindness: a duty for those who ward off (evil).

Then again, we find some provisions on talaq in chapter 4 of the Quran under the heading, 'The Women':

The Women

Surah 4, 35

If you fear a breach between them appoint one arbiter from the people of the man and one from the people of the woman. If they wish to have a settlement then Allah will reconcile them, for Allah is all knowing and cognisant.

Surah 4, 128

If a woman fears ill-treatment from her husband or his tiring of her, there is no harm if they make a peaceful settlement, and peace is an excellent thing. Yet avarice is part of man's nature. If you do good and fear Allah, Allah is cognisant of all that you do.

Surah 4, 130

If both (decide to) separate, Allah in his largesse will provide for them; for Allah is infinite and all wise. The again, in the chapter 'The Allied Troops' we find:

O you who believe, when you marry believing women, then divorce them before having (sexual) contact with them, you have no right to demand observance of the 'waiting period' of them. But provide suitably for them, and let them go with honour.

In chapter 65 of the Quran there are also some provision on talaq.

Divorce

Surah 65, 1

O prophet when you divorce women, divorce them at their appointed period, and calculate that period, and fear Allah, your lord. Do not expel them from their houses, nor should they go away themselves, unless they are openly guilty of adultery. These are the limits set by Allah. And any one who exceeds the limits set by Allah sins against his own self.

Surah 65, 2

When they have reached their appointed time, then either keep them lawfully or let them go honorably; but have two witnesses from among you, and give truthful evidence for (being acceptable to) Allah. This is to warn him who believes in Allah and Last Day. Allah will furnish a way out for him who fears Him.

Surah 65, 4

As for your women who have lost hope of menstruation, and in case you have a doubt, the prescribed period (of waiting) for them is three months, as also those who have not menstruated yet. As for those who are pregnant, their prescribed period is until the delivery of the child. Allah will make things easy for him who is mindful of Allah.

Surah 65, 6

House the (divorced) women where you live, according to your means; but do not harass them so as to reduce them to straitened circumstances. If they are pregnant, then spend on them until they give birth to the child. And if they suckle the child for you, then make the due payment to them, and consult each other appropriately. But if you find this difficult, let some other woman suckle (the child) for her.

If we go through the uttering of the Quran on divorce then we can mention different modes of divorce. The contract of marriage in Islam may be dissolved in any one of the following ways: (i) by the husband at his will, without the intervention of the court; (ii) by mutual consent of the husband and wife, without the intervention of the court; and (iii) by the judicial decree at the suit of the husband or wife. The wife cannot divorce herself from her husband without his consent, except under a contract whether made before or after marriage, but she may, in some cases, obtain a divorce by judicial decree.

We are to remember that when the divorce proceeds from the husband, it is called talaq; when it is affected by mutual consent, it is called Khula or mubara'at according to the terms of contract between the parties. And Muslim of sound mind, who has attained puberty, may divorce his wife whenever he desires without assigning any cause.

A talaq may be effected (i) orally (by spoken words), or (ii) by a written document called a teleqnama.

In oral talaq, no particular forms of words are prescribed for affecting a talaq. Some Mohammedan jurists argue that if the words are expressed (saheeh) or well understood as implying divorce no proof of intention is required. It is the words are ambiguous (kinayat) the intention must be proved. This argument has been given in some cases like Ma Miv. Kallandar Ammal, Spura; Asha Bibi v. Kadir (1909) 33 Mad. 22,31. C. 730.

On the other hand, it is not necessary that the talaq should be pronounced in the presence of the wife or even addressed to her. What is required most is to name the wife. In a Calcutta case (Furzund Hussain V. Janu Bibee (1878) 4 Cal. 588) the husband merely pronounced the word 'talaq' before a family council and this was held to be invalid as the wife was not named. If the talaq pronounced in the absence of the wife takes effect though not communicated to her, but for purpose of mahr it is necessary that it should come to her Knowledge (Fulchand

V. Nazib ali, Supra and her alimony may continue till she is informed of the divoree (Ma Mi V. Kallandar Ammal, supra; Abdul Khader V. Azeaza Bec (1994) I.M.L.J. 17, 214 IC 38, (1944) A.M. 227).

Talaq in Writing

A talaqnama may only be the record of the fact of an oral talaq; or it may be the deed by which the divorce is effected. The deed may be executed in the (a) presence of the Qazi or of the (b) wife's father or of (c) other witnesses. The deed is said to be in the customary form if it is properly super scribed and addressed so as to show the name of the writer and the person addressed. If it is not so super scribed and addressed it is said to be in unusual form. If the deed is in customary form and manifest, the intention to divorce is presumed. Otherwise, the intention of the divorce must be proved. It is to be noted here that communication within a reasonable time is not necessary and the talaqnama operates from the date of execution. If an acknowledgement of divorce is made by the husband, the divorce will be held to take effect at least from the date upon which the acknowledgement is made. (Asmat Ullah V. Khatun-un-nisa [1939] All. 763)

Malik (1987: 144) and Hidayatullah (1972: 297) discussed divorce under three broad headings: ahasan talaq, hasam talaq and talaq-al-bida.

To divorce his wife, according to the most acceptable form, a *hasan talaq,* the husband utters a single word, talâq and abstains from marital intercourse with her for a period of three months during which reconciliation is possible and the divorce revocable. If the husband explicitly revokes it by resuming co-habitation, the effect of the talaq is nullified and the marriage continues. If the husband does not revoke the talaq during the said period, the divorce becomes final at the end of the three months.

Hidayatullah (1972) argues that when the marriage has not been consummated, a talâq in the ahsan form may by pronounced even if the wife is in her menstruation. Where the wife has passed the age for periods of menstruation the requirement of a declaration during the tuhr (period between menstruation) is inapplicable; furthermore, this requirement only applies to an oral divorce and not a divorce in writing.

The less approved form of divorce (*hasan talaq*) involves a procedure by which the husband pronounces a talaq once a month for three consecutive months. According to some Mohammedan jurists, this consists of three pronouncements made during successive tuhrs, no intercourse taking place during any of the three tuhrs. The first pronouncement should be made during a tuhr, the second during the next tuhr, and the third during the succeeding tuhr.

The most reprehensible form of divorce and, by far, the most common (talaq-ul-bidaat or talaq-i-badai) is when the husband simply makes three pronouncements immediately during a single tuhr either in one sentence, e,g., "I divorce three thrice", or in a separate sentence, e.g. [Amir-ul-din V. Khatun Bibi (1917) 39 All. 39. I.C. 513].

The Hanafi recognizes two kinds of talaq, namely:

(a) *Talaq-us-sunnat,* that is, talaq according to the rules laid down in the *sunnat,* i.e., traditions of the prophet, i.e., or Talaq–us-sunnat is two kinds, namely, (i) ahsan, that is most proper, and (ii) hasan, that is, proper. In the case of talaq ahsan and talaq hasan, the husband has an opportunity of reconsidering his decision, for the talaq in both these cases does not become absolute until a certain period had elapsed, and the husband the option to revoke it before then.

(b) *Talaq-ul-biddat,* i.e., new or irregular talaq. Some jurists call it talaq al-bid'ah, i.c. innovative form of divorce. Talaq-ul-biddat was first introduced by the Omeyyade monarchs in the second century of the Mohammedan era. Some scholars argued that talaq-ul-biddat is good in law, through bad in theology, and it is the most common and prevalent mode of divorce among the Sunni Muslims in our country.

It is not that all agreed in its practice. There are the differences among the great Islamic jurists regarding its permissibility. Imam Abu Hanafi and Imam Malik, two great jurists of Islam, argue that the three divorces in one sitting in bid'ah i.e. an innovation and so this form of divorce not permissible. Whereas Imam Shafa'I, the fourth great Imam and jurist, thinks that this form of divorce is permissible and is the husband's right.

From this general understanding of divorce or talaq we may ask the question of when does talaq become irrevocable. These are as follows:

A talaq is the *ahsan* mode becomes irrevocable and complete or the expiration of the period of iddat.

A talaq in *hasan* mode becomes irrevocable and complete or the third pronouncement.

A talaq in the *badai* mode becomes irrevocable immediately after it is pronounced. There is no need for waiting the iddat period in this case. As it becomes irrevocable immediately, it is called talaq-i-bain, that is, irrevocable talaq.

Women's Right to Divorce

Islam also recognizes the women's right to divorce. In Islam a marriage may be dissolved not only by talaq which is the arbitrary act of the husband. A dissolution of marriage by agreement may take the form of *Khula or mubara'at*. This type of divorce is accepted by an offer from the side of the wife to compensate the husband if he releases her from his marital rights and acceptance by the husband of the offer. Once the offer is accepted by the husband, it operates as a single irrevocable divorce i.e. talaq-i-bain and its operation is not postponed until execution of the Khulanama (deed of the Khula).

A divorce by Khula is a divorce with the consent, and at the instance of the wife, in which she gives or agrees to give a consideration to the husband for her release from the marriage tie. In such a case, the terms of the bargain are matters of arrangement between the husband and wife and the wife may, as the consideration, release her dyn-mahr (dower) and other rights or may make any other agreement for the benefit of the husband (this kind of judgement was given in the case of Monshee Buzul-ul-Rahim V.Luteefutoon-Nisa (1861) 8 M.I.A.

379,395). Failure on the part of the wife to pay the consideration for the divorce does not invalidate the divorce [(1861) 8 M.I.A. 379, 397-398 SUPRA], though the husband may sue the wife for it.

Regarding talaq the Prophet had a mixed reaction. The teaching of the prophet Mohammed on the general subject of divorce is expressed in the traditions as follows:

The thing which is lawful but disliked by Allah is divorce. There are three things which whether done in jest or in earnest, shall be considered serious and effectual, namely, marriage, divorce and taking a wife back.

The prophet is reported to have conveyed his indignation to a man who pronounced three talaqs in one sitting (Nasa'i) and annuled a talaq pronounced three times without intervals (Ibn Hanbal). The prophet is reported to have also disapproved women demanding talaq from their husbands without sufficient reasons. A tradition laid down that the three talaq should be pronounced during the three period of purity (i.e., the non-menses period) and the husband should not have any intercourse during period to make the talaq binding and irrevocable (Bukhari) (Lokhandwala 1987:71).

But in reality there is a wide divergence between theory and practice regarding marriage and divorce. We have conducted a survey on divorced and separated Muslim women living in two Gram Panchayats in two districts of West Bengal i.e. Panchthupi Gram Panchayat in Murshidabad district and Mongolkate Gram Panchayat in Barddhaman dictrict.

Seventy divorced/separated Muslim Women were interviewed in Monglokate Gram panchayat among whom 31 respondents were divorcees and 39 separated. In panchthupi Gram Panchyat 58 respondents were interviewed among whom 36 respondents were divorcees and 22 were separated. For gaining an understanding of the problem it is imperative to analyze at first the nature of the two categories of the population i.e. 'divorced and separated Muslim women'.

"Divorced' Muslim women are those whose talaq or release from marriage has occurred in the presence of legal authorities or local elderly people. Here legal authorities mean Moulana,

Mauluvi, Imam, while local elderly people mean those who have their authority for witnessing such action. It also includes those cases in which release from the marriage tie has occurred in the court.

On the other hand, 'separated' Muslim women are those who at present are living with their parents and do not have any connection with their husbands. These women however, may harbour the fond hope that their husbands would one day give due recognition to them and take them back with honour.

Divergence between theory and practice will be very evident if we examine the three broad perspectives of marriage and talaq, i.e. consent of the bride for marriage, mahr (bride money) and iddat (three menstrual cycle).

It is to be noted here that Islamic law makes it compulsory to obtain the consent of the bride for marriage. Her marriage depends on her approval being given on her own conditions. The proposal comes from the man and the acceptance is made on behalf of the woman by her wali (The marriage guadian). The ijab and qubul-as the consent of the marrying parties is called-are mandatory; though differences exist in the modalities of obtaining consent. However, our survey reveals that only 16 out of 58 parents (roughly 27.6%) in Murshidabad took the consent of their daughters for marriage. The corresponding figure for Barddhaman is much higher, nearly 71.5 per cent (the above figure relates to information provided by the divorced women themselves. When the parents were interviewed, the same question evoked a different response. However, the differences can be ignored). This is a clear indication that in Murshidabad, in particular, there is wide divergence between theory and practice regarding marriage. We may rightly observe that:

.... The jaliliyah practice of contracting marriage by her wali (marriage guarding) on her behalf re-established itself and her approval was reduced to a mere nod or silence. From playing an active role in marriage she came to be relegated to a passive position.

As far as divorce is concerned, it was observed that knowledge of rules and regulation about talaq as laid down in the Quran and Haditts was limited to a very small group of interviewees in Barddhaman. Strangely enough, none of the interviewees from Murshidabad all divorced/separated Muslim women-possessed any information about the religious viewpoints.

The Quran is very specific on the question of iddat (i.e. three menstrual cycles). The condition of a woman during iddat is dealt with only in Surah al-Baqarah, chapter 2 of the Holy Quran but in the Surah Al-Talaq, chapter 65. The relevant provisions are as follows:

Surah 2,228

Women who are divorced have to wait for three monthly periods, and if they believe in Allah and the Last Day they must not hide unlawfully that Allah has formed within their wombs. Their husbands would do well to take them back in that case, if they wish to be reconciled. Women also have recognized rights as men have, though men an advantage over them. But Allah is all-mighty and all-wise.

Surah 2,231

When you have divorced our wives, and if they reached the end of the period of waiting, then keep them go with honour, and do not detain them with the intent of harassing lest you should transgress. He who does so will wrong himself. Do not mock the decrees of Allah, and remember the favours Allah has bestowed on you, and revealed to you the Book and the law to warm you of the consequences of doing wrong. Have fear of Allah, and remember, Allah is cognisant of everything.

Surah 2,232

When you have divorced your wives and they have completed the fixed term (of waiting), do not stop them from marrying other men if it is agreed between them honorably. This warning is for those among you who believe in Allah and the Last Day.

This is both proper and right for you, for Allah knows and you do not know.

Surah 65,1

When you have to divorce women, pronounce divorce only when they are in free state (i.e. free from menses or pregnancy).... Do not turn them out of their houses....Allah may perhaps bring about reconciliation between you.

Surah 65,2

And when they reach their prescribed term, either retain them with kindness or part from them in a just or gentle manner. Take two upright witnesses to the transaction.... Allah will show a way to the righteous for honorable reconciliation or an honorable parting.

Surah 65,4

The prescribed term of waiting is three months except for pregnant women whom time is extended till they have laid down their burden...

Surah 6 5,6

Lodge them (women in iddat) where ye yourselves lodge and let them live in a style ye yourselves live....

In our field study, we found that no one in Murshidabad or Barddhaman has observed the tenets laid down in the Quran. If we look a bit deeper into the data collected, the said divergence between theory and practice regarding divorce becomes even more marked.

Wide variation is also to be found in case of mahr. In Islam, marriage is a contract between persons belonging to two opposite sexes. The consideration of the contract is mahr gift too the bride, the amount of which, not being fixed by law varies from dinar upwards. Without mahr a marriage can not be said to have been properly solemnized. It is the exclusive right of the woman or bride to determine the amount. And the mahr belongs to the wife alone. The mahr money has been given to the bride as a token of love, fidelity and sincerity. The Quran (24,4)

> 'And give women their dowries as free gift. But if themselves be placed to give you portion thereof, consume it with enjoyment and pleasure'.

Mahr is defined as a sum of money or other property which the wife entitled to received from the husband in consideration of the marriage. Paras diwan(Shah Bano Case) has contradicted this view. He criticizes this definition on the ground that mahr is not payable "in consideration of marriage", but is an obligation imposed by law on the husband as a mark of respect for the wife, as is evident from the fact that non-specification of mahr at the time of marriage does not affect the validity of marriage.

Without entering into the debate, we are here concerned with finding out whether mahr is an amount payable by the husband to the wife on divorcé. the main reason behind our confusion is that, the amount of mahr is usually split into two parts, one of which is called "prompt", which is payable on demand, and the other is called 'deferred', which is payable on the dissolution of marriage by death or divorce. But the fact is that deferred mahr payable at the time of the dissolution of marriage, can not justify the conclusion that it is payable on divorce.

It is usually asserted that the mahr is a good security for the woman in case of any difficulties in her marital life, and when she is divorced the mahr money has to be given to her. However, we see from our data that only two out of 128 women interviewed got mahr. Can there be any better evidence of the gulf of difference between theory and practice of divorce in the Muslim community of West Bengal?

REFERENCES

Abdul Samad, S.V. AIR 1926 Cal. 1144.

Aga Mohamed, A.R.V. 1893. 21, 1A, 56.

Bhatty, Z. (1976), 'Status of Muslim Women and Social Change'. in B. R. Nanda (ed.). *Indian Women: From Purdah to Modernity*. New Delhi: Vikas Publishing House.

Engineer, A. A. (1992), *The Right of Women in Islam* New Delhi: Sterling Publishers Privet Limited .

FakherJung, S. Q. V. AIR 1953, Hyd. 6

Fyzee, A.A.A. (1963), A Modern Approval to Islam, New Delhi: Asia Publishing House.

Fyzee, A.A.A (1987), *Outlines of Mohammedan Law*. 4th ed. Delhi, Oxford.

Hanfi, A. M. A. (1954), *Al Mar 'ah-fialsh'ar al jahili*, Cairo

Hidayatullah, M. (1972), *Mulla Principles of Mohammedan Law*. Bombay: N.M. Tripathi Pvt. Ltd.

Imtiaz A. (2003) (ed.), *Divorce and Remarriage among Muslim in India:* New Delhi, Manohar.

Lokhandwala, S. T. (1987), 'The Position of Woman under Islam'. In Asghar Ali Engineer (ed.), *Status of Women in Islam*, New Delhi: Ajanta Publication.

Malik, R. (1987), *Nari Samaj O Islami Siksha* (in Bengali), Dhaka: Islamic Foundations.

Moinuddin, S. A. H. (2000), *Divorce and Muslim Women*. Jaipur and New Delhi: Rawat Publication.

Mumtaj Begum, M.Y.V. AIR (1936), Lah. 1716.

Pickthall, M. (1930), *The Meaning of the Glorious Quran. Text and Explanatory Translation*, Karachi: Tax Company Limited.

Rashid, S. K. (1999), *Muslim Law*, Lucknow: Eastern Book Company.

Sanai Badar, F. A.V. AIR (1923), Nag 262.

Shah Bano Case (1986), *Shariat and the Muslim Women (Protection of Rights on Divorce)* Act,Published by the Judical Department, Govt. of West Bengal.

Shushtery, A. M. A. (1972), *Outlines of Islamic Culture*. Bangalore:The Bangalore Printing and Publishing Company Ltd.

Yusuf Ali, A. A. (1982), *The Meaning of the Illustrious Quran*, New Delhi: Kitab Bhaban.

Zahedunnissa, M.V. AIR (1941), Cal. 657.

Section Four

Women in Politics

9

Women and Politics in India–Quotas as Antidote to Marginalization

SWAPAN KUMAR PRAMANICK

The debate relating to the nature of political representation of women and the issue of quotas has pervaded the political arena in India during the last one decade. Ever since the constitution (73rd Amendment) Bill was accepted in 1993 giving one third right of representation to women in Panchayat Raj institutions (local self government bodies), the debate has been continuing on whether and how far women are capable of exercising this right; whether this right is to be extended to Assemblies and Parliament, the highest legislative bodies in India and whether reservation is a correct method of enhancing the political participation of women.

Against this debate, this paper is concerned with the examination and analysis of three important but related issues connected with the participation of women in politics in India, viz, (1) the increasing marginalization and peripheralization of women in politics in India accompanied by a situation where politics itself is getting marginalized due to nonparticipation of all decent people, including women; (2) the paradoxical attitude of male dominated politics and political parties towards the question of reservation for women in the political arena. This is the result of a situation where 75 per cent of men and 79 per cent of women favour active participation of women in politics and reservation for them in legislatures[1] but where, in actuality, only 7.9 per cent of seats are held by women in the Indian Parliament. The argument is that it is the result of widespread depoliticization of our society; and (3) the nature and effect of 33 per cent reservation of seats and offices for women in Panchayats. The analysis has been made, with reference to empirical studies done in rural areas in a few states in India, particularly in the state of West Bengal.

Unlike in many western countries, right to equal political participation for women including their right to vote was granted to women in India almost automatically with independence. Not only that women did not have to fight for that but also there was a large measure of sympathy and support for women. This support for women's rights was the result of a historical legacy where women participated in the political process and fought valiantly along with men against British rule. They participated extensively, in urban and rural areas alike, drawing thousands of them from the working classes and the peasantry as also from the urban middle classes to fight against British rule and to undergo all sorts of tortures, including imprisonment, as a consequence of that. Mahatma Gandhi had a big role to play in encouraging women to participate in the freedom movement. To him the struggle for women's equality was an integral part of the movement for *Swaraj*. His method of non-violent *Satyagraha* as a form of movement was also particularly suitable for women. It is no accident that women joined in large number in this form of movement as compared with the radical stream of movement as sponsored by the extremists[2]. So, not only the elitist sections of women, ordinary women joined in thousands as the forms and messages of movement were nearer their heart and corresponded their experience. Nehru has said on this point "our women came to the forefront and took charge of the struggle. Women had always been there, of course, but now there was an avalanche of them which took not only the British Government but their own menfolk by surprise. There were women, women of the upper and middle classes, leading sheltered lives in their houses, peasant women , working class women, rich women-pouring out in their tens of thousands in defiance of government orders and police lathis".[3] As a result of this, the women's movement reached its peak in the 1930's and 1940's.

From this high position, women's participation in politics began to decline since independence. Even in 1952, when a large number of women freedom fighters were active and in the fray, the Congress Party had only 14 women members elected to Parliament. They constituted no more than 4.4 per cent of the total members of Parliament. In spite of their tremendous contributions to the Congress Party, they were marginalized even within the Congress and had hardly any control over the decision making apparatus. Here again perhaps Gandhiji's influence worked as he demanded that women should enter the public life in a spirit of selfless sacrifice and their motto should be more service to society than grabbing of power. As he said in an inimitable style, "And you sisters, what would you do by going to Parliament? Do you aspire after collectorships, commissionerships or even the viceroyalty? I know that you would not care to, for the viceroy has got to order executions and hangings, a thing that you would heartily detest".[4]

As a result of all these, politics in India got masculinised along with its increasing bureaucratization, criminalization and corruption. What is more worrying is that this was not the result of women withdrawing from public life. In fact, with increasing literacy and spread of consciousness among women, they established themselves in every walk of life. They became successful lawyers, doctors, architects, bureaucrats, executives, engineers. Though they were lesser in number compared with men, they proved their capacities beyond doubt. But as far as politics was concerned, either they were not interested or they were not given entry. If politics means service to the community, then women were certainly interested, as they joined in large number in transformative politics, in community based action programmes and in associating themselves with

NGOs and voluntary organizations. But they have not shown their interest in institutionalized or electoral politics. The nature of political process in post independent India, the adverse attitude of the major political parties towards granting position to women in politics and the norms of patriarchy–all combined to alienate women from politics. As Madhu Keshwar has stated, " marginalization of women (in politics) is integrally linked with the marginalization of all decent people from our party politics".[5] As regards the representation of women in Parliament given by the major political parties, she says, "Even after all the major parties had promised 33 per cent reservation for women in legislatures, they all reverted back to tokenism when it actually came to giving party tickets for the 1996 Lok Sabha election. The Congress (I) fielded only 49 women out of a total of 530 candidates. The BJP gave tickets to 23 women out of a total of its 477 candidates. The CPI (M) gave five seats to women out of 77, while the CPI fielded four women out of 43 candidates. The Janata Dal fielded 11 women out of 220 candidates".[6]

FIGHTING AGAINST DEPOLITICIZATION THROUGH PANCHAYATS

The process of depoliticization of women continued inspite of constitutional provisions stipulating equal rights for women in every sphere of life. Increasing awareness and concern about women's lack of power became a major public issue since the 70's. In 1977 the Government of India appointed a committee on the status of women in India to undertake a "Comprehensive examination of all the questions relating to the rights and status of women". The committee noted the failure of the earlier policy to induct women into local government bodies through reservation of a few seats as a form of tokenism and recommended the establishment of statutory rights of women in panchayats at the village level to ensure greater participation on their part. Several other factors like the International Women's Year in 1975, International Women's Decade 1975–1985, the formulation of a National Perspective Plan for women (1988) and the establishment of a National Commission for

Women in 1992 along with the demand of the society including women activists to grant more space for women in public life –all contributed to this increased awareness about the political empowerment of women.

The case for women entering in large number in political decision making bodies would ensure the demands of equity and justice for them. The other effects of women entry are, as stated by Nanivadekar that "they will change the whole texture of present day politics. They will bring different values, preferences and perspectives into the political arena. Women's issues will find high priority on the agenda of political parties. Women's presence in decision making positions will lead to the elimination of discrimination against women".[7]

It was a result of all these that the 73rd Constitution Amendment Bill was passed in 1993. But the development was not sudden as even before that in various commission/ committee reports, recommendations were there for granting more space to women. The Balbantrai Mehta Committee (1957) did not give much of attention to the question of women participation in Panchayats. But the committee on the status of women (1974) favoured the establishment of statutory all women Panchayats at the village level with resources for the management and administration of women and child development programmes. The Ashok Mehta Committee (1978) recommended reservation of two seats for women in Panchayats and to co-opt them, if they did not come through elections in order to ensure 'greater representation of women in the panchayat bodies and participation in the elective process'. The National Perspective Plan (1988), on the other hand, recommended 30 per cent reservation for women in all local self government agencies and a similar reservation for executive posts in all the three tiers of panchayats.

Many states had also introduced reservation of seats for women through legislative changes before the 73rd Amendment Act though the percent of reservation varied from 10 per cent as in Madhya Pradesh to 33 percent as in West Bengal. In Kerela, through an Act of 1984, there was a 30 per cent reservation for women in the District Councils of Kerela. In

Orissa, 30 per cent reservation of seats for women in panchayats was introduced in 1990. In West Bengal, through the West Bengal Panchayat (Amendment) Act, 1992, provision was made for compulsory reservation of one third of the total seats in Panchayats for women. In Karnataka, through an Act of 1985, 25 per cent of seats had to be reserved for women in the Panchayat.[8]

The 73rd constitution Amendment Bill provided for 1/3 reservation of women in the three tiers of Panchayat in all the elective seats and offices. It also envisaged a significant structural change in the process of decentralisation of power and development planning at the local level by assigning to Panchayats (a) preparation of plans for economic development and social justice; (b) implementation of schemes for economic development and social justice in relation to matters listed in the XI th Schedule (which includes 29 items).[9]

It is interesting to note that the same Parliament which passed this Bill guaranteeing 1/3 reservation of seats in Panchayats has faced political paralysis in so far as the question of extending 1/3 reservation of seats in Parliament and state legislatures is concerned. In spite of providing lip service to the issue, most of the political parties has faced dissensions within their rank on this question. In view of the potential threat to the position, power and privileges of a male dominated Parliament, the Bill has been shelved for the last seven years. It seems that so far as granting powers to women at the level of Panchayats are concerned, this can be done without much of debate but in so far as vital decision making bodies like the Parliament or the state legislatures are concerned, women cannot be granted that much of power-sharing right. Attempts are now being made to reduce the quota from 1/3 to a lower figure acceptable to all the parties. As the Prime Minister has told the Parliament that 'legislation of such social importance cannot be enacted without a consensus' as it requires 'persuasion and accommodation'. So without minimising the significance of women's participation at the level of the Panchayats, it may be argued that the dominance of 'Patriarchy' in our society is proved by the fate of the Bill on Women's reservation in Parliament.

DEBATE ON GENDER QUOTA AS AN INSTRUMENT OF EMPOWERMENT

Doubts are often raised about the effectivity of gender quota as an instrument for equity and equality for women. An interventionist strategy like enforcing women's reservation may not be helpful for women themselves, it is argued. What is necessary, is to build up a congenial social environment wherein women will feel empowered. Political power will automatically come out of that. As it has been said 'to try and push reforms without necessary social support is mere adventurism, mere symbolism ... the damaging impact of ill thought intervention, even if the intention is noble, is no less serious than inaction and paralysis'[10]. The real issue is to address the underlying causes of women's exclusion rather than enforcing a reservation. Secondly, questions are also raised about the 'representational' character of women. Given their multiple and different locations in the polity, can there be a common status of women as a group? Will it not trap women in their identity as women? And what will happen about other identities based on class, religion or caste, for example? Thirdly, it is also argued that too much identification with organs of the state smacks of a 'growing statism' wherein a simple equation is drawn between reservations in the Parliament and empowerment of women. Empowerment is a multidimensional phenomenon, an insignificant part of which is in the sphere of political empowerment. In fact, it can be argued that if in the social and economic spheres there is dependence, then political empowerment will only result in proxy figures. As Keshwar has stated "the presence of such proxy figures in Parliament... is actually harmful. Political socialization of such women legislators, required for being an effective member of state assemblies and parliament, cannot take place smoothly when women members remain filially attached and politically dependent on the male party leaders".[11] Such proxies, instead of improving the position of women would further undermine their position as, basically, the proxies serve the patriarchal interests of the family and as such their participation in politics is itself patriarchal. Furthermore, proxies enter into the political arena for protecting the constituency of their male relatives and are prepared to vacate the same, once dereserved. Thus, their involvement in politics is not a means of self actualization and self-expression.[12]

But the arguments for gender quota in the context of the prevailing socio-economic situation in India are far more relevant. In a forceful argument for introducing quota for women, Vina Majumdar has stated that institutionalised inequalities require ' institutionalised counter measures' in the form of reservation. She argues that this legislation has brought about 'political dynamism' of women voters.[13] On the issue of identity of women as a group, it is true that women have also identities other than women. But the idea of group representation promotes the interests of smaller or less powerful groups under a system of majority rule. One has also to make a distinction between 'mirror representation' and 'elected representation'. The point is that women representatives will act as 'elected representatives'. The legitimacy of representation guarantees a certain freedom and flexibility on the part of the representatives to represent the heterogeneity of interests and not simply a particular form of identity. Thus, while identifying with women as women in some arenas of public life, working women can still identify with working men in other (overlapping) areas of public life.[14] Regarding the capacity of women to act independently, one is reminded of the famous statement of J S Mill that a child cannot walk, cannot be an argument of why he must not be allowed to learn to walk. The experience of elected women representatives show that in spite of some initial ambivalence, they have excellently adapted themselves to the requirements of the situation. In any case, "the presence of women benefited by their family connections should be treated as an inevitable part of the initial stage of the process of empowerment and should not be used as a tool against the policy of reservation. We find an equally large number of male politicians benefited due to the political connection of their family. ... This may be a transient phenomenon that will disappear with growing involvement of a large number of women in politics. Special measures will be necessary to reduce the proxy element in the women relatives of male politicians"[15]. As a result of reservation, hundreds of thousands of women have been elected in various responsible posts. There are enough evidences to show that women can stand on their own, demonstrate their political ability, acumen and far-sightedness and can take effective leadership position. The failures, if there are any, are not gender specific.

DEBATE ON MECHANISM OF RESERVATION

Even while admitting the logic of reservation for women, there is a debate on the mechanism of this reservation. The mechanism which has been prescribed in the realm of local self government and which is sought to be extended in the spheres of Assemblies and Parliament is that this one/third seats and offices will be allotted by rotation to different seats /wards on a random basis. So every third seat will be rotationally allotted to women at the time of every election. There are several arguments of why this arrangement militates against the principle of representational politics.

Firstly, this will have a tendency to Ghettoise women's politics in that only women will be pitted against women. Women thereby will be confined within a limited world and not allowed to compete with men. As Madhu Keshwar says, "confining women to fight elections only against other women, amounts to declaring that women are not competent to face men. Leadership acquired in such a manner will be seen as unnatural, artificial and as having been foisted on the electorate"[16]. Second, this will result in a forcible unseating of two thirds of the incumbents in every general election. This compulsory unseating militates against the very basic principles of democratic representation. Since the legislators do not know whether they can retain their seat next time, accountability to their own electorate will reduce. The process of building up a rapport between the electorate and their representative will be hampered as a result. A. M. Singhvi says, "A change of constituency every five years ... would snap that fundamental link between the electorate and the elected and completely eliminate all incentive and interest in the development, nurturing and continued prosperity of the constituency which every representative must have and which is the very essence of representative democracy. It would make the very purpose of women's representation empty and devoid of substance" [17].

The same applies to women representatives also. Nursing their constituencies on a long term basis will not be fruitful, because after the dereservation of that constituency after one term, they are not likely to get a ticket for the same seat. This may be a strong disincentive for them. The principle of accountability in politics will be lost. Men, being unseated at the last moment, may have a tendency to put their relatives as dummies who will retain their seat till the next election when they can reclaim their seat. This has been known in Indian politics as the ***biwi-beti*** (wife-daughter) syndrome. This is neither honourable for women nor helpful for representative democracy.

The alternative which is being suggested is either the introduction of multi-seat or dual member constituencies or the system of voluntary, party based quotas as it is found in many democracies of Northern Europe and Scandinavia with extremely successful result.

In a multi-seat constituency there can be a clubbing of three members, one of which has to be a female member, the other two being elected from those male or female, getting highest number of votes. "The proposal involves the creation of multi-seat constituencies with one-third quota reserved for women. For instance, three constituencies could be clubbed together to make one and each clubbed constituency can be represented by three people, one of whom must be a woman"[18]. The advantage of this system is that representatives, either male or female, would not be compulsorily delinked from their constituencies and that electoral accountability can be enforced, while ensuring representation for women.

The other alternative is that, instead of identifying any particular constituency as reserved for women, mandatory regulations for political parties may be made that at least one third of their nominees must be women candidates, leaving it to them to choose the constituencies for their women candidates. This would prevent a situation of Ghettoisation where women candidates are pitted only against women candidates. The system would result in 'equality of opportunity' through party based quotas. The example of Norway is suggested, where through the Equal Status Act 1988, it is required that the contesting parties must field at least 40 per cent candidates of both sexes on all public boards, councils and committees. Gender quotas have operated at the level of political parties in Germany also. The 'Greens' operate a 50-50 system whereas the Social Democrats in Germany, reserve 40 per cent of party posts for women. Similarly the Labour Party in UK recently 'twinned' constituencies ensuring one female representative in every two for the Scottish Parliamentary elections[19]. This being the experience in many Western countries, the argument being made is that this system is better than compulsory selection on a rotation system of one-third of the women representatives as it is followed in India in the case of Panchayat election. It appears to the present author that the mandatory regulation on political parties is better than mandatory rotational reservation of constituency as it gives greater freedom to the political parties and to the electorate without compromising the necessity of enhanced representation of women.

RESERVATION: A POLITICAL SPACE

It is with this background about the issues involved in reservation that we can now analyse the effects and implications of reservation of seats for women in Panchyats. The obvious benefits of this may be summed up as follows:

1. It has created a space for women to operate in the political sphere and has induced hundreds and thousands of them to join in politics which, other wise, they would not have done. In West Bengal, for example, in the Panchayat election for 1998, about 25000 seats were reserved for women in the three different tiers of Panchayat and assuming an average

of three women per constituency, the number was a staggering 75000. That alone justifies reservation, whatever its other side effects may be.

2. A large number of women belonging to the underprivileged sections of society have entered the political arena and have been elected to Panchayats. The social base of representative democracy has widened as a result of that.
3. It has legitimized and reinforced the role of women in the public sphere, particularly in formal governmental structures. This is likely to change the prevalent notions of power in a hierarchical patriarchal society. The idioms of politics are likely to change as a result of that. Instead of being based on attributes like conflict, violence and aggressiveness, it is likely to give importance on values like love, sharing and caring etc.
4. The process has increased self-esteem, confidence and motivation of women. "It has started creating cross hierarchies that have the potential for challenging the hierarchies of patriarchy in the long run".[20]

ALLIED ISSUES

But reservation per se does not guarantee much substantial things to women unless this is associated with other features. Several other complementary processes need to be initiated in order to make reservation meaningful. Nanivadekar says, "An artificial measure like reservation will ensure only quantitative participation of women. There is no guarantee that these women would behave in a way conducive to the overall empowerment of women"[21]. In a thought provoking work, Anne Phillips argues that in the sphere of politics, the question of what is being represented is being overshadowed by who is being represented. 'The separation between 'who' and 'what' is to be represented, and the subordination of the first to the second, is very much up for question. The politics of ideas is being challenged by an alternative politics of presence"[22]. The dominant concern of politics should be sharing of ideas -

political beliefs, goals, aspirations and not who the persons are, like Hindu or Muslim or brahmin or dalit or man or woman. The argument goes on that the presence of collectivities like women or SCs or STs may be necessary in view of the contextuality of the situation but these must not overshadow the substantive issues, viz, the goals or ideals which are being pursued.

So reservation of seats for women is related with such other important issues like the extent of power and effectivity of Panchayats, the goals which the Panchayat is pursuing and the nature of composition of the leadership structure of the Panchayat. Only when the issue of reservation is viewed in the perspective of these aspects, we can assess the effect of reservation.

THE SITUATION IN WEST BENGAL

It is against this backdrop that we can analyse the performance factor of women Panchayat members in different states of India, more particularly in West Bengal. In West Bengal, the most noticeable feature is the massive participation of women in the 1993 and 1998 Panchayat elections. Whereas in Pre 1993 Panchayats, women representation was just 2 per cent of the total, in 1993, out of a total of 71,120 seats in the three tires of Panchayats, 24,895 seats were reserved for women, a staggering 35 per cent of the total seats. All these seats were filled up through multi-cornered contests. Certainly this added a new dimension to the political empowerment of women. This is in contrast to Karnataka, for example where though officially 1/3 reservation was made for women, many of the seats could not be filled up. As it has been said, "But it is sad that most of the seats (in Karnataka) were vacant due to lack of women candidates. Of the 200 seats reserved for women in North Canara, for example, 162 seats were vacant."[23] The second important aspect in West Bengal is the nature of the socio-economic background of the women representatives. Almost all the studies made in the field have shown that Panchayat representatives including women come from lower socio-economic classes. While talking about the 1993 Panchayat election in West Bengal, Bhattacharyya wrote, "the fourth panchayat poll has filled a third of panchayat seats with SC/ST and women representatives. This surely marks a significant change in the pattern of base-level rural representation .... The rural poor's struggle will surely benefit from every articulation of their experience and aspiration and every assertion of their specific interests and identities".[24] Dutta writes, "There is no notable study as yet on either the social background of women members or on the role played by women in panchayats. But one can say on the basis of social background of all members studied by a number of scholars that most of the women members come from poor families. One micro-study done by the State Institute of Panchayats on the educational background of women in one block in the district of Burdwan shows that a good number of them have either acted as voluntary trainers or as participants in the literary programmes".[25]

Significant increase in the number of women panchayat members have had their impact on the functional aspects of panchayats-in that panchayats are giving more attention than hitherto upon welfare and developmental functions. The focus of the panchayat has now been on drinking water, school education, health care and dealing with problems relating to sanitation and fuel. They have also begun to address some of the social evils like alcoholism, domestic violence and child marriages. Expectedly, while dealing with these issues, many faced initial hostility not only within the village community, but also within the family. The struggle is not an easy one but the process of empowerment indicates that the struggle has began[26]. Nirmala Buch writes, "The participation (of women) in panchayats has had an impact on their sense of self. The data on their perceptions, recognition, respect, enhanced status, confidence levels, enhanced levels of mobility and exposure, their increased political aspirations and community's perceptions and evaluation o. their performance are seen as markers of empowerment process for this long disadvantaged group."[27] To illustrate these points, one can cite a few case studies on the West Bengal situation.

G. K. Lieten, in a study of the socio-economic background of the Panchayat leaders in one Block in Birbhum district in West Bengal has cited the instance of one Alema Bibi, a secondary school teacher, who was elected to the 1983 panchayat. But after her husband was murdered, she was forced to resign by her father with the argument that muslim ladies should not take part in public life. Fortunately, she revoked that decision and volunteered to be a candidate for the next election as well. He also gave the example of one Malati Tudu who was a tribal illiterate but became the ***upapradhan*** (vice – chairman) of a panchayat.[28]

Such instances before 1993 were in the nature of exception but have now become fairly common. In line with women's participation in other states, movements like the Chipko movement in Himachal Pradesh or the Gangha madhan agitation against BALCO in Orissa or the movement against Arak in Andhra Pradesh. In West Bengal also, in the Kultikuri panchayat, which was an all women panchayat, the panchayat took an active part in organizing protests against and in dismantling the liquor dens to stop alcoholism of men, in fighting against superstitions like the practice of witch hunting, in taking up issues like health and hygienic standards and in taking up development projects for women and children like the DWCRA project through which women are being helped to be engaged in small scale agro based industries to encourage self employment programme among women.[29]

The study of Esther Duflo and Raghabendra Chattopadhyay, who worked on 65 gram panchayats in the district of Birbhum West Bengal, compared the types of public goods provided in reserved and unreserved panchayats. They have shown that reservation for women increases female participation and the investment priorities differ. In the reserved panchayats there are more investments in road construction, recycled fuel equipment and drinking water.[30]

In another Survey the following aspects were noted (a) it was found that 87 per cent of the women respondents were the first member of the family to get represented so the charge of women as substitute members for their males do not hold good; (b) 78 per cent of the respondents stated people come to them directly for the redressal of their grievances, not through their family or through the party; (c) the rate of attendance of women members and their participation in the decision making process was also found to be very high and effective.[31]

The study made by Dilip K. Ghosh on the background and performance of women members of panchayat in the district of Birbhum similarly shows that they participate in large number irrespective of caste, creed or religion. Mostly women of younger age group come to the panchayats. But the educational status of women members are comparatively low vis-à-vis male members. This sometimes creates barriers in effective interaction. Regarding their economic condition, it was found that of the 408 women members, 42.65 per cent have no land of their own and 44.12 per cent have land holdings upto 2.5 acres. Thus there was a convergence of lower caste-lower class syndrome in the women members of the panchayat.[32]

Of course, all the studies on the level of participation of women in panchayats in West Bengal do not reflect this optimistic situation. In one such study in the district of South 24 Parganas, it was revealed that, among 92 elected women representatives, less than 25% used to take part in discussions at the meetings and those who participated seldom used to speak against the elders. The performance of more than 50% of women was not satisfactory. Family pressure, lack of literacy, lack of awareness-all these factors accounted for this situation.[33]

SITUATION IN OTHER STATES

Such a mixed situation in regard to the women's empowerment in Panchayats is to be found in other states as well. A study of 12 all women Panchayats in Maharashtra showed that though men generally welcomed the entry of women, there were anxieties also about the impact of this role reversal on the part of women.[34] A study in Haryana has shown how the male relatives of the women members rise in prominence in the eyes of the government. A report from Orissa shows the positive impact of women's participation on other aspects of their lives.

Studies on Kerela show how women are fighting against the traditional patriarchal values and are asserting their rights to stay in office. The story of Bhanwari, a woman panchayat member from Bassi Block in Jaipur district of Rajasthan is now fairly well known who was gang raped for fighting against the evil practice of child marriage and who had also to face boycott by ***Sarpanches*** of the panchayats in that area. [35] So the profiles and experiences of the women panchayat members are varied. Though one does not get a neat and consistent picture, it is clear that the norms and values of a patriarchal society are being challenged by this type of political empowerment.

CONCLUSION

One has to remember that political empowerment of women is not an end in itself- it is just a means to an end. The over all socio-economic milieu in our society still continues to be discriminatory. Norms of patriarchy are wide spread. Poverty and illiteracy are widespread phenomena and women particularly are the victims of that situation. Women, who come in under gender and caste reservation, "have come in with their social and economic disadvantages- mostly non literate, with little productive assets, largely dependent on wage labour and belong to a society that has fixed places for various castes and gender. These cannot be changed by a wave of the constitutional amendment Wand".[36]

Admitting that women's position in panchayats has significant outcome, it would be too much to believe that it would be a sufficient weapon to fight against social injustice or poverty. Women have class and caste identity, not just a gender identity. In fact, "gender as a phenomenon hardly ever appears in a pure form. It is almost always alloyed with caste, class and religious factors. In matters where there is a clash between gender and caste or class, we cannot expect women to align themselves with other women, going against their caste or class loyalties".[37]

On the basis of the experience of Kerala, Thomas Issac said that 33% reservation is a necessary but not a sufficient condition for women's empowerment. This has to be accompanied by capacity-building programme and an enabling environment within the Panchayats themselves.[38] An artificial measure like reservation will ensure only quantitative participation of women. Capacity building implies both qualitative improvement among women representatives and a conducive social environment. Massive efforts for comprehensive political education and gender sensitization are necessary.[39] It is true that despite the change in the role of women in the public sphere, their role in the private sphere has not changed. Proposals for training women in panchayat work are met with the typical refrain, 'who will make ***chapatis***'? Even in West Bengal, G. K. Lieten has observed, 'the unwillingness to alter the division of labour at home and apprehension that the entry of women into the public domain would mean passing on household chores to males,' is to be found.[40] These are the hard realities of a patriarchal society and women as well as men have to confront the situation if women's participation has to be made meaningful.

The role of women's own organisations and the role of NGOs may be made very relevant in such an enabling programme. Women, particularly from poorer households, need their own organisations to help them break the barriers of inequality, invisibility and powerlessness and expand the base for their 'participatory development' (like SEWA in Ahmedabad, WWF in Chennai, CWDS or AIWC). These organisations can generate necessary awareness as well as increase the bargaining capacity of women and can confront/cooperate with other organisations to represent the collective interests of women. The NGOs can also be tremendously helpful. Many of the NGOs run training programmes involving leadership development, capacity building, group dynamics and the like. Some of the NGOs have organised training specifically for PRI members (e.g. SEARCH and UMA in Karnataka, FRCH in Maharasthra, CINI in West Bengal, YIP in Andhra Pradesh).[41] In West Bengal, the State Institute of Panchayats also organize such training programmes.

Women's representation in panchayat will not initiate fundamental changes in society. But that does not minimise the issue of women's representation. Local government can be made much more meaningful through participatory process and in that process, women's participation is a necessary, though not a sufficient condition for ensuring a smooth transformation to a better social order.

NOTES AND REFERENCES

1. *India Today*, 31.8.1996.
2. See, his Article in *Harijan*, Feb., 24, 1940.
3. Jawaharlal Nehru. *The Discovery of India*, Oxford University Press: New Delhi (1982).
4. Tendulkar, G. D. *Mahatma*, Vol. III, P. 61 (Publications Division, GOI).
5. Keshwar, Madhu (1996), Women and Politics: Beyond Quotas, *Economic and Political Weekly*, Vol. 31 (43), October, p. 2869.
6. *Ibid*, p. 2867.
7. NaNivadekar, Medha (1998), Reservation for Women: Challenge of Tackling Counter Productive Trends, *EPW*, July II.
8. Dutta, Prabhat (1998), *Major Issues in Development Debate* (New Delhi: Kanishka).
9. Sharma, Kumud (1998), Trusformative Politics: Dimensions of Women's Participation in Panchayati Raj, *Indian Journal of Gender Studies*, (5:1).
10. Singh, T. (1997), Empowering Women: A Symposium on Political Reservation for Women, *Seminar*, 457, pp. 12–12.
11. Keshwar, Madhu (1996). *Op. cit*, p. 2873.
12. NaNivadekar, Medha (1998), *Op. cit*, pp. 1815–18.
13. Majumdar, Vina (1997), Historical Soundings, *Seminar* 457, September, pp. 14–19.
14. Dhanda, Meena (2000) Representation for Women: Should Feminists Support Quota? *EPW*, 12.8.2000, p. 2969.
15. NaNivadekar, Medha (1998), *Op.Cit*, p. 1816.
16. Keshwar, Madhu (2000), Equality of Opportunity *Vs* Equality of Results, *EPW* Nov, 18, p. 4152.

17. Singhvi, A. M. (1997), The Women's Reservation Bill, *Seminar*, 457, pp. 25-30.
18. Kishwar, Madhu (1996), *Op. cit*, p. 2870.
19. Dhanda, Meena (2000), *Op. cit*, p. 2971.
20. NaNivadekar, Madha (1998), *Op. cit.*, p. 1818.
21. *Ibid*, p. 1818.
22. Philips, Anne (1995), The *Politics of Presence* (OUP), p. 5
23. Bhargava, B. S. and Subba, K *Energing Trends in Panchayati Raj in India*, p. 115.
24. Bhattacharyya, Dipankar (1993), New Challenges for Bengal Left: Panchayat Poll Pointers, *EPW*, July 17-24, p. 1494.
25. Dutta, Prabhat (1998), *Major Issues in the Development Debate* (New Delhi, Kanishka), p. 52.
26. Pillai, Sudha (2001), Can Panchayati Raj Improve the Scene? *Yojna*, August, p. 45-47.
27. Buch, Nirmala (2001), Panchayats and Women, *Kurukshetra*, April Also, Dutta, Prabhat, Women in Panchayats, *Kurukshetra*, Dec., 2001, pp. 30-33.
28. Lieten, G. K. (1988), Panchayat Leaders in a West Bengal District, *EPW*. Oct., p. 2072.
29. Ghosh, B. N. (1999), Women Leaders in Gram Panchayat: Prospects and Constraints, *Socialist Perspective*, Vol. 27, Nos. 1-2 p. 38-39.
30. World Bank Webcast *Women's Leadership and Policy Dicisions: Evidence from a Nation wide Randomised Experiment in India*, Nov. 2001.
31. Dutta S., Bandyopadhyay, S. and Pakrasi, K. (1998), Impact of Women Empowerment: A Pilot Study of West Bengal Panchayats (Joshi, Adhikari Instt. of Social Studies, West Bengal).
32. Ghosh, D. K. (1997), Grassroot Women Leaders: Who are they? A Study in a West Bengal District, *Journal of Rural Development*, Vol. 16 (2), pp. 291-311.
33. Pramanick, S. K. and Nandi, N. C. (2000), Empowerment of Women in Panchayat Raj: A Case Study of Mograhat II Development Bank, West Bengal, *Socialist Perspective*, Vol. 28, Nos. 1-2.

34. Dutta, Brinda (1995), Who will Make the Chapatis?
35. For a Review of the Situation in Various States, see *Journal of Rural Development,* Vol . 16 (4) (1997).
36. Vyasulu, P and Vyasulu, V. (1999), Women in Panchayati Raj: Grass roots Democracy in Malgudi, *EPW,* Dec. 25, p. 3684
37. *Ibid,* p. 3684.
38. Quoted in Ghosh, Anjan and Chakravorty, Basabi (1998). Women in West Bengal Panchayats: A Challenge Ahead, *Society and Change,* Ap-June, p. 66.
39. NaNivadekar, Medha (1998) *op. cit* (*EPW*) p. 1819.
40. Lieten, G. K. (1996), Land Reforms at Centre Stage: The Evidence on West Bengal, *Development and Change,* Vol. 27, No. 1, p. 25.
41. Vyasula P. and Vyasulu V. (1999), *Op. cit.*

10

Women and Compensatory Justice: Populism Through Reservation

SOUMYAJIT PATRA

The issue of women empowerment, in contemporary India, revolves around, to a large extent, the question of reservation. The fundamental changes, taken place in viewing the problems of the women, have brought the concept of participation to the fore. As soon as it is realized that mere welfare measures could not bring in sufficient changes in their position in the society, emphasis is given on sharing power equally with their male counterparts. And it is the right point aimed at.

Participation here means involvement outside home which relieves the women from their traditional bonds with the domestic activities. If the position of an individual is determined, as has been envisaged by Veblen, by her or his position in the economic and technological spheres, the social exclusion of the women could bring little grace for them. The confinement of women in what has been termed by Finch (1996) 'private sphere' makes her indifferent of the changes taking place in the wider society. When it is believed that 'a strong sense of identity and self-esteem' is a necessary requisite for building up a new type of male-female relationship, participation of women in collective organizing action has no alternative (Helen: 1994).

The strategic shift from 'women and development approach' to empowerment has pointed to two important spheres in which women should participate: economic and political. It is believed that women's economic and political participation will automatically reorganize power relations which empowerment entails. This view, however, has been criticized by many on the ground that in countries like India the difficulties to eradicate gender inequities lie in peculiar belief pattern and value system (Manna and Patra: 2001). Mere participation, without changes in the mental make up of both sexes and also in the normative order of the society, would do little to empower 'the biggest oppressed minority in the world' (Forbes: 1999). The issue has got prominence in recent years as a result of the constant debate regarding the reservation of seats in various statutory bodies for the women.

The idea of participation of women in the realm of politics as instrumental to empowerment has naturally given rise to two antagonistic stances. Those who believe that social marginalization of women could be prevented by ensuring their political participation, demand reservation of seats for them in formal political system. The argument is that changes in the composition of political authority would gradually reduce patriarchal dominance in other spheres of life as well. The notion of political participation of women gets importance in anti-reservation discourses also. But they argue that without changing the attitude of the society towards women, mere reservation of seats in election will hardly bring any positive impact. I will extend this argument in subsequent sections.

II

Admitting the problem of relativism in studying women problems that emphasises on the 'limitation of speaking of women's identity in singular', it can be said that women of different sections of the society face problems which are different in nature and degree (Giri: 2001). The subjugation of educated working women is less severe than that of the illiterate, poor women. Similarly, as women's movements in India are confined largely to 'urban, westernized middle and upper-middle-class women', the women of these categories enjoy more liberty in their day to day life (Beteille: 2000). But the same is not true in case of the vast majority of women who can not even take decision on matters related exclusively to their own lives. Therefore top-down imposition of any measure considering the 'women' as a unified category, having an absolute invariant identity, is bound to fail to be effective.

This aspect of the problem is related directly or indirectly to what is known as patriarchal domination. But there is another facet too, which points to the attitude of the women themselves. In a famous article, 'Feminism: Indian Ethos and Indian Convictions', Suma Chitnis has pointed to 'their relative inability to tune in to the demands for equality and personal freedom' (emphasis added), (Chitnis 1988). The Social construction of self of the women is done in such a way that they internalize the value of submissiveness even at the cost of their personal choice and freedom from the very beginning of their life. Unlike most of the western countries where equality is given top most priority, Indian society nurtured the notion of hierarchy for thousands of years. Unless changes in values, belief systems and cultural practices take place, superficial administrative reforms would be meaningless. At the same time it should be remembered that it is more important to bring changes in the attitude of the women than that of the men, who themselves nurture and sustain the tradition (Sharma: 2000). The supporters of reservation policy should remember the peculiarities of gender relations in our country.

It is true that an honest and sincere implementation of three-tier panchayati raj in West Bengal has been very much effective in bringing the previously excluded communities under the domain of the mainstream politics. No one denies that in this state a good number of women are participating in rural reconstruction programmes of the government after being elected at the grass roots levels. Even there are also women-run panchayats in West Bengal (for example Bankra III Gram

Panchayat of Howrah District) where all the elected members are the women (2003 Panchayat Election). In 2008 Panchayat election of West Bengal the CP1 (M) had given nominations to a large number of women to involve them in local politics. This is a good sign of course. But forced reservation for the women can not be an effective measure so long as they have to work under male domination almost in every sphere of life. The observation of B. S. Baviskar (2002) is worth mentioning.

> Have the new Panchayats, following the 73rd amendment proved to be more inclusive? Are they more effective in including the excluded? Although two elections have been held during the last nine years, in most states the answer in not clear.

The newly emerged groups of house wife-turned-politicians, as a consequence of compulsory or forced reservation policy, are often proxy figures. How is it possible for quota system to be the antidote to the social marginalization of women in a country which is basically undemocratic? It is not to question their political potentiality, but to admit that the political empowerment of women is related to a number of factors on which they themselves have no control. The author has witnessed a number of occasions in which the women Panchayat Pradhans are constantly dictated by their husbands or local male leaders during the time of interviews. There are people who remain satisfied with the numerical presence of the women in politics. But the sociologists should analyze the implications of any attempt to change a deep-rooted cultural practice by mere administrative reform or constitutional amendments like reservation.

Political participation requires some sort of political motivation which in turn is related to a number of factors. These are mostly social, like the educational level, familial background, group membership, economic self sufficiency etc. Contemporary social scientists have opined that ' political participation is not natural; it has...to be learnt' (Mukhopadhyay: 1992) . In a recent work, in three districts of Assam, namely Sonitpur, Cachar and Nalbari, it is found that the elected women-panchayat members are mostly unaware of and indifferent to the local issues. Some of them even do not know the nature of the problems of the people of her panchayat (Hazarika: 2006). Therefore if any one (either male or female) is forcibly given nomination to fulfill quota, the institution is bound to suffer in the last analysis. Are the proponents of reservation sure that the women, who are mostly confined to household duties from morning to evening to night have developed the political motivation necessary for a political career? It seems a planned attempt to divert the attention from the root of the problem. Feminist movements should attack the cultural practices which help perpetuate cruel patriarchal domination first. Are the male members of pro-reservation camp ready to accept gender equality in every sphere of life- in family, in politics, in religion, in economy every where? Beteille (2002) has rejected such a policy saying that if the burden of empowerment is placed on the quota system it would be a 'heavy burden 'for the smooth functioning of total system. He also points out that such preferential treatment is at odds with the idea of 'citizenship'.

III

Apart from the ethnic, caste, educational or religious differences being important in studying the problem of women's political participation, there is another issue which is very closely related to their political empowerment. It is the question of the degree and nature of their economic dependence. The experience of our country suggests that so long as the women remain economically dependent, no move for their emancipation becomes fruitful. Two examples can be cited here. It is not true that women's liberation movement is new in India. Even during the medieval period of Indian history various religious movements (known as Bhakti movement) involved women and tried to bring them in the frontline. This movement started among the Hindus during seventh to tenth century A.D. Bhakti movement produced some prominent women like Andal, Meerabai, Akkamahadevi. Srinivas (2000) in a recently published article opines that this movement created 'hope of salvation' among low caste people and women. Though this article is not directly related to women problem but it provides a necessary clue for our present analysis.

The Bhakti movement became very popular among a section of population but it failed to reach the desired end. The reason is that this movement could not bring changes in the economic position of the women. Similarly, the participation of women in national freedom struggles helped them move outside the domain of home management but could not empower them in the true sense. Not only in India, but also in countries like South Africa, national struggles are considered as a landmark in the women liberation movement. But in our country until there was ramification of modern occupation which opened the door for the women also, the traditional position of women was hardly affected.

To say that economic self sufficiency of women is instrumental to their political career is not to undermine the socio-cultural factors related to deep-rooted patriarchy. As Beteille points out, 'shifts in the balance of economic power between classes, between communities, and between men and women have been taking place, but they rarely, if ever lead to the empowerment....' This is because empowerment is a total concept which demands a holistic approach of analysis. And so it is difficult for the women to achieve in a patriarchal set up. Historian Nihar Ranjan Roy (1993) in his monumental work *Bangalir Itihas* has opined that Indian society as a whole was oriented mostly to patriarchy with the spread of Aryan culture. The Aryans were patriarchal and they came approximately around 1750 B.C. The advocates of reservation should admit the historical root of the problem, before suggesting any administrative measure.

The historicity and pervasiveness of the problem of subjugation not only suggest that the policy of reservation is superficial and inadequate but also point to the unwillingness of the government to eradicate gender discrimination in reality. Contemporary sociologists have categorically said that any sort of positive (or protective) discrimination also creates negative discrimination which helps perpetuate the difference. A sincere attempt should, on the contrary, aim at changing the value system, belief pattern and cultural practices and internalization of these though proper socialization. One major step towards this radical transformation may be the introduction of gender studies right from the primary level of formal education. What Sharma (2000) has called 'conscientisation' can be initiated in this way. Would the pro-reservation camp wholeheartedly move for such a necessary step?

There is a more fundamental question. If we move for gender equality, then, on what grounds can we argue for reservation? Doesn't it go against our basic objective? When there are some special seats reserved for some special categories of people, there are chances that a potential candidate is deprived of being nominated and instead a less qualified and less capable one will take the opportunity of reservation. Therefore it denies justice. Every society should have a proper procedure for role allocation in order to get the maximum service from that position. Thus from a functional point of view also reservation is unscientific. While there is serious doubt about the effectiveness of quota system, it is sure that society suffers from the problem of mediocracy as a consequence. Beteille (2000), who never supports quota system, elsewhere points to dialectic between the principle of equality and reservation. I would like to quote him at length in this regard.

> Positive discrimination may be described as a way of reducing social disparities by creating special opportunities for some in addition to the equal opportunities created for all. Obviously there is a tension between the two principles-equal opportunities for all and special opportunities for some... . (Beleille: 2000).

The anomalies and ambiguities inherent in the concept of 'reservation' itself give rise to conflicting stances even among its supporters. While some contemporary feminists demand one third seats in the Assembly and Parliament for women as such, there are others who went further to ensure the representations of the backward communities. The latter camp accuses the former of being Brahminical in its approach and outlook. They even see casteist bias in the demands of the so called feminists regarding reservation.

Thus if the process of allotting quotas within quota goes on and the reservation facility is being extended to the women of all backward classes in order to ensure their representation in the political bodies, the social composition of the authority structure would be a true reflection of the population, but there is serious doubt about its effectiveness, on which depends the institutional well-being. I have already pointed out that political role performance depends on a number of factors. Therefore, in a democratic political set up it is desirable that the entire electoral system is open, secular and rational. And through this process an effective ruling class comes up.

IV

Most of the states in this country, except a few like Bihar, have completed at least 'one-five year term' till 1993 when the bill was passed. At present thousands of women are working in local panchayats as representatives of their respective communities (see Table 1 for detail state wise description). But in reality they are not politically independent in the sense that even in minute matters their husbands or brothers interfere as if they are not able to perform the duties for which they have been elected. Veteran Journalist Bharat Dogra (2002) observes many such examples:

> It is easy to point out numerous examples of women who have worked entirely according to what they were told by their husbands or other male members of their families. In some eases elected women remained at home while their husbands attended the panchayat meetings and carried out official transactions on their behalf.

Is it political empowerment? This type of reservation, in fact, gives birth to a group of shadow politicians who exercise power from behind the backdrop. It seems a new strategy to perpetuate male domination while showing sympathy to the movement for women empowerment.

Table 1
State wise Elected Women Panchayat Representatives in the Three Tiers: 2002

State	*Gram Panchayat*	*Intermediate Panchayat*	*District Panchayat*
Andra Pradesh	68736	4919	364
Arunachal Pradesh	-	-	-
Assam	7851	746	117
Bihar	-	-	-
Chattisgarh	41913	906	95
Delhi	-	-	-
Goa	457	-	17
Gujrat	41180	1312	274
Hariyana	18356	842	109
Himachal Pradesh	6822	562	87
J & K	-	-	-
Jharkhand	-	-	-
Karnataka	35922	1375	339
Kerala	4801	629	105
Madhya Pradesh	106491	2159	248
Maharashtra	77548	1407	658
Manipur	611	-	22
Meghalaya	-	-	-
Mizoram	-	-	-
Nagaland	-	-	-
Orissa	31414	2188	296
Punjab	26939	813	89
Rajasthan	39450	1908	364
Sikkim	322	-	-
Tamil Nadu	26181	1770	173
Tripura	1895	106	28
Uttaranchal	-	-	-
Uttar Pradesh	-	-	-
West Bengal	11497	1923	156
Union Territories			
Andaman & Nicobar Islands	261	25	10
Chandigarh	55	6	3
Dadra & Nagar Haveli	45	0	4
Daman & Diu	17	0	10
Lakshadeep	30	0	8
Pondichery	-	-	-
Total	548794	23596	3605

N.B.: In Meghalaya, Mizoram and Nagaland Traditional Councils exist. In Delhi Panchayati Raj system is yet to be revived.

Source: India, Ministry of Statistics and Programme Implementation, Central Statistical Organisation 2003.

CONCLUSION: 'DEVELOPMENT AS FREEDOM'

No social institution exists without some structure of authority, in which some exert power over others. This natural phenomenon becomes a problem when the social composition of this authority structure becomes gender biased. A good balance of gender is healthy and desirable in so far as it is achieved through capacity building. Contemporary sociologists agree that only capacity building can bring about empowerment. Such an approach is desirable for the good performance of the institution also. In Sen's analysis capacity building is essential for freedom which is the single most important criterion of development (Sen : 1999). This approach leads us to rethink the issue of reservation of seats in formal political structure for women from a new perspective: whether the move leads to increase the freedom of the women or not. If the answer is no, such administrative steps could not be termed as development at least.

REFERENCES

Baviskar, B. S. (2002), 'Including the Excluded: Empowering the Powerless', *Sociological Bulletin*, Vol. 61, No. 2, pp. 168-174.

Beteille, A. (2000), *Antinomies of Society: Essays on Ideologies and Institutions*, New Delhi: Oxford University Press.

Chitnis, S. (1988), "Feminism: Indian Ethos and Indian Conviction" in R. Ghadially (ed), *Women in Indian Society*, New Delhi: Sage Publication, pp. 81-95.

Doera, B. (2002), *www.goodnewsindia.com*

Finch, J. (1996), 'Women, The Family and Families" in T. Cosslett *et. al* (eds.), *Women, Power and Resistance: An Introduction to Women Studies, Buckingham* Open University Press, pp. 13-22.

Forbes G. (1999), *Women in Modern India*, Cambridge: Cambridge University Press.

Giri, A. K. (2001), 'Civil Society and the Limits of Identity Polities'. *Sociological Bulletin*, Vol. 50, No. 2, pp. 266-285. Oving Hazari K., S.D. from p. 232.

Hazarika, S. D. (2006), 'Political Participation of Women and the dialectic of 73rd Amendment', *The Indian Journal of Political Science*, Vol. LXVII, No. 2.

Helen, O. (1994), *Women and the Family,* London: Zed Books Ltd.

Manna S. and Patra, S. (2001), 'Women Empowerment. Civil Society and Institutional well-being', *Journal of the Department of Anthropology,* Vol. 7, No. 1 and 2, pp. 117-122.

Mukhopadhyay, A. K. (1992), *Political Sociology,* Calcutta: K. P. Bagchi & Co.

Sen, Amartya (1999), *Development As Freedom,* New York, OH, P.

Sharma. S. L. (2000), *'Empowerment Without Antagonism: A Case for Reformulation of Women's Empowerment Approach', Sociological Bulletin,* Vol. 49, No. l, pp. 19-39.

73rd Amendment', pp. 245-260.

11

Political Participation Among Women in West Bengal-Its Nature and Extent

Sandip Kumar Ghatak

No discussion about the nature of any political system can be completed without an analysis of the nature of political participation among its people. For political participation, political power is considered as most important ingredient which is monopolized by the elites. It cannot be denied that the rulers invariably try to involve the people in the affairs of the state and thereby try to legitimize their political power. Whatever may be the character of the political system, even in a modern dictatorial regime, political participation has great importance. And traditional democratic theory generally regards participation by the individual in political activity as a virtue of its own rights. In fact, participation has been seen as a civic duty, as well as a sign of political health.

The concept of political participation has been defined variously. Thus, according to Ali and Sharma (1983: 140) "Political participation is the involvement at various levels in the political system. Involvement expresses itself in various kinds of overt or manifest political activities"

By political participation, Huntington and Nelson (1970: 67) also mean: "Simply an activity by private citizen designed to influence governmental decision-making".

Thus, political participation refers to those legal activities of the people which affect the governmental decision making and actions.

According to Huntington and Nelson (*ibid*: 1970) "Knowledge about politics, interest in politics, feeling of political competence, and efficiency, perceptions of the relevance of political all these may often be closely, related to political action, but at other times they are not. Their study and measurement also require techniques that differ significantly from those needed to study behavior along."

So, in their opinion, subjective political attitudes are not equivalent to political participation. On the contrary, they are separate variables.

Mathews and Protho (1966:37) define political participation as, "all behavior through which people directly express their political opinions."

Hence, "Participation is the principal means by which consent is granted or withdrawn in a democracy and rulers are made accountable to the world" (McCloski 1968: 253).

But this does not mean that in every democracy, the rate of political participation is very high. In fact, there is great difference among diverse political system in this regard.

Thus while the rate of political participation in Australia, New Zealand, and Great Britain is very high but in U.S.A. this is relatively low. This reveals the complexity of the phenomenon which is greatly influenced by a number of variables.

So, it can be said that political participation denotes a number of voluntary activities which have significant influence upon the political system regarding issues like the selection of rulers and the formation of public policy.

The ingredient of candidature for elections to representative bodies of various levels is also a very important mode of political participation. Particularly in a democratic polity, the individual has a greater chance to take part in politics, to influence the decision making process and to take active part in making of major decisions by participating in the election process. Thus, through this ingredient the individual can more directly relate himself with the political affairs of the state. As a candidate, the individual closely attaches himself with the political parties, public meetings etc. and thereby extends his political awareness. Even as an independent candidate having no formal connection with any political party he can influence the electorate, can win the elections, and can become a member of the legislature. Since in every democratic polity, citizens have the right to participate in the election process, this is also an effective way by which the individual can participate in the political system. Thus, the ingredient of candidature in the elections also widens the scope for political participation.

Thus individuals of participate in the political system in various ways, and their degree or extent of participation are not the same. That is why we find different forms of political participation in any given state. Again, the extent of political participation also depends upon some variables like income, occupation, sex etc. Ghosh (2002:2) opines:

> One important determining factor is obviously gender difference. Gender is now considered to be a category of discrimination. It has been observed that the process of development has failed to improve the social position of the unprivileged sections in general and of women in particular. Greater participation in development is considered as an important factor in reversing the present trend which signifies unequal social, economic and political position of men and women. In the economic sphere it has been observed that most of the manual and non-technical work is done by women, while men operate new agricultural machines and control inputs as well as the produce. In the production process of economy the role of women is not properly recognized. Only child bearing, rearing and domestic activities have been considered by the society as non-productive, non-economic and feminine. The traditional socio-economic culture has legitimized the outlook by

sustaining the gender relationship of dominance and subordination.

The pattern of gender relationship is equally true in the political sphere also. Although, barring nine countries, (New land: 1975) women now enjoy legally equal political status open to men in all democratic countries of the world, this does not mean automatic enjoyment of the rights conferred there in. Studies in this perspective bear evidence of the fact that women are still second class citizens in spite of the equal rights conferred on them (Mann 1972: 8).

In India, the demand for voting rights of women had started in pre-independence period, when the Indian women were active and organized a deputation to Lord Chelmsford and Mr. Montague for their equal voting rights like men. They also appealed to all organizations including the Indian National Congress to stand in favour of them.

> In 1918 the Provincial Conferences of Bombay and Madras passed resolution to remove sex disqualification from the reform bill. Similar resolutions were approved by the Andhra Provincial Conference, the Bombay Special National Congress Session, the India Home Rule League, and the Muslim League (Forbes 1998: 73).

In the special session of Congress held in Bombay in August 1918, Sarojini Naidu delivered her speech in favour of women's suffrage. Mrs. Naidu held the view and also presented before the audience that the voting rights of the women was not only rational but also politically and scientifically sound, compatible with tradition, and consistent with human rights.

In the Thirty-Third session of the Indian National Congress, Saraladevi Choudhuri strongly established her view regarding the voting rights of women. According to Saraladevi, women should have equal rights with men so that they can chart their own destines. Because, according to Saraladevi, the present age was characterized by human rights, justice, freedom, and self-determination. She contended that "Sphere of women included comradeship with men in the rough and tumble of life and to being the fellow-workers of men in politics and spheres (Report of the Thirty Third sessions of INC 1918).

Provincial and district Congress Conferences and women's organizations also stood firmly behind the demand for women's franchise. To raise the demands for women's franchise in its zenith, the condition of Dorothy Jinarajadasa and Margaret Cousins-two British women were immense behind the scene.

In 1918 the Southborough Franchise Committee visited India with a view to collect the information regarding the case of women's suffrage. Though they accepted petitions and talked with women from only two provinces-Bengal and Punjab (Cousins: 1919) but the Southborough Committee failed to accept the plea in favour of women's franchise, while on their tour in India they overlooked the fact in their findings that women were already serving on municipal councils and other local bodies. Against the resolutions of the Southborough Committee, Annie Besant and Sarojini Naidu went to England and presented all the evidences in favour of them before the Select Committee.

In fact, there is a long history of the movement for women's rights in India. The personalities like Annie Besant, Sarojini Naidu, Herabai, Tata and her daughter Mithan, fought against the attitude of most of the British men who believed that Indian women were uneducated and living in seclusion. These personalities repeatedly demanded for equal citizenship and equal opportunities which were regarded as the most important factors for the successful working of a parliamentary democracy.

Again another sad story is that some of the Nationalist leaders also challenged the women's rights to vote. "In his first article on Women in 'Young India.' Gandhi raised his voice and wanted that women should take their proper place by the side of men but he would not support a vote for women campaign. The time was wrong. India needed to struggle against the British and the franchise campaign would waste their energy. Women should use their energies helping their men against the common foe (Forbes : 1998).

But, after a long struggle of the women for their right to vote, Bombay and Madras were the first provinces to recognize women's right to vote in 1921; followed by the United Province in 1923, Bengal and Punjab in 1926; and finally Assam, Bihar, Orissa and the Central Provinces in 1930.

The issue of the political participation is of crucial importance from the context of socio-economic development of a country and also from the context of international peace.

"Women's participation in politics is without doubt an important step towards social equality, economic development and national and international peace. But opinions differ regarding the nature of participation and the indicators used to measure it. Due to the lack of a gender sensitive non-discriminatory approach, the relevance of this issue is often obfuscated by the absence of a formal barriers to women's participation and this tends to make us overlook certain realities (Kumar and Kidwai: 4-5).

In this connection, it should be mentioned here that regarding the measurement of the nature and extent of political participation, other important factors like party membership, attending public meeting, casting votes, political discussion with the neighbourhood, reading newspaper and magazine regularly etc. are also to be taken into account.

The position of women in their respective political parties, both in the National and State level is not very encouraging. No political party gives equal share to women with the men while they nominate their candidates in any election. Even the top most position of the party is also monopolized by the men. The picture of the women's presence in top decision making committees in all the political parties is also very dismal. The percentage of women in top decision making committees in all the political parties is very negligible (Chatterjee 2001: 384). "Parties that led the national movements against colonial powers were compelled to mobilize women's support. As a result, many of them formed women's organization within the parties as part of their overall effort to combat colonialism. However, once in power, these women's wings were more or less marginalized and assigned areas that primarily dealt with women and children. Women's organizations thus ended up playing a supportive role to the male leadership in power, and leaders of such organizations were seldom women with independent political parties" (*ibid*: 2001).

Women's participation at the local level is not also satisfactory. Before 1990 women in local politics were generally either politicians who had lost membership of higher institutions, or those who were given such an opportunity to serve the purpose of publicity. In most of the cases, the motive was partially also to satisfy the aspiration of these few women, since they could then be kept under virtual political control and denied higher aspiration.

Table 1
Participation of Women in Eight Leading Political Parties

Name of the Party	*Percentage Women members West Bengal*	*Members in the highest decision making body (state-level)*	*Number of women in the highest decision making body*
RSP	15	15	1
FB	Not available	12	1
CPI	14.66	9	1
BJP	30	11	1
CPI(ML)	10	31	2
INC	50	80-	27
CPI(M)	9.6	85	8
ATMC	Not available	Not available	Not available

Source: The Changing Status of Women in West Bengal, 1970-2000: The Challenge Ahead; Jasodhara Bagchi (ed), Sage Publication, New Delhi, 2004, p. 89.

Women's participation in the local-self government increased quite radically after 1993 due to the enactment of the legislation which acknowledged 33 per cent reservation of seats for women in local bodies. The laws regarding the Panchayati Raj and its effective implementation slightly changed women's participation in local-self government. In West Bengal also the position of women in the local-self government also changed after the enactment of legislation which guaranteed 33 per cent of seats reserved for women in local bodies. Women's participation in Zilla Parishad, Panchayat Samiti and Gram Panchayat in West Bengal has increased significantly.

The present literature will review the issue of the political participation of women of West Bengal on the basis of the study of the women's participation in Parliament and Assemblies. While considering the nature and extent of women's participation in both the National and State Legislature in West Bengal, it should be borne in mind that in the developed countries the rate of women's participation in the legislature is only 14% whereas, in the developing and underdeveloped countries it is about 9% (Dutta 2007). Whenever we analyse the representative politics of our country we will find a very dismal picture of women's participation both in Parliament and Assemblies. The total number of women members in the First Lok Sabha with 499 seats was 22. It has only increased to 44 by 1998. The number of women MPs in the Lok Sabha touched the lowest point with 19 MPs in 1977, the year of the Congress debacle; the highest point was reached with 44 women MPs in the Eighth and Twelfth Lok Sabha (1984 and 1988). There has been on an average 30 women MPs in all Lok Sabha till 1998. Since 1984 a downward trend is visible in women's representation in Lok Sabha. Congress reverses have affected women's representation as the Congress used to field larger number of women candidates. The representation in the Rajya Sabha has ranged from 14 to 29 in a house membership of 240, which is 5.8 per cent to 11.8 per cent of the total strength of the House. The general trend in the Rajya Sabha has been that of a steady increase, in contrast to the Lok Sabha. From 1976 onwards the presence of women has been over 9.8 per cent excepting in 1993. The average representation in India of women in Parliament is much below the average of many other countries (Chatterjee 2001).

Table 2 clearly reveals that up to the seventh Lok Sabha election, the number of women representatives in the Lok Sabha from West Bengal was confined within 2. From eighth Lok Sabha election (except Ninth Lok Sabha election) the number was within five. So, out of total 44 seats in Lok Sabha in West Bengal the women's representative was only five. The number is not at all encouraging.

The scenario of West Bengal is not very different from the rest of the country. Though the women's participation in the Panchayats is somewhat encouraging but, whenever we are concerned with the women's participation in the legislative assembly as well as in the Parliament the picture is not very satisfactory.

Table 2
Representation of Women Members from First to Thirteenth Lok Sabha

Lok Sabha	*Total Seats*	*No. of Women Contested (all India)*	*No. of Women elected (all India)*	*Percentage of Women (all India)*	*No. of Women elected from West Bengal*
First (1952–57)	499	Not Known	22	4.4	1
Second (1957–62)	500	45	27	5.4	2
Third (1967–71)	503	70	34	6.7	2
Fourth (1967–71)	523	67	31	5.9	2
Fifth (1971–76)	521	86	22	4.2	2
Sixth (1977–80)	544	70	19	3.4	2
Seventh (1980–84)	544	142	28	5.1	2
Eighth (1985–90)	544	164	44	8.1	5
Ninth (1990–91)	517	198	27	5.2	2
Tenth (1990–96)	544	325	39	7.18	3
Eleventh (1996)	544	599	40*	7.18	4
Twelfth (1998)	544	271	44*	.8	5
Thirteenth (1999)	542	NA	48	8.86	5

* One member was nominated by the President.

Source: The Changing Status of Women in West Bengal, 1970–2000. The Challenge Aheadl; Jasodhara Bagchi (ed), Sage Publication, New Delhi, 2004, p. 87.

As shown in Table 3, in 1971 only six women were elected in the legislative assembly and in 1996 the number went up to 22. But in 1971 no woman was included in the ministry of West Bengal Government. In 1952 the percentage of women ministers in the state government was 6.66 and in 1996 it went up to 8.33. Thus, the level of women's representation both in the Lok Sabha and State Assembly is really very poor in comparison with the men. The all India scenario is not very different from the State of West Bengal.

In fact, women's representation in the legislature both in the Centre and the State to a large extent depends upon their position in their respective political parties. Women's position in the highest decision making body in all political parties is not very satisfactory. As a result this section of the community stands far away from both the National and State decision making bodies.

Table 3
Women MLAs from West Bengal, 1971-96

Year	*Total No. of Seats*	*Total No. of Women MLAs*	*Percentage of Women MLAs in State Legislative Assembly*
1971	280	6	2.14
1973	280	5	1.78
1977	294	4	1.36
1982	294	7	2.38
1987	294	12	4.08
1991	294	23	7.82
1996	294	22	7.40

Tabl 3a
Women Minister in West Bengal Government

Year	*Cabinet Minster*	*Minister of States*	*Deputy Minister*	*Total no. of women*	*Total no. of Minister*	*Percentage of Women minister in the State Govt.*
1952	1	-	1	2	30	6.66
1957	-	1	1	2	30	6.66
1962	2	-	3	5	37	13.51
1967	-	-	-	-	19	0
1967	-	-	-	-	3	0
1968	-	-	-	-	17	0
1969	1	1	-	2	31	6.45
1971	-	-	-	-	26	0
1972	-	-	1	1	28	3.57
1977	-	1	-	1	30	3.33
1982	-	2	-	2	45	3.4
1987	1	-	-	1	32	3.12
1991	1	3	-	4	44	9.09
1996	1	3	-	4	48	8.33

Source: The Changing Status of Women in West Bengal, 1970-2000: The Challenge Ahead; Jasodhara Bagchi (ed), Sage Publication, New Delhi, 2004 p. 88.

With a view to improve the position of the women in the lawmaking body an active role should be played by the political parties. Women's representations in all section of the party organization have to increase. Poor women representation in the legislature is not at all a good sign for the betterment and success of any democratic society.

REFERENCES

Ali, A. and Sharma, L.N. (1983), '*Political Sociology*', Madras University Press.

Chatterjee, B. (2001), 'Women & Politics in India', in '*Politics India': The State-Society Interface,* Chatterjee Rakhohari (ed.), South Asian Publishers, New Delhi.

Cousins, H. (1919), (Letter from M. Cousins to A. Besant (June 4, 1919), Theosophical Society Archives, Madras.

Dutta, P. (2007), Seminar Lecture on 'State Democracy and Development", in Samajbiggyan Mahasammelan, Deshbandhu Chittaranjan Mahavidyalaya, Chittaranjan, Burdwan, 18-20th January.

Forbes, G. (1998), *The New Cambridge History of India, Women in Modern India:* Cambridge University Press, NewDelhi.

Ghosh, J. (2002), '*Political Participation of Women in West Bengal–A Case Study*. Progressive Publishers.

Kumar, A. and Kiwai, S. (1999), '*Crossing the Sacred Line: Women's Search for Political Power*', Orient Longman, New Delhi.

Mann, J. (1972), *Women in Parliament*, Odhans Press, London.

Mathew, D.R. and Protho J.W. (1966), 'Negroes and the New Southern Politics', New York, Har Court, Brace & World.

Mcclosky, H. (1968), 'Political Participation', in *International Encyclopedia of the Social Sciences*, New York, Collier, Macmillan, Vol. 12.

Newland, K. (1975), 'Women in Politics: A Global Review', *Worldwatch*, Paper 3, December.

Huntington, P.S. and Nelson, H.J. (1970), '*No Easy Choice*', Cambridge University Press.

Report of the Thirty Third Session of the Indian National Congress, Delhi, December 26-31-1918, pp. 118-121.

Index